INTRODUCTION
TO
EVANGELISM
Delos Miles

BROADMAN PRESS
Nashville, Tennessee

To my friend, Dr. C. E. Autrey, a Barnabas,
who nearly twenty years ago
encouraged me to stay in the work of evangelism
long enough to make an impact

© Copyright 1983 • Broadman Press

All rights reserved

4262-39

ISBN: 0-8054-6239-2

Dewey Decimal Classification: 269

Subject Heading: EVANGELISTIC WORK

Library of Congress Catalog Card Number: 82-73078

Printed in the United States of America

Preface

This volume is designed for use as an introductory textbook on evangelism. While its intended readers are students of evangelism, I hope it will also serve the larger Christian community.

A ditchdigger was asked, "Why did you dig this ditch?"

He answered, "I dig the ditch to make the money to buy the bread to give me the strength to dig the ditch." If your goal is that confused, you will not be very effective in evangelism.

The content of this book is about equally divided between the theoretical and the practical aspects of evangelism. I have been guided in my writing by three objectives: (1) to confront the reader with his or her personal responsibility to make Christian disciples who will become responsible members of the church; (2) to equip the reader to be a more effective witness to Jesus Christ and his kingdom; and, (3) to give the reader the necessary inspiration and information to equip others to intentionally share their faith. I am very much in agreement with A. C. Archibald who said: "Without an evangelism that works, Christianity is doomed."[1]

You and I need to be confronted with our personal responsibility to self-consciously bear witness to Jesus Christ. Also we need some assistance with what has come to be called the equipping ministry (see Eph. 4:12). Dwight L. Moody told a big truth when he said, "The successful preacher is he who can get the most work out of his members." Evangelist Sam P. Jones put the same truth this way: "The more I can get them to do, the lighter my labors are."[2] That's a large part of what this volume is about.

One student, who took two courses with me, said to me after finishing the second course: "Now I know you can't teach evangelism in a classroom setting!" I've thought about that comment long and hard. It is true that ultimately one can't learn how to evangelize by sitting in a classroom. You can, in the final analysis, learn how to evangelize only through on-the-job training. Evangelism is one of those fine arts which can be mastered only through field work.

Nevertheless, there are some things which can be taught about evangelism in a classroom. Modeling is one of them. If it is true that evangelism is caught more than it is taught, then it is both caught and taught more through modeling than any other way. The student needs to be exposed to living role models among his or her teachers and fellow students. These role models ought to embody the love of God for the church and the world. They should endeavor to be living examples of God's intention in world evangelization.

There was a time when we could get by in our seminaries without designated teachers of evangelism. But to say today of evangelism, "Everybody teaches it," is to talk about a house which nobody owns.

My perspective on evangelism comes from thirty-eight years as a Christian, ten of those years as a pastor, fifteen as a denominational executive in evangelism, and five as a professor of evangelism. While I write as a Southern Baptist practitioner and theoretician of evangelism, I believe evangelism is ecumenical and eclectic both in its methodology and its theology.

Strictly speaking, there is no such phenomenon as Southern Baptist or United Methodist evangelism. The great divide in evangelism comes along the lines of the nature of saving grace. If you believe saving grace comes through hearing the gospel and responding in personal faith to what is heard (see Rom. 10:8-17), you will tend to take one approach to evangelism. On the other hand, if you believe saving grace is mediated through the sacraments of the church duly administered by those who are in proper apostolic succession, you will tend to take a different approach to evangelism.

The time is ripe for us to abandon our false stereotypes of evangelism. An evangelist is not one who grabs people by the lapels and forces them to listen to a testimony or to the Roman-road plan of salvation. We don't have to love persons to do that. Real evangelism is reaching out in love to the persons who are in our world of influence.

Evangelism is certainly worth promoting, but it is a passion rather than promotion. When evangelism is a passion, it is concerned primarily with the salvation of persons. When evangelism is a promotion, its primary concern is with statistics.

When evangelism is a passion, it is used to advance the kingdom of God. When evangelism is promotion, it is used to enlarge an institution.

When evangelism is a passion, joy and exhilaration are present in its performance. When it is promotion, pressure and strain exist in its application.

When evangelism is a passion, it is an exercise of the loving heart. When it is promotion, it resorts to ecclesiastical gimmickry to achieve religious success.[3]

I believe in the orchestra approach to evangelism. C. B. Hogue, the former evangelism leader for Southern Baptists, was expressing that kind of approach when he said: "Christians are witnesses in different ways: by word of mouth (whether to individuals, small groups, or large crowds); by print; by picture; by good works of love; by a Christ-centered home; by a transformed life; and even by an almost speechless excitement about Jesus."[4]

Not much is said in what follows about the role of various church program organizations in evangelization. My opinion is that the first function of religious education in the local church is to create an atmosphere conducive to an acceptance of Christ as one's Savior. Pastor Herschel H. Hobbs spoke my sentiment when he said, "Soul-winning is the responsibility of every organization within a church."[5]

If we think of evangelism as ebbing and flowing like the tides, I see our time as the tide coming in. Evangelism is now approaching a high-tide mark in this last quarter of the twentieth century.

There are two persons to whom I owe a special debt of gratitude for this book. First, I should like to thank my wife, Nada, for patiently typing the manuscript, most of it through several drafts. Also, I am grateful to Paul M. Pridgen III, my fellow and Master of Theology student. Pridgen created the three indexes and assisted me with the proofing.

Notes

1. Arthur C. Archibald, *New Testament Evangelism: How It Works Today* (Philadelphia: The Judson Press, 1946), p. 13.

2. Both sayings are quoted by Mrs. Sam P. Jones and Walt Holcomb, *The Life and Sayings of Sam P. Jones* (Atlanta, Ga.: The Franklin-Turner Co., 1907, 2nd. rev. ed.), p. 78.

3. Morris Chalfant, "Passion: The Indispensable Ingredient," *Ministry,* Vol. 55, No. 7, July, 1982, pp. 18-19.

4. C. B. Hogue, "A Vision of Witnessing and Winning," Max Caldwell, compiler, *Witness to Win: Positive Evangelism Through the Sunday School* (Nashville: Convention Press, 1978), p. 13.

5. Herschel H. Hobbs, *New Testament Evangelism* (Nashville: Convention Press, 1960), p. 94.

Contents

Section I
The Meaning of Evangelism:
What Is It?

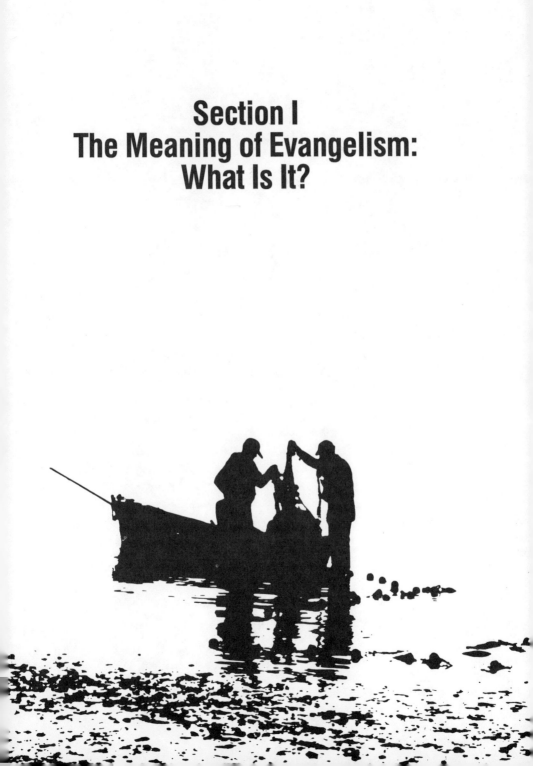

1
Biblical Clues to the Meaning of Evangelism

Genesis 12:1-3; Galatians 3:6-9

Introduction

Galatians 3:8 tells us that "the scripture . . . preached the gospel beforehand to Abraham, saying, 'in you shall all the nations be blessed.'" What a truly remarkable statement!

Some 4,000 years ago the gospel was preached to our father Abraham. That led John R. W. Stott to comment: "the Bible does not just *contain* the gospel; it *is* the gospel. Through the Bible God is himself actually evangelizing, that is, communicating the good news to the world. . . . All Scripture preaches the gospel; God evangelizes through it."[1]

Seen in that light, the Bible itself offers us a model for evangelizing. God makes himself known to us through Scripture without losing his identity. Likewise we Christians are to make God known to others without losing our identity.

Furthermore, God accommodated himself in Scripture to the languages which humans could understand. For example, the New Testament was written in *koine* Greek, the language of the common person in the first century. If we model our evangelism after that of divine revelation and inspiration through the Bible, we too shall accommodate our good news to the languages which persons can understand.

Therefore, the Bible is our best source book for understanding evangelism! I invite you to look with me at ten biblical clues to the meaning of evangelism.

The Proclamation of the Gospel

The first of these clues is that evangelism is the proclamation of the gospel. Whatever else may be said about

19

evangelism, it must be said that it has to do with the gospel. Our English word *evangelism* is in fact a transliteration, and not merely a translation, of the Greek word for *gospel.*

That close identification of the English word *evangelism* with the Greek word for *gospel* may account for a common definition of evangelism as the proclamation of the gospel. Mark 1:14-15 summarize the ministry of Jesus in terms of proclaiming the gospel of God.

What we actually have in the Greek New Testament is a cluster of words which relate etymologically to our words *evangelism, evangelize,* and *evangelist.* The first Greek word in this cluster is *euaggelion.* That noun appears some seventy-seven times in the New Testament. This is the main substantive. It is usually translated *gospel* in our English versions. A good example of this word's use is Mark 1:14-15.

The second of these Greek words is *euaggelizō,* which occurs in one form or another fifty-five times in the New Testament. This is the main verb form of the cluster. It is usually translated *proclaim* or *preach* in our English versions. An example of this word's use is Revelation 14:6.

The third of these words is the Greek *euaggelistēs.* That is another substantive of the Greek cluster and is usually translated *evangelist.* This word occurs only three times in the New Testament. Timothy is told to "do the work of an evangelist" in 2 Timothy 4:5. Ephesians 4:11 refers to the gift of "evangelists." That reference uses the plural number rather than the singular. Then, in Acts 21:8 Philip, one of the seven mentioned earlier in the Book of Acts, is called "the evangelist."

I find it suggestive that the only person whom the New Testament calls *the* evangelist was one of the seven. If the seven of Acts 6 were the first deacons, that would mean that Philip was a layman. Hence, the only person whom the Bible calls "the evangelist" was a layman.

The title of "evangelist" in our present-day language would correspond to district missionaries wrote Herschel H.

Hobbs in 1960.[2] The word is also sometimes used to refer to the writers of the four Gospels.

If we were able to literally translate these three words *euaggelion, euaggelizō,* and *euaggelistēs,* we might construct a sentence reading something like this: "The gospeler *(euaggelistēs)* gospelizes *(euaggelizō)* with the gospel *(euaggelion).*" Another possible literal translation might be: "The evangelist evangelizes with the evangel."

Some Christians insist that evangelism is simply the proclamation of the gospel. They do that on the basis of the etymology of our words *evangelism, evangelize,* and *evangelist.* Moreover, they do it because of the way the Bible uses the above cluster of Greek words.

Making Disciples

A second biblical clue to the meaning of evangelism is that it is making disciples. The Great Commission in Matthew 28:19 says, "Go therefore and make disciples of all nations." Those words "make disciples" are a translation of the Greek word *mathēteusate* which comes from the Greek word *mathēteuō,* meaning "I disciple." It appears here in the imperative mood. That accounts for the imperative "make disciples."

Some years back I used that phrase "make disciples" in a speech on evangelism. Afterwards, a lady chastised me for my language. She felt that only God could make disciples and that we should not use such language of ourselves. Yet that is the actual biblical phrase, and it is used in the Great Commission to command Christ's followers to disciple the nations. If we believe those disciples were a microcosm of the church, then the command to make disciples applies to us twentieth-century disciples also.

Again, as was the case with the word *gospel,* what we really have in this word *disciple* is a cluster of words. The Greek cluster includes such words as *mathēteuō, mathētēs,* and *mathētria.* Those words cover such English terms as *disciple, learner,* and *pupil.* The Greek verb form also carries the connotation of to teach or to instruct. That accounts for the way the King James Version translates the phrase "make disciples" (RSV) as "teach all nations."

That word *mathētria* is a female disciple. Tabitha of Joppa, for example, is called a *mathētria* in Acts 9:36. One of the clearest ways to define a disciple is to remember that he or she is the opposite of a teacher.

Jesus is the Teacher, the *didaskalos*; we are his disciples, his learners. He went about making disciples while here on earth. After his resurrection from the grave and before his ascension into heaven, he commanded his disciples to make disciples of all nations. That command has never been rescinded. It is still our mandate.

That is the reason many think of evangelism as making disciples. I seriously doubt that one can arrive at a solid biblical foundation for understanding the meaning of evangelism apart from discipleship.

Bearing Witness to Jesus Christ

A third biblical clue to the meaning of evangelism is that it is bearing witness to Jesus Christ. Another form of the Great Commission is found in Acts 1:8. That verse uses the word *witness* instead of the word *disciple* to describe the work of the disciples: "and you shall be my witnesses in Jerusalem and in all Judea and Samaria and to the end of the earth."

Again the New Testament presents us with a cluster of words, such as *witness, testimony, testify, martyr.* These are some of the English words used to translate a cluster of Greek words, such as *marturia, marturion, martureō, marturomai,* and *martus.*

Both the Gospel of John and 1 John (see especially 1 John 5:6-12) make much of the word *witness.* Seven witnesses to Jesus Christ are mentioned in John's Gospel. Five of these are found in the same chapter (ch. 5) and the other two in one chapter (ch. 15).

Jesus bore witness to himself: "I bear witness to myself" (John 5:31). While that reference is quickly passed over in John 5, John 8:13-19 makes it clear that the witness which Jesus bore to himself is corroborated by the witness of the Father and is therefore a true witness.

The Father does bear witness to the Son: "And the Father who sent me has himself borne witness to me" (John 5:37). John 5:32 is an allusion to the Father's witness: "there is another who bears witness to me, and I know that the testimony which he bears to me is true." John 8:16-19 emphasizes that the One sent is attested by the sending Father.

John the Baptist bore witness to Jesus, the Christ: "You sent to John, and he has borne witness to the truth" (John 5:33). Besides those words about the witness of John in John 5:33-36, we have the prologue of John's Gospel: "There was a man sent from God, whose name was John. He came for testimony, to bear witness to the light, that all might believe through him. He was not the light, but came to bear witness to the light" (1:6-8). Remember it was John the Baptist who said of Jesus, "Behold, the Lamb of God!" (John 1:36). What a witness he was. Well might we use him as a model for our own witness to Jesus Christ.

The works of Jesus bear witness to him: "for the works which the Father has granted me to accomplish, these very works which I am doing, bear me witness that the Father has sent me" (John 5:36). Other passages in John's Gospel which refer to the witness of Jesus' works are 10:25; 14:11; and 15:24. John 15:24 describes these works of Jesus as "the works which no one else did."

Another witness to Jesus, as stated in John 5, is the Scriptures: "You search the scriptures, because you think that in them you have eternal life; and it is they that bear witness to me" (v. 39). It is at this point that Jesus claimed Moses as one of his witnesses: "It is Moses who accuses you. . . . If you believed Moses, you would believe me, for he wrote of me" (vv. 45-46). Interestingly enough, something of this same point is made by Jesus in the story of the rich man and Lazarus. Father Abraham says, "They have Moses and the prophets; let them hear them" (Luke 16:29). Eternal life, therefore, is not in the Scriptures. Rather it is in Jesus Christ. But the Scriptures do, indeed, bear witness to the Savior of the world.

If we will move from John 5 to John 15, we can see a sixth and seventh witness to Jesus in this Fourth Gospel. The Holy Spirit bears witness to Jesus: "But when the Counselor comes, whom I send to you from the Father, even the Spirit of truth, who proceeds from the Father, he will bear witness to me" (John 15:26). John 16:7-15 enlarges upon the witness of the Holy Spirit to the Son. Jesus is reported to have said, "No one can come to me unless the Father who sent me draws him" (John 6:44). Much of the Bible teaches us that the Father draws persons to the Son through the Holy Spirit.

Finally, the apostles were witnesses to Jesus Christ: "and you also are witnesses, because you have been with me from the beginning" (John 15:27). I am struck by the way the writer of the Fourth Gospel brings his story of Jesus to a close by saying in part, "This is the disciple who is bearing witness to these things, and who has written these things; and we know that his testimony is true" (John 21:24). Insofar as you and I follow in the train of the apostles, we also will bear witness to the things which we have seen and heard and otherwise experienced about Jesus the Christ. May we not call such intentional witnessing evangelism? A careful searching out of the word *witness*, along with its cognates, will reveal much about the biblical foundation of evangelism.

Fishing for Men

A fourth biblical clue is that evangelism is fishing for persons. As Jesus was walking by the Sea of Galilee he saw Simon and Andrew, his brother, casting a net in the sea, "for they were fishermen." Jesus said to them, "Follow me and I will make you become fishers of men" (Mark 1:17). The full passage is Mark 1:16-20, and its parallel is Matthew 4:18-22. Two Greek scholars say that Jesus was "allegorically connecting their present and future vocations."[3] The call to discipleship was a call to follow Jesus and let him make them "fishers of men."

Have you ever set the call of Simon and Andrew alongside the "third" postresurrection appearance of Jesus in John 21:1-14? If we interpret that postresurrection appearance of Jesus in the light of Mark 1:16-20 and Matthew 4:18-22, it certainly has symbolical significance and also fits the allegorical connection referred to above. Peter said, "I am going fishing." Thomas, Nathanael, James, and John went fishing with Peter. That night "they caught nothing" (John 21:3). The next morning on the instruction of Jesus they caught 153 large fish. Was that incident intended as a reminder to Peter of his call to be a fisher of men rather than a fisher of fish?

Although Luke's Gospel does not have an exact parallel to the word in Mark and Matthew about fishing for persons, there is a similar word in Luke 5:1-11. Verse 10 quotes this word from Jesus to Simon, "Do not be afraid; henceforth you will be catching men." Those words were uttered immediately following a great catch of fish. The full Greek phrase is *apo tou nun anthrōpous esē zōgrōn*. Literally translated, it is: "from the now you will be catching men." The sense of the phrase is: "from now on instead of catching fish, you will be catching men."

That word translated *catching, zōgrōn,* comes from the root *zōgreo* meaning "I capture alive, or I capture for life."[4] Joseph Henry Thayer says it means "to take alive" in classical Greek. He translates the phrase from Luke 5:10 as "thou shalt catch men, i.e. by teaching thou shalt win their souls for the kingdom of God."[5]

This phrase is the basis of a book on "individual soulwinning" by Charles Gallaudet Trumbull entitled, *Taking*

Men Alive. Trumbull calls to our attention that the word *zōgreo* is used only twice in the New Testament, once in Luke 5:10 and once in 2 Timothy 2:26. Interestingly enough, Trumbull suggests that both Christ and the devil are in the business of taking men alive.[6]

The devil captures persons alive in order to destroy them; whereas Christ and his disciples catch them in order to liberate them from sin and destruction. There is no implication of trickery or deceit in the disciples catching persons alive. It may help us to recall that those fishermen whom Jesus called to catch men were catching fish with a net rather than with a hook. Therefore, Mennonite Arthur G. McPhee is correct in comparing faith sharing to net fishing rather than angling.[7]

Being the Salt of the Earth

A fifth biblical clue to the meaning of evangelism is that it is being the salt of the earth. One of the oldest written references to salt is in the Book of Job: "Can that which is tasteless be eaten without salt?" (Job 6:6a). Some think Job to be the oldest book of the Bible. If so, that may well be the oldest reference to salt in the Bible.

When we get to the New Testament, we hear Jesus saying, "You are the salt of the earth" (Matt. 5:13a). He was speaking to his disciples. Like salt they were to give taste to the earth and to create a thirst for the Water of life among people. As salt penetrates the food, preserves the meat, and flavors what we eat, so we Christians are to penetrate the earth, preserve that which is good, and give flavor to every aspect of life. Salt can heal; so can we when we are the salt of the earth.

Two other points strike me about our being salt. First, we are to be the salt of the *earth*. That corresponds to what is said later about our being the light of the *world*. We are not merely the salt of the church or of the respective communities where we happen to live. We are the salt of the earth.

That's a bit heavy, isn't it? Perhaps it implies something about the universality of our mission.

Second, we are told by our Lord that the salt can lose its taste. It can become savorless (see the remainder of Matt. 5:13). The Dead Sea has no outlets. Water flows into it but not out of it. Too much salt is concentrated in one place. We Christians are to be the salt of the earth, not merely the salt of our Jerusalem. It is possible for us to create a religious "Dead Sea."

Salt may also become savorless by lack of use, overuse, or misuse. Salt which is not used to the glory of God may become savorless through lack of use. Overuse of salt may produce burnout. Misuse of salt may destroy the health of a human body or a part of the body of Christ.

The really good news on this last point is that it is possible to recycle savorless salt. We can count on the Holy Spirit to aid us in this process. We can strive for integrity in our service of Christ. Integrity rules out the use of trickery in any form. Surely we cannot afford to say, as one preacher did, "Let's get people saved even if we have to trick them to do it."

Being the Light of the World

A sixth clue to the biblical meaning of evangelism is that it is being the light of the world. Jesus said to his disciples, "You are the light of the world" (Matt. 5:14; see also vv. 15-16). Then in another place he said of himself, "I am the light of the world" (John 9:5).

There need be no conflict between those two statements. Ambrose reminds us that the church is like the moon, which has no light of its own. Just as the moon reflects the light of the sun, so the church should reflect the light of Christ. Indeed, is not the same analogy true of the Christian? Christ is *the* light of the world. We are the light of the world only as we reflect the light of Christ which shines upon us.

The story of *Rudolph, the Red-Nosed Reindeer* helps us to understand the meaning of the Christ event. Rudolph was a rejected little reindeer whose nose would light up and shine in the darkness. Instead of remaining an outcast, he became the leader and showed the way. So it is with Jesus Christ. He is the true Light who shines in the darkness and shows others the way.

What if the Christmas carols are true? What if the candlelights do represent the Light of the world? Then, we bear witness to a Light which no government can put out. Then the candlelight of Christmas burns more brightly than the fires of Hiroshima and Nagasaki.

Few biblical metaphors, if any, yield so much gold for evangelism as those of light and darkness. "Sir, if you would put a larger bulb in your socket, we could see the way by your light." So spoke an elderly Indonesian to William Schweer, a former missionary to Indonesia. Remember it was our Lord himself who said, "Let your light so shine before men, that they may see your good works and give glory to your Father who is in heaven" (Matt. 5:16).

Paul's mission from the risen Lord used the words, "to open their eyes, that they may turn from darkness to light and from the power of Satan to God" (Acts 26:18). Paul had seen a light from heaven brighter than the noonday sun (see Acts 26:12-13). He was blinded by that light. When the scales fell from his eyes, that is to say when his eyes were opened, he was commissioned to open the eyes of others who yet lived in the land of darkness. Note also in Paul's commission how the power of Satan is connected with darkness and blindness, whereas light and open eyes are associated with God.

Furthermore, we might recall that the writer of 1 Peter expressed the mission of the new people of God, the church, in these words: "that you may declare the wonderful deeds of him who called you out of darkness into his marvelous light" (2:9*b*). Again, see how both metaphors of light and darkness are used to tell us about the church's advertising.

Like salt, one role of light is penetration. Nothing can penetrate darkness like light.

Light not only penetrates darkness but also drives darkness away. One spring morning I awakened at 5:00 AM. The birds were already singing, serenading the arrival of morning and heralding the dawn. Even the birds know how to welcome the coming of the light and the driving away of the darkness.

Light also illuminates the darkness and makes it possible to see clearly. If you want to know how dark the darkness is, expose it to the light. "For every one who does evil hates the light, and does not come to the light, lest his deeds should be exposed" (John 3:20).

Furthermore, light has a medicinal quality. It heals and purifies. Nowadays, surgeons are using concentrated laser beams to perform delicate surgery.

Therefore, whenever one seeks to define evangelism as being the light of the world, we should be able to resonate with that. It is so biblical. We are the light of the world, geographically, morally, vocationally, and spiritually.

W. Randall Lolley, president of Southeastern Baptist Theological Seminary, expressed his conversion in terms of a lamp lighting. "It was as if the Lord Christ turned on the light in my young life. What had been dark and scary now became bright and peaceful. I was aglow on the inside of my life—saved, forgiven, redeemed, died for!"[8]

Bearing Fruit that Remains

A seventh biblical clue to the meaning of evangelism is that it is bearing fruit that remains. Two verses in John 15 may be cited: "By this my Father is glorified, that you bear much fruit, and so prove to be my disciples" (v. 8). "You did not choose me, but I chose you and appointed you that you should go and bear fruit and that your fruit should abide" (v. 16).

Nature has a law which says that everything produces after its own kind. An apple tree bears apples. Pear trees bear pears. Cows bear cows. Should not Christians bear Christians?

Bob gave his testimony at a revival meeting. It went something like this:

Suppose I said I was a farmer? You might ask me, "What do you grow? Do you grow corn on your farm?"

I would say, "No, I don't grow any corn."

Then you might ask, "Well, I suppose you grow wheat then?"

"No, I don't grow any wheat."

"You grow grass then and raise cows?"

"No, I don't grow any cows."

You might finally say, "Are you sure you are a farmer?"

I might say, "Well look here at my deed. It says this is a farm. And see these papers which certify I am receiving farm subsidies from the government. Don't these items prove I am a farmer?"

My friend answers, "If you don't grow anything, I don't believe you are a farmer!"

Isn't it about the same in the Christian life? If we don't grow and produce any fruit, it is questionable whether we are really Christians, is it not? Paul expressed his desire to "have some fruit" among the Romans "even as among other Gentiles" (Rom. 1:13, KJV).

Perhaps Jesus was referring in John 15 to the role of *agape* love. Nor should we ever think that we can bear the fruit which pleases God in and of ourselves. It is even possible that the fruit of which he spoke is the fruit of the Spirit in Galatians 5:22-23. But may it not also be a reference to the fruit of the womb of the church? Isaiah 54:1 (quoted in Gal. 4:27) may be our best clue for understanding the fruit that remains.

Paul in his great love hymn told us that faith, hope, and love abide (1 Cor. 13:13). We can also be certain that those Christian disciples for whom we travail, like a woman giving birth to a child, will abide forever. Most of the fruit which we store up here on earth will perish, but that fruit which we bear in doing the will of God will forever remain. "They shall be mine, saith the Lord of hosts, in that day when I make up my jewels; and I will spare them, as a man spareth his own son that serveth him" (Mal. 3:17, KJV).

Being the Aroma of Christ

An eighth biblical clue to the meaning of evangelism is that it is being the aroma of Christ. Christians do not just live differently, act differently, speak differently, and think differently. They also smell differently. Paul said "we are the aroma of Christ" (2 Cor. 2:15).

Evangelism is bearing the fragrance of the knowledge of God everywhere (see 2 Cor. 2:14). The gospel scent which we give off through our life-styles and our lips is "a fragrance from life to life" for those who are being saved. It is by the same token "a fragrance from death to death" for those who are perishing. That is very heavy stuff. Little wonder Paul cried out, "Who is sufficient for these things?" (2 Cor. 2:16).

Next time you think of evangelism, bring to your mind the sweetest most pleasant smell you can recall. That wonderful fragrance is evangelism. You and I and the rest of Christ's disciples are the perfume which makes the world smell good. Any stinking odor which we give off, any stench which we may have, belongs to the old nature and is not a part of the new creation.

Moreover, those who prefer to perish and those who choose death over life will perceive our fragrance as death and judgment. They will not welcome our smell or want our precious perfume. It will be offensive to them. Some persons are so messed up that they can't smell properly. The Christ perfume is a name brand which doesn't set well with the powers of darkness.

The Ministry of Reconciliation

A ninth clue to the biblical meaning of evangelism is the ministry of reconciliation. The incomparable passage on reconciliation is 2 Corinthians 5:17-21. God has given to the new creation the ministry of reconciliation. He was in Christ reconciling the world to himself. He has entrusted to us the message of reconciliation. We are ambassadors for Christ. God now makes his appeal to the unreconciled through us. We are to beseech the unreconciled to make friends with God.

Wars and rumors of war, even a possible nuclear war, make *reconciliation* an apt word for evangelizing in our time. There is so much reconciliation needed between persons and God, between persons and other persons, between our split selves of Dr. Jekyl and Mr. Hyde, and between humans and nature that the biblical *shalom* seems almost impossible. Nevertheless, the faithful God who makes all things possible to his ambassadors sends us forth to reconcile the world to himself. His plan for the fullness of time is to unite all things in heaven and on earth in Christ (see Eph. 1:9-10). The Lord of history calls us to the great work of being peacemakers (see Matt. 5:9).

Advertising the Deeds of God

A tenth biblical clue to the meaning of evangelism is that it is advertising the wonderful deeds of God. First Peter 2:9-10 describes the church as the new people of God, tells us what the mission of the church is, and adds a kind of postscript which reminds us that it was through no merit of our own that we became God's people. The particular words which give us our clue for the meaning of evangelism are: "that you may declare the wonderful deeds of him who called you out of darkness into his marvelous light" (1 Pet. 2:9*b*).

This is clearly a reference to Isaiah 43:21, "the people whom I formed for myself that they might declare my praise." Much as the same titles of privilege which applied to Israel are now applied to the church in 1 Peter 2:9*a*, so the mission originally given to Israel is assigned to the church. The New Covenant people of God are to declare the wonderful deeds of God. That word "declare" is translated "shew forth" in the King James Version. It really means to advertise, to make visible, to lift up.

We are to advertise to the world what God has done through Jesus of Nazareth. Certainly those deeds would include the crucifixion and the resurrection. Perhaps they would also include the incarnation, the ascension, and the second coming. Whatever else the church may be doing, if she isn't advertising to the world what God has done through Jesus of Nazareth to liberate humanity from the darkness of sin and death, then she isn't fulfilling her mission. That advertising is evangelism.

Suggestions for Further Reading

"Biblical Background" in C. E. Autrey, *Basic Evangelism* (Grand Rapids: Zondervan Publishing House, 1959), pp. 26-39.

"The Evangel" in Michael Green, *Evangelism in the Early Church* (Grand Rapids: William B. Eerdmans Publishing Co., 1970), pp. 48-77.

John R. W. Stott, "The Biblical Basis of Evangelism," in J. D. Douglas, ed., *Let the Earth Hear His Voice* (Minneapolis: World Wide Publications, 1975), pp. 65-78.

Notes

1. John R. W. Stott, "Scripture: The Light and Heat for Evangelism," *Christianity Today,* Vol. XXV, No. 3, Feb. 6, 1981, p. 28.

2. Herschel H. Hobbs, *New Testament Evangelism* (Nashville: Convention Press, 1960), p. 3. I prefer the term *pioneer missionary* to Hobbs' "district missionary."

3. William F. Arndt and F. Wilbur Gingrich, *A Greek-English Lexicon of the New Testament and Other Early Christian Literature* (Chicago: The University of Chicago Press, 1957), p. 37.

4. Alexander Souter, *A Pocket Lexicon to the Greek New Testament* (Oxford: The Clarendon Press, 1953 ed.), p. 105.

5. Joseph Henry Thayer, *A Greek-English Lexicon of the New Testament* (New York: American Book Co., 1886), p. 273.

6. Charles Gallaudet Trumbull, *Taking Men Alive* (New York: Fleming H. Revell Co., 1938 ed.), esp. p. 29.

7. Arthur G. McPhee, *Friendship Evangelism: The Caring Way to Share Your Faith* (Grand Rapids: Zondervan Publishing House, 1978), pp. 44-49.

8. W. Randall Lolley, "Testimony," *Outlook,* Vol. XXXI, No. 1, September-October, 1981, p. 2.

2
Selected Definitions

2 Kings 7:9; Luke 5:10

Introduction

There are about as many definitions of evangelism as there are evangelists. John R. Mott in 1939 cited thirty-one different definitions in one chapter of the Tambaram Series.[1] Let us cite and interpret five representative definitions.

1918 Anglican Definition

First, look at the 1918 Anglican definition: "To evangelize is so to present Christ Jesus in the power of the Holy Spirit, that men shall come to put their trust in God through Him, to accept Him as their Saviour, and serve Him as their King in the fellowship of His Church."[2] This succinctly worded and widely quoted definition originated in 1918 through the Archbishops' Committee of Inquiry on the Evangelistic Work of the Church. It was quoted, accepted, and interpreted by the Archbishops of Canterbury and York in 1943. Canon Bryan Green built his popular 1951 volume, *The Practice of Evangelism*, upon it.[3] Some have associated this definition with Archbishop William Temple, although I cannot at this time substantiate that association.

The 1938 International Missionary Council (I.M.C.) basically adopted the Anglican definition. They did give it a more ecumenical and "churchy" twist. Also the word "King" is changed to *Lord*. Other than that, the I.M.C. definition is almost the same word for word.[4]

Surely this is one of the most beautiful and wholistic definitions of evangelism. I also think it is one of the best.

35

Bryan Green did find a certain narrowness in it. He acknowledged that it should be placed in a larger context, whereby Christ chooses to proclaim himself to the world through the "whole life" of his church "in her corporate being." That "whole life" addition led Green to differentiate between preevangelism and evangelism and between pastoral work and evangelism. He saw evangelism proper as sandwiched between preevangelism and pastoral work.[5] You will note that no such distinctions are made in the definition.

The definition came long before sexism became an issue in the church. Therefore, the word "men" is used in the generic sense. Nowadays we use the word *people*. I prefer *persons*.

"King" is a very appropriate word for British subjects to use. Here it refers to Jesus Christ as King. Most likely the way "King" is used in the definition is a reference to the kingdom of God.

There is a certain dynamism or energy in the definition: "Evangelism is so to present. . . . " That fits the word of Paul to Timothy, "do the work of an evangelist" (2 Tim. 4:5). Evangelism is work, probably some of the hardest work we shall ever do. George E. Sweazey was right when he wrote, "A church always tends to drift away from evangelism, never toward it."[6] That drifting away is due in part to the painstaking work required for success.

Note the phrase "in the power of the Holy Spirit." The better definitions of evangelism always have some reference to the role of the Holy Spirit. Evangelism is spiritual work which requires spiritual persons who have spiritual power.

I see an emphasis on education, growth, and development in the definition. It does not view evangelism as an instantaneous act but as a process. That allows us to take a systemic approach to evangelization. There is also a strong emphasis on individual responsibility.

The definition calls for us to "present Christ Jesus" and not ourselves or our theories. Paul said, "For what we preach is not ourselves, but Jesus Christ as Lord, with ourselves as your servants for Jesus' sake" (2 Cor. 4:5).

One final point to note about the definition is that it defines evangelism in terms of achieved results, which amounts to saying that the essence of evangelizing is producing converts. J. I. Packer in his book, *Evangelism & the Sovereignty of God,* criticizes that part of the definition. Packer thinks evangelism should be defined in terms of a message delivered, but not in terms of an effect produced in our hearers. He sees evangelism as our work and the giving of faith as God's.[7] So long as we are careful not to remove the intentionality of evangelism from our definitions, I have no problem with Packer's objection to defining evangelism in terms of results. Especially do I like this definition and the writings of evangelical Anglicans, such as Bryan Green, John R. W. Stott, Michael Green, David Watson, and J. I. Packer.

D. T. Niles's 1951 Definition

Another of the most widely quoted definitions of evangelism is D. T. Niles's 1951 definition: "It is one beggar telling another beggar where to get food." We usually see it in its paraphrased and more abbreviated form of "one beggar telling another beggar where to get bread."

Perhaps we can better grasp this definition by seeing it in its fuller context in Niles's book, *That They May Have Life*:

> Evangelism is witness. It is one beggar telling another beggar where to get food. The Christian does not offer out of his bounty. He has no bounty. He is simply guest at his Master's table and, as evangelist, he calls others too. The evangelistic relation is to be "alongside of" not "over against." The Christian stands alongside of the non-Christian and points to the Gospel, the holy action of God. It is not his knowledge of God that he shares, it is to God Himself that he points. The Christian Gospel is the Word become flesh. This is more than and other than the Word become speech.[8]

Niles defined evangelism in several ways in that one volume.[9] Mott had cited another of his definitions in the 1939 Tambaram Series.[10] Actually all of Niles's definitions of evangelism are more like pithy vignettes than formal attempts to define. It so happens that the one vignette which caught the ear was "one beggar telling another beggar where to get food."

My guess is that the vignette is based on 2 Kings 7 and John 6. The four leprous beggars came to the hastily abandoned Syrian camp. They found food and other precious items. After gorging themselves and hiding much of their bounty, they said to one another: "We do not well: this day is a day of good tidings, and we hold our peace: if we tarry to the morning light, some mischief will come upon us: now therefore come, that we may go and tell the king's household" (2 Kings 7:9, KJV). John 6:35 quotes Jesus as saying, "I am the bread of life; he who comes to me shall not hunger."

All persons are beggars. Some are beggars in rags. Others are beggars in velvet. Christians are also beggars in Christ. We are all hungry, hungering for that which satisfies. All persons hunger for Eden. And, as Simone Weil says, one thing you can't do is persuade a hungry soul that he is not hungry.

The difference between us Christians and all other beggars is that we have found in Christ the Bread of life. We know where the "wonder" Bread is. Christian evangelism is showing others where they can get that Bread which satisfies completely. We have some good news to share with the world's beggars. There is "wonder" Bread for the world's hunger. "O taste and see that the LORD is good!" (Ps. 34:8a).

A 1977 Church Growth Definition

Donald A. McGavran and Winfield C. Arn, in 1977, gave us a church growth definition of evangelism in their book, *Ten Steps for Church Growth*: "to proclaim Jesus Christ as

God and Savior, to persuade people to become his disciples and responsible members of his church."[11] McGavran is the father of the modern church growth movement and founding dean of the School of World Mission at Fuller Theological Seminary in Pasadena, California. Arn was one of McGavran's doctoral students and is the founder of the influential Institute for American Church Growth located in Pasadena.

There is ample evidence that this formal 1977 definition had been the operational definition of evangelism which McGavran espoused at least as far back as 1955, the date which is now used to mark the beginning of the church growth movement. The earlier church growth literature frequently used some of those very words and phrases to define church growth and mission.

Several features stand out in the definition. First, look at the high Christology in that first clause, "Jesus Christ as God and Savior." Second, see the twin emphases on "proclaim" and "persuade." Church growth leaders make much of the three *p*s in evangelism: presence, proclamation, and persuasion. Third, note the emphasis on "disciples" rather than decisions. Church growth is concerned with Great Commission evangelism and missions, such as is found in Matthew 28:18-20. Finally, note the emphasis on responsible church membership in the definition. Church growth wants to see new disciples incorporated into the church.[12]

The 1974 Lausanne Covenant Definition

The International Congress on World Evangelization was held in Lausanne, Switzerland in July of 1974. That body drew up The Lausanne Covenant, which has become one of the important documents on evangelism as we look toward the next century. The Lausanne Covenant defines evangelism in these words:

To evangelize is to spread the good news that Jesus Christ

died for our sins and was raised from the dead according to the Scriptures, and that as the reigning Lord he now offers the forgiveness of sins and the liberating gift of the Spirit to all who repent and believe. Our Christian presence in the world is indispensable to evangelism, and so is that kind of dialogue whose purpose is to listen sensitively in order to understand. But evangelism itself is the proclamation of the historical, biblical Christ as Savior and Lord, with a view to persuading people to come to him personally and so be reconciled to God. In issuing the Gospel invitation we have no liberty to conceal the cost of discipleship. Jesus still calls all who would follow him to deny themselves, take up their cross, and identify themselves with his new community. The results of evangelism include obedience to Christ, incorporation into his church and responsible service in the world.[13]

John R. W. Stott was the guiding architect behind The Lausanne Covenant. Following the congress, Stott wrote an exposition and commentary on that document, five pages of which are devoted to the nature of evangelism.[14]

I find the definition too lengthy and wordy. Stott himself says it "begins with a definition, and goes on to describe the context of evangelism, namely what must precede and follow it."[15] It does lift up the content of the gospel in a fuller way than the previous definitions at which we have looked. I see that as the most commendable feature of the definition. A part of that content is that Jesus is "the reigning Lord." That interjects the kingdom of God into the definition.

"The liberating gift of the Spirit" is language which would fit evangelism into the stream of liberation theology. The words "presence," "proclamation," and "persuading" show the pervasive influence of church growth theoreticians upon the definition. Dialogue and listening are coupled with Christian presence. Therefore, there is some recognition of the dialogical nature of evangelism.

Nevertheless, The Lausanne Covenant definition views

evangelism proper as proclamation and persuasion. Christian presence and dialogue are more in the category of preevangelism. Moreover, there is a kind of postevangelism in the definition which includes identification with and incorporation into the church and responsible service to the world. J. I. Packer must have been pleased that the heart of the Lausanne definition did not define it in terms of its results.[16]

George Hunter's 1979 Definitions

George W. Hunter gave us three definitions of evangelism in his 1979 volume, *The Contagious Congregation*:

Evangelism is what WE do to help make the Christian faith, life, and mission a live option to undiscipled people, both outside and inside the congregation.

Evangelism is also what JESUS CHRIST does through the church's *kerygma* (message), *koinonia* (fellowship), and *diakonia* (service) to set people free.

Evangelism happens when the RECEIVER (receptor, respondent) turns (1) to Christ, (2) to the Christian message and ethic, (3) to a Christian congregation, and (4) to the world, in love and mission—*in any order.*[17]

Hunter taught evangelism at the Perkins School of Theology of Southern Methodist University in Dallas, Texas, prior to becoming the executive in charge of evangelism for the United Methodist Church. He studied with D. A. McGavran and sought to apply some of the church growth concepts to evangelism.[18] His definition deliberately builds upon the church growth emphasis on disciples as over against decisions.

Hunter identifies five approaches to Christian ministry in our day, each of which is frequently called evangelism. The first approach basically says, "Let us help you." Mother Teresa is an example of this approach. Colin Williams is one writer on evangelism who supports this approach. Probably the late Dorothy Day and the Catholic Worker Movement would also belong in this category.

A second approach says, "Let God help you." Hunter places the late Kathryn Kuhlman, Oral Roberts, and Robert Schuller in this category.

A third approach says, "Hear the Word." Much radio and television ministry belong here. Hunter includes J. I. Packer and John R. W. Stott also.

A fourth approach says, "Make a decision." Most crusade evangelism belongs here. The Campus Crusade approach and Billy Graham are examples of this type of ministry.

The fifth approach says, "Become Christian disciples." The church growth movement belongs to this group. Hunter posits his definitions to incorporate the best of each of these five approaches and to correct what he considers weaknesses in each of the first four approaches. Evangelism to Hunter is more than saying: "Let us help you"; "Let God help you"; "Hear the Word"; or, "Make a decision." The heart of it is "Become Christian disciples." Only that evangelism which has as its objectives making lifetime followers of Jesus Christ and incorporating them into the church is classical, apostolic, Great Commission evangelism, according to Hunter.[19]

Note that Hunter defines evangelism in terms of what *we* do, what *Jesus Christ* does, and what the *receiver* does. This is an action definition which takes a systemic approach. Hunter also sees evangelism operating inside the congregation, as well as outside of it. That would make room for what church growth leaders call E-O evangelism, or the evangelization of lost church members. There can be no question about Hunter's commitment to church evangelism. An anonymous quotation, which A. C. Archibald passed on to us, makes the point: "Now abideth church evangelism, interchurch evangelism, and extrachurch evangelism, but the greatest of these is church evangelism."[20]

Hunter's definition sees the need for four turnings, but don't overlook his belief that these may come *in any order.* Some persons do turn to Christ after they have turned to a Christian congregation. Methodist evangelist Sam P. Jones, for example, has related how one man was converted *after* he joined a small Georgia church. Jones urged the man to join the church along with his wife. He was trying to start a new congregation on his Newberne circuit. The man told Jones he would never join the church until he got religion. Jones replied: "Would you know religion if you were to see it coming down the road?" To Jones's surprise both the man and his wife joined the church. He kept on coming, but felt something was missing.

One Saturday night Jones was visiting with this man. They got to talking about what it meant to be truly Christian. The man said he would be willing to go to work in the church if his pastor desired. He agreed to be the Sunday School director or a class leader or a steward, whatever the pastor wanted. Then, all of a sudden, like a bolt of lightning out of the blue, the gentleman said: "Glory to God, I've got it now, I've got it now!" Out there in the field, when that fellow made up his mind to serve God, the Lord graciously and gloriously saved him.[21]

Summary

We have examined seven definitions of evangelism: the 1918 Anglican definition, D. T. Niles's 1951 definition, a 1977 church growth definition, The Lausanne Covenant definition of 1974, and George Hunter's three 1979 definitions. The first of those came from the Anglican communion in England. The second came from an ecumenical leader who at one time was a district evangelist for the Methodist Church in Ceylon. Number three came from the fountainhead of the church growth movement. D. A. McGavran was for more than thirty years a third-generation missionary in India with the Disciples of Christ. Winfield C. Arn held a leadership position with the Evangelical Covenant Church prior to founding the Institute for American Church Growth. Number four bears the mark of an evangelical Anglican, John R. W. Stott. But it also is indelibly stamped by the church growth movement. The last three are from a United Methodist. Five of the seven are church growth-type definitions.

Suggestions for Further Reading

John R. Mott, compiler, "What Is Evangelism?" in *Evangelism*, Vol. 3, The Tambaram Series (London: Oxford University Press, 1939), pp. 48-62.

"Definitions of Revival and Evangelism" in Edwin B. Dozier, *Christian Evangelism: Its Principles and Techniques*, Vol. 1 (Tokyo, Japan: The Jordan Press, 1963), pp. 1-9.

"The Task of Evangelism" in Bryan Green, *The Practice of Evangelism* (New York: Charles Scribner's Sons, 1951), pp. 1-15.

"What Is Evangelism?" in David Watson, *I Believe in Evangelism* (Grand Rapids: William B. Eerdmans Publishing Co., 1976), pp. 25-39.

"Getting Our Bearings" in George E. Sweazey, *Effective Evangelism* (New York: Harper & Brothers Publishers, 1953), pp. 19-25.

Notes

1. John R. Mott, "What Is Evangelism," in *Evangelism*, Vol. 3 of The Tambaram Series (London: Oxford University Press, 1939), pp. 48-62. This is but one volume of a seven-volume series on the 1938 International Missionary Council Meeting at Tambaram, Madras, India.

2. Commission on Evangelism, Report of a Commission on Evangelism Appointed by the Archbishops of Canterbury and York Pursuant to a Resolution of the Church General Assembly Passed at the Summer Session, 1943, *Towards the Conversion of*

England (Westminster: The Press and Publications Board of the Church Assembly, 1944), p. 1.

3. Bryan Green, *The Practice of Evangelism* (New York: Charles Scribner's Sons, 1951), pp. 1 and 7.

4. *Evangelism,* p. 407.

5. Green, pp. 7-10.

6. George E. Sweazey, *Effective Evangelism* (New York: Harper & Brothers, 1953), p. 26.

7. J. I. Packer, *Evangelism & the Sovereignty of God* (Downer's Grove, Ill.: Inter-Varsity Press, 1961), pp. 37-41.

8. D. T. Niles, *That They May Have Life* (New York: Harper & Brothers Publishers, 1951), p. 96.

9. Ibid., pp. 17, 33, 51, 66, 82.

10. Mott, p. 52.

11. Donald A. McGavran and Winfield C. Arn, *Ten Steps for Church Growth* (New York: Harper & Row, Publishers, 1977), p. 51.

12. Delos Miles, *Church Growth—A Mighty River* (Nashville: Broadman Press, 1981), pp. 124-134, for a fuller account of the contributions of church growth to evangelism.

13. J. D. Douglas, ed., *Let the Earth Hear His Voice* (Minneapolis: World Wide Publications, 1975), p. 4. This is the official reference volume of papers and responses of the International Congress on World Evangelization held in Lausanne, Switzerland, July, 1974.

14. John Stott, *The Lausanne Covenant: An Exposition and Commentary* (Minneapolis: World Wide Publications, 1975), pp. 20-24.

15. Ibid., p. 20.

16. Packer, pp. 37-41.

17. George G. Hunter, III, *The Contagious Congregation* (Nashville: Abingdon, 1979), pp. 26, 28, 30-31.

18. Donald McGavran and George Hunter III, *Church Growth Strategies that Work* in the Creative Leadership Series, Lyle E. Schaller, ed. (Nashville: Abingdon, 1980).

19. Hunter, pp. 21-25.

20. Arthur C. Archibald, *New Testament Evangelism* (Philadelphia: The Judson Press, 1946), p. 8.

21. Mrs. Sam P. Jones and Walt Holcomb, *The Life and Sayings of Sam P. Jones* (Atlanta, Ga.: The Franklin-Turner Co., 1907, 2nd rev. ed.), pp. 80-81.

3
A New Definition of Evangelism

Genesis 15:5-6; Acts 16:25-34

Introduction

Evangelism is being, doing, and telling the gospel of the kingdom of God, in order that by the power of the Holy Spirit persons and structures may be converted to the lordship of Jesus Christ. That is my present definition of evangelism. It has been in process for nearly two decades. And while I am not completely satisfied with it, I am willing to live by it and to defend it.

Guidelines for a Definition

It seems to me that several guidelines should be followed by those who seek to define evangelism. First, the heart of that definition ought to be the good news about the kingdom of God. We are not called to bear witness to ourselves, but to Jesus Christ our Lord. The good news that Jesus Christ is Lord over all—over the physical universe, over history, over all the rulers of the nations, and over us all—is the essence of our message. Whatever else we may need to say about evangelism, we really have nothing more to say about it until we say it is sharing the good news that the rule of God has come, is coming, and will come through Jesus Christ.

Second, a definition of evangelism ought to be wholistic without claiming hegemony over turf which does not rightfully belong to its domain. What we want is a definition which will fit the whole person with the whole gospel of the whole Christ by the whole church in the whole world for the whole of time and eternity. Nothing more or less than that will suffice.

Third, the definition ought to make theological sense. For example, does it fit the Trinitarian experience of the biblical witness to God as Father-Creator, Son-Redeemer, and Spirit-Sanctifier? Does it make room for a doctrine of creation, as well as for a doctrine of the new creation? Does it have to do with God's kingdom or some other kingdom? Does it make allowances for what God, we, and unbelievers are, do, and say? Is it relational in its conception?

Fourth, we probably should ask ourselves of any definition: does this definition have a sharp cutting edge? Those definitions which dull the cutting edge of evangelism are suspect. Biblically based evangelism is analogous to a fine tempered sword with a sharp point and two razor-sharp cutting edges. It cuts both ways. That accounts for what persons mean when they say there is also an element of bad news in evangelism.

The good-news side of the sword of evangelism cuts to heal and bring wholeness. Shalom, peace, integration, health, joy, and safety are its goal. However, the other side— the bad-news side, if you please, cuts to announce the wrath and judgment of God upon the powers of darkness: "For the wrath of God is revealed from heaven against all ungodliness and wickedness of men who by their wickedness suppress the truth" (Rom. 1:18).

If that analogy of the sword of evangelism is too painful for you, try to soften it with "the aroma of Christ" about which Paul wrote (see 2 Cor. 2:14-16). Even so, that aroma is a fragrance from life to life among those who are being saved, but a fragrance from death to death among those who are perishing. We should make every possible effort to share our faith without being offensive. But we have no right to remove the built-in offense of the incarnation and the crucifixion.

I have sought to keep the preceding guidelines in mind while building my new definition. You may be the judge as to how well I have followed them. Now, I invite you to consider the affirmations which the definition makes about evangelism.

Evangelism Is Three Dimensional

Evangelism is three dimensional. It is being, doing, and telling the gospel. That *being* corresponds to what the Bible calls *koinonia,* the *doing* to the biblical *diakonia,* and the *telling* to the biblical *kerygma.* What we are, along with our deeds and our words, reveal the three faces of evangelism.

This part of the definition fits some of the biblical clues to the meaning of evangelism. Evangelism is being the salt of the earth, the light of the world, and the aroma of Christ. There is the being dimension. Evangelism is fishing for persons, bearing fruit that abides forever, and engaging in the ministry of reconciliation. There is the dimension of doing. Evangelism is the proclamation of the gospel, bearing witness to Jesus Christ, and advertising the wonderful deeds of God in Christ. There is the telling dimension.

Let us be very clear on this point. We evangelize through being the good news, doing the good news, and telling the good news. Making disciples is a task which always includes those three aspects of life, love, and lips. To be sure, one dimension may be in the forefront and the others in the background, depending upon the methodology utilized. Nevertheless, an evangelism with integrity will attempt to achieve a wholesome balance among being, doing, and telling. If any dimension is totally missing for long in any evangelistic method, a state of asymmetry and disproportion will occur. Effective evangelism has to be incarnated in the servant's life-style. It has to go about doing good in the name of Jesus Christ. And it has to proclaim the good news of the kingdom of God.

Evangelism Tied to the Gospel

This new definition ties evangelism to the gospel. The key clause in it is "the gospel of the kingdom of God." Later, in chapter 4, I shall more precisely define the content of the gospel. Suffice it to say here that it is the good news that God sent Jesus Christ into the world to redeem it. The King has come; if you want to be a part of his rule, you'll have to turn from your sins and believe this good news that he has ushered in a new age.

Every time we read the word *gospel,* or any other word in that family of words, we can read into it the word *evangelism* because our English word *evangelism* is built upon the Greek word *euaggelion.* Evangelism and the gospel are connected both etymologically and theologically.

The basic content of evangelism is the good news about God's government. Evangelism is God's good news for man's bad news.

An interesting implication to tying evangelism to the gospel may be that the parameters of evangelism are synonymous with those of the gospel. Wherever the gospel begins, there evangelism begins. By the same token, wherever the gospel ends, there evangelism ends. If we tie up evangelism with the gospel, we shall better understand its limits.

A Kingdom-of-God Enterprise

This new definition sees evangelism as a kingdom-of-God enterprise. Perhaps the heaviest phrase in it is "the kingdom of God," and that is a part of the foundational clause, "the gospel of the kingdom of God." Later, toward the end of the definition, "the lordship of Jesus Christ" is also a euphemism for the kingdom of God. Herschel H. Hobbs contends that only in the light of the lordship of Jesus Christ "can first-century evangelism be understood, or twentieth-century evangelism be effective."[1] I wholeheartedly agree.

C. S. Lewis saw our world as "enemy occupied territory." Satan is the god of this world. Evangelism, seen in that light and in the light of the kingdom of God, is bruising the head of that old serpent, the devil. It is wresting territory from a pretender and usurper and restoring it to its rightful Owner and Sovereign.

Evangelism is in some ways a counterculture movement. While it does not always change one's status and position, it does transform relationships and attitudes. Luke described the early Christian messengers as those who turned the world upside down (see Acts 17:6). The gospel went contrary to some customs of Jews, Romans, and Greeks (see Acts 16:20-21).

The goal of evangelism is the kingdom of God:

> Thy kingdom come,
> Thy will be done,
> On earth as it is in heaven (Matt. 6:10).

Those words from the Model Prayer articulate that goal. It follows then that evangelism at its best is both *extensive* and *intensive*. It extends outward to all persons and peoples and places. But simultaneously, it intends to touch and transform all facets of human experience and to bring all of life under the lordship of Jesus Christ. That is what has been called respectively evangelism-in-depth and in-depth evangelism.

Dependent Upon the Holy Spirit

Evangelism is dependent upon the power of the Holy Spirit. The phrase, "by the power of the Holy Spirit," points to that dependency. Evangelism is spiritual work by spiritual persons who have spiritual power. George W. Peters was aiming in the right direction when he said: "Spiritual work can be accomplished only by the Holy Spirit."[2] Ultimately, that is certainly so.

The greatest need we have in our evangelism is the power of the Holy Spirit in its programs and strategy. Perhaps we do need some new programs, but most certainly we need a new spirit—the Holy Spirit.

Some of us are majoring on mechanics and minoring on dynamics in our evangelism. The chief dynamic of evangelism is the Holy Spirit. If we are going to major on either of these, it ought to be on dynamics. If our dynamics are strong enough, they can be counted on to create whatever mechanics are necessary.

The Holy Spirit opens doors for evangelization. He opened the prison doors for the apostles in Acts 5:19. He opened the door of the Ethiopian eunuch's heart in Acts 8. He opened the door of the continent of Europe to the gospel (Acts 13:2; 16:6 *ff.*). We can be sure that he is still opening doors today.

Seeks to Convert

The intention of evangelism is to convert persons and structures to the lordship of Jesus Christ. That fits the last part of the new definition. The evangelist is a change agent, dealing first and foremost with that change called repentance. The most profound change any person can ever experience is biblical repentance. Conversion is a fundamental change in persons (see Matt. 12:33). It is a cleansing from the inside out (see Matt. 23:26). Our agenda is not hidden. We are out to change the minds and hearts of persons. We also seek to change the attitudes and actions of individuals.

Evangelism seeks to make new persons. It has to do with the new person and the new creation, which begins with the new birth. The business of evangelism is to convert tadpoles into bullfrogs and caterpillars into butterflies. I understand one musical star who converted to the Christian faith has a song about tadpoles becoming bullfrogs and caterpillars becoming butterflies. That is what conversion is like. Every bullfrog used to be a tadpole. He once looked more like a minnow than a frog. But gradually he began to change from the form of a fish into the form of a frog.

Every butterfly used to be a caterpillar. She was once a worm crawling around on leaves. Now, she has undergone a miraculous metamorphosis and become a beautiful, fluttering butterfly. What liberation! What a marvelous transformation.

A word of caution is needed here. Evangelism does not seek to convert persons merely through a once-for-all experience. There is a definite turning in conversion. But salvation in the Bible is more of a process than a once-for-all experience. Sin is ever present; therefore, there must be a continuous turning away from sin. Repentance is always needed. The Christian life is, in fact, a constant turning away from sin and setting our face toward God. That turning from sin we call repentance. That setting our face toward God we call faith.

Evangelism also seeks to convert structures to the lordship of Jesus Christ. Certainly the family structure needs to be converted. The family, we should remember, is a pre-fall divine institution. Its salvation should always concern us. The New Testament refers to whole families, or complete households, becoming Christians. If it is good to convert one member of a family to Christ, it is even better to convert the whole family. That way provides a support system for the believers in the family.

Apart from that, we need a definition of evangelism which fits the whole world and the whole church. Most of the world and much of the church is more conscious of the corporate nature of life than we are in our highly individualized Western culture. Evangelism seeks to convert the nuclear family, the extended family, the tribe, the caste, the clan, and all the ethnic groupings of humanity. The church has also grown through people movements and group conversion (see Acts 9:35). Western individualism may not be the highest norm or the absolute ideal. Some think household evangelism to be a higher norm in the New Testament than Western individualism.[3] That is a part of what I mean by the conversion of structures.

Another structure which I believe continuously needs to be converted to the lordship of Jesus Christ is the church itself as an institution. The Protestant principle says the church is always in need of reformation. Many of the churches I know need more than reformation. They need transformation and conversion. One well-known missiologist put it this way:

> The New Testament . . . demands the "Conversion" of the church. Such conversion is not an easy matter, yet a mental and practical conversion from being introverted to becoming extroverted must take place if the church is to grow. The church must be turned inside out if it is to turn the world upside down. Outreach must characterize the church that would fulfill the Great Commission whether that is in Jerusalem and in Judea or in the uttermost part of the earth.[4]

The polarity of converting souls or structures is an illusion. It is unreal. And *if* there is a polarity, the poles should be seen in terms of a tuning fork. The poles of a tuning fork vibrate each other. Each pole of the fork acts as a complementary opposite, and only in this sense are they polar opposites.

Let me bring all of this to a head by quoting and interacting with two outstanding world Christian leaders. "To truncate the Christian mission simply to the changing of social structures," said Carl F. H. Henry, "profoundly misunderstands the biblical view of human nature and divine redemption."[5] I heartily agree. If that kind of reductionism does happen, we could lose sight of the individual persons for whom all social structures exist. Nevertheless, I should argue just as strongly that to truncate the Christian mission simply to the changing of individual persons profoundly misunderstands the biblical view of sin and of the demonic powers and principalities, as well as the biblical view of the kingdom of God.

Our Western models of evangelism tend to truncate the gospel and divide the needs of persons into social and spiritual. I agree with Stanley Mooneyham of World Vision International: "When we stop treating people as if they were souls without bodies, and when we start treating the gospel as the instrument for holistic redemption and change, our message will gain a new, powerful credibility."[6]

Recapitulation

To recapitulate, I have defined evangelism as being, doing, and telling the gospel of the kingdom of God in order that, by the power of the Holy Spirit, persons and structures may be converted to the lordship of Jesus Christ. I have also suggested four guidelines to follow in defining evangelism. These are: first, the heart of that definition ought to be the good news about the kingdom of God; second, a definition of evangelism ought to be wholistic without claiming hegemony over turf which does not rightfully belong to it; third, the definition ought to make theological sense; and, fourth, we probably should ask ourselves of any definition: does this definition have a sharp cutting edge?

Next, I lifted up five affirmations which are made by the new definition: (1) evangelism is three dimensional; (2) evangelism is tied closely to the gospel; (3) evangelism is a kingdom of God enterprise; (4) evangelism is dependent upon the power of the Holy Spirit; and, (5) evangelism seeks to convert persons and structures to the lordship of Jesus Christ.

Suggestions for Further Reading

"The Necessity of Conversion" in Bryan Green, *The Practice of Evangelism* (New York: Charles Scribner's Sons, 1951), pp. 16-42.

"Evangelism Is Essential in Kingdom Building and Christian Living" in Roland Q. Leavell, *Evangelism: Christ's Imperative Commission* (Nashville: Broadman Press, 1979 rev. ed.), pp. 40-54.

David H. C. Read, *Go & Make Disciples* (Nashville: Abingdon, 1978), pp. 1-69.

"What's Evangelical about Evangelism?" in Ralph W. Quere, *Evangelical Witness: The Message, Medium, Mission and Method of Evangelism* (Minneapolis: Augsburg Publishing House, 1975), pp. 11-24.

Notes

1. Herschel H. Hobbs, *New Testament Evangelism* (Nashville: Convention Press, 1960), p. 78.
2. George W. Peters, *A Theology of Church Growth* (Grand Rapids, Michigan: Zondervan Publishing House, 1981), p. 89.
3. Ibid., p. 234.
4. Ibid., pp. 210 and 212.
5. Carl F. H. Henry, "American Evangelicals in a Turning Time," *The Christian Century,* Vol. XCVII, No. 35, Nov. 5, 1980, p. 1062.
6. W. Stanley Mooneyham, "Getting More Hooks in the Water Is Not Enough: World Evangelization Requires the Right Tackle," *Christianity Today,* Vol. XXV, No. 16, Sept. 18, 1981, p. 20.

Section II
The Message of Evangelism:
What Should We Share?

4
The Gospel

Isaiah 53:4-6; 1 Corinthians 15:1-11

Introduction

This division centers around the *message* of evangelism. It addresses the question, What should we share? The big point I want to make in answer to that question is that we are to share the gospel. That is our message. But what is the gospel?

Gabriel Fackre of Andover Newton Theological Seminary says that Christians today have two things in common with the church at the end of the apostolic age. There is "on the one hand, a major mobilization for mission, and, on the other hand, a lack of clarity about the content of the gospel."[1]

Some of you may be able to identify with the pastor who said in desperation: "We don't need more evangelists, or techniques for evangelism. We need to know the evangel."[2] What is *the* story, *the* good news, *the* way, *the* Word?

Good News

Etymologically speaking, the gospel is the good news. Our English word *gospel* comes from the two Greek root words *eu* and *aggelia,* meaning literally well (or good) message. Hence, the gospel is good news. Albert Outler of Southern Methodist University's Perkins School of Theology catches the gist of the gospel when he defines evangelism as "God's good news for man's bad news."

The gospel is good news. Robert G. Bratcher called his translation of the New Testament, *Good News for Modern*

59

Man. He wrote it on about a fourth-grade level. The gospel is good news, good news for all persons and for every person everywhere: good news for the poor; good news for the rich; good news for the illiterate; good news for the intelligentsia, good news for the captives; good news for the blind; good news for the prisoners; good news for the slaves; and good news for the masters. "So if the Son make you free, you will be free indeed" (John 8:36).

The gospel is the good news that the power of God is made perfect in the weakness of persons. That power which raised Jesus from the dead will liberate the poor and oppressed of this world from their bondage to the evil one.

Good news can lift us up much as bad news can weight us down. The gospel is the best news we shall ever hear or share. It lifts persons up out of the very pit of hell. Such good news is the Jesus story that it can raise from the dead those who are dead in trespasses and in sins. This good news about the kingdom of God so uplifts us that it puts us into the orbit of God.

A Word

Etymologically the gospel is good news. But the gospel in a word is Jesus Christ. Apparently, the oldest creed of the church was, "Jesus is Lord" (1 Cor. 12:3; see Phil. 2:11).

The gospel is the Christ story. The next time you hear the words "the Gospel of Matthew," translate that into "the Christ Story by Matthew." The same is true of each of the four Gospels. "The story of Christ is . . . not the greatest story ever told, but the only story ever told. It is the story from which all other stories receive their meaning and significance," wrote Henri Nouwen. "The story of Christ makes history real."[3]

What is the gospel? Is it not in the final analysis Christ himself? Some have strange notions that the gospel is their view of the atonement or their view of the Bible or even their view of Jesus Christ. No! While the gospel may be related to

all of these, it is synonymous with none of them. "I teach . . .
that *Christ Himself Is His Gospel*," said A. C. Archibald. "And
by Christ himself I mean all he is in his person and all he is
in his works."[4]

If the gospel were a particular view of this doctrine or
that one, we could reduce it to a creed, encompass it into a
formal statement, or lay it out into a neat set of propositional
truths. However, we must remember that the Word became
flesh and not merely a word or words. Such reductionism
runs a grave risk of turning faith into mere credulity or
mental assent.

One is saved by trusting in the living Lord Jesus, by
attaching oneself in obedience to the person of Christ. Faith,
in order to be saving faith, must move beyond mental assent
to trust in the person whom we call the Lord Jesus Christ. If
we believe in the right person, he will in due time give us the
right feeling, the right doctrine, and the right conduct.
Again, the gospel in a word is Jesus Christ.

A Sentence

The gospel is the good news about Jesus Christ. If we
wanted to summarize the gospel in a biblical sentence, that
sentence might be: "God was in Christ, reconciling the world
unto himself" (2 Cor. 5:19, KJV).

Gabriel Fackre gives some content to the gospel when
he says of Christ, "He brings forgiveness for our sins, but
more; he liberates from oppression, but more; he brings
knowledge and light to our night, but more; he conquers
our last enemy, death." In short, it "is nothing less than to say
He is Lord and Savior."[5]

A Paragraph

The gospel, therefore, is the good news that God was in
Christ reconciling the world unto himself. If you want it in a
biblical paragraph, let me suggest 1 Corinthians 15:3-5. The
gospel which Paul delivered was "that Christ died for our

sins in accordance with the scriptures, that he was buried, that he was raised on the third day in accordance with the scriptures, and that he appeared to Cephas, then to the twelve." That one paragraph refers to Christ's death, burial, resurrection, and two of his postresurrection appearances.

Paul emphasized that the gospel which he preached was that same gospel which he had received. There can be only *one* gospel. Any different gospel than that received through the apostles is not another gospel. Instead, it is a perversion which merits a curse upon those who preach it. The true gospel is no man's gospel. It is a revelation of Jesus Christ. It is the gospel of God (see Gal. 1:6-12). This one gospel is in fact the old gospel which was preached beforehand to Abraham saying, "In you shall all the nations be blessed" (Gal. 3:8; see Gen. 12:3).

Negatively speaking, the gospel is not the gospel of circumcision which the Judaizers proclaimed, "Unless you are circumcised according to the custom of Moses, you cannot be saved" (Acts 15:1). That's what the Jerusalem conference in Acts 15 was all about. Paul refused to glory in anything except the cross of Christ. To him, neither circumcision nor uncircumcision counted anything; only the new creation mattered (see Gal. 6:14-15). Those who add works, even religious works, to the gospel today are to be opposed as vigorously as Paul did the Judaizers.

Evidently there were several attempts to pervert the gospel in the apostolic age. Gnostic heretics, or their forerunners, apparently denied the reality of Christ's humanity. Hence, the writer of 1 John said, "every spirit which confesses that Jesus Christ has come in the flesh is of God" (1 John 4:2). The three witnesses who agreed: the Spirit, the water, and the blood, also contradicted the incipient Gnostic heresy (see 1 John 5:6-8).

The Thessalonian letters may have been written to counter a misunderstanding about the second coming of Christ (see 2 Thess. 2:1-12). First Corinthians 15 was written to correct those who denied the bodily resurrection and who may have substituted the immortality of the soul for the resurrection of the body (see 1 Cor. 15:12-58). "In greater or lesser degree," said Herschel H. Hobbs, "every epistle in the New Testament was designed toward keeping the gospel pure."[6]

A Book

If you want the gospel in a biblical book, you will find it in either, or all, of the four Gospels—Matthew, Mark, Luke, and John. Each of the four evangelists, as they are sometimes called, gave us the gospel in an inspired book.

You will note as you read the Gospels that each is different, although there are many similarities in them. Their central figure is Jesus Christ. They tell about his birth, life, ministry, teachings, death, and resurrection. In short, they recount God's mighty deeds through Jesus of Nazareth for the salvation of humankind and the world. Their evangelistic intent is most clearly articulated by John's Gospel: "these are written that you may believe that Jesus is the Christ, the Son of God, and that believing you may have life in his name" (John 20:31).

These four Gospels are not biographies of Jesus, as we customarily use that term, so much as they are evangelistic autobiographies and biographies of faith. The witness of the Gospel writers itself becomes a part of their good news. The authors wrote from a faith stance and most likely represented communities of faith in the apostolic and early church. Accordingly, both their content and style are laden with theological meaning.

I used to think Paul was the great intellectual of the New Testament. For some reason, I tended to pit him against the "simple" writers of the four Gospels. My professors opened my eyes to see that the writers of the four Gospels were intellectual giants and every bit as sophisticated as Paul.

That moves me to the point of saying that those who want the gospel in a book may also discover it in the Book of Romans. Paul wrote to the church at Rome: "For I am not ashamed of the gospel; it is the power of God for salvation to every one who has faith, to the Jew first and also to the Greek. For in it the righteousness of God is revealed through faith for faith; as it is written, 'He who through faith is righteous shall live'" (1:16-17).

The following outline of Romans, which has spoken to me through the years, shows how the book unveils the gospel:

- What is the gospel? (1:1-17)
- Why do persons need salvation? (1:18 to 3:20)
- How then are persons saved? (3:21 to 4:25)
- What are the benefits of salvation? (chs. 5—8)
- But what of those who refuse this gospel? (chs. 9—11)
- What shall be the daily life of those saved by faith? (chs. 12—15)[7]

The Kerygma

Another place to see the gospel is in the preaching, or the kerygma, of the apostolic church. If you analyze the sermons and speeches in the Book of Acts, you may notice that they tend to follow about the same outline. Most of them gather around the incarnation, crucifixion, resurrection, ascension, and second coming of Christ. There may also be a reference to the outpouring of the Holy Spirit.

Look with me, for example, at the following summary of the gospel in Acts 2:22-24, "Jesus of Nazareth, a man attested to you by God with mighty works and wonders and signs . . . this Jesus, delivered up according to the definite plan and foreknowledge of God, you crucified and killed by the hands of lawless men. But God raised him up." So preached Peter at Pentecost.

"Is there any better summation of the gospel than that?"

asked Herschel H. Hobbs. We see in them the humanity of Jesus, God's approval, Jesus' power, humanity's wickedness, God's redemptive purpose, Jesus' death and resurrection, and God's judgment upon sin and death. Moreover, we may add to these God's promise of Jesus' ultimate victory at his second advent (Acts 2:34-35); and the lordship and savior-hood of Christ (Acts 2:36).[8]

A Creed

Finally, if you want the gospel in a creed, you may find it in the second article of the Apostles' Creed. That is the oldest creed of the church outside the Bible.

Some of you may feel about creeds like Sam P. Jones, an itinerant Methodist evangelist of the late nineteenth and early twentieth century. Jones never wasted much time on creeds. He would say: "It is the skin of the truth, dried and stuffed with sand and sawdust. If I had a creed, I would sell it to a museum."[9]

Nevertheless, article 2 of the Apostles' Creed succinctly sums up the content of the gospel which we preach and teach. This is an early and worthy effort to verbalize the good news about Jesus Christ which is at the heart of our evangelistic message.

Ponder these words:

> And in Jesus Christ his only Son our Lord:
> Who was conceived by the Holy Ghost,
> Born of the Virgin Mary:
> Suffered under Pontius Pilate,
> Was crucified, dead, and buried:
> He descended into hell;
> The third day he rose again from the dead:
> He ascended into heaven,
> And sitteth on the right hand of
> God the Father Almighty:
> From thence he shall come to judge
>   the quick and the dead.

Summary and Conclusion

I have sought to suggest that the message of evangelism is the gospel. Seven answers have been offered to the question, What is the gospel? The gospel is the good news. It is in a word, Jesus Christ; in a sentence, "God was in Christ, reconciling the world unto himself" (2 Cor. 5:19, KJV); in a paragraph, 1 Corinthians 15:3-5; in a book, one of the four Gospels or the Book of Romans; in the kerygma of the early church, Acts 2:22-24; and in a creed, the second article of the Apostles' Creed.

Jesus said, "I will give you the keys of the kingdom of heaven" (Matt. 16:19). Those keys are the gospel by which the gates of heaven are to be opened or kept shut to the human race. Our binding or loosing the gospel determines to a great extent who is saved and who is lost. What an awesome thought![10]

Therefore, preach the gospel. It will win when everything else fails. When we preach the gospel, we have a monopoly. If we preach it faithfully, we shall succeed.

Suggestions for Further Reading

"What Is the Evangel?" in Ralph W. Quere, *Evangelical Witness* (Minneapolis: Augsburg, 1975), pp. 25-43.

"Proclaiming the Incarnation" in James S. Stewart, *A Faith to Proclaim* (New York: Charles Scribner's Sons, 1953), pp. 11-47.

"Mission and the Message" in Clifford Christians, Earl J. Schipper, and Wesley Smedes, eds., *Who in the World?* (Grand Rapids: Wm. B. Eerdmans Publishing Co., 1972), pp. 15-36.

Notes

1. John Rodman, "Old-Line Churches Rally to Evangelism Banner Again," *Christianity Today*, Vol. XXVI, No. 7, April 24, 1981, p. 41.

2. Quoted by William H. Willimon, "What I Learned at School," *The Christian Century,* Vol. XCVIII, No. 23, July 15-22, 1981, p. 738.

3. Henri Nouwen, "A Self-Emptied Heart," *Sojourners,* Vol. 10, No. 8, August, 1981, p. 20.

4. Arthur C. Archibald, *New Testament Evangelism: How It Works Today* (Philadelphia: The Judson Press, 1946), p. 88. Italics and caps are Archibald's.

5. Quoted by John Rodman, p. 41.

6. Herschel H. Hobbs, *New Testament Evangelism* (Nashville: Convention Press, 1960), p. 82.

7. This is an adaptation from Chester Warren Quimby, *Paul for Everyone* (New York: The Macmillan Co., 1944 ed.), pp. 114-138.

8. Hobbs, p. 82.

9. Mrs. Sam P. Jones and Walt Holcomb, *The Life and Sayings of Sam P. Jones* (Atlanta, Ga.: The Franklin-Turner Co., 1907, 2nd rev. ed.), p. 86.

10. Hobbs, p. 74.

5
The Gospel of the Kingdom of God

Psalm 145:10-13; Mark 1:14-15

Introduction

Earlier I sought to define the gospel message which we are commissioned to bear in our evangelization. We defined the gospel in terms of its etymology and in a word, a sentence, a paragraph, a book, a creed and the kerygma of the early church. Now I should like to further circumscribe the gospel message by emphasizing that it is the gospel of the kingdom of God which we are called to share.

Jesus began his ministry with a proclamation of the kingdom of God: "Jesus came into Galilee, preaching the gospel of God, and saying, 'The time is fulfilled, and the kingdom of God is at hand; repent, and believe in the gospel'" (Mark 1:14-15). We now need to examine the phrase "the kingdom of God" to see how it gives content and context to the gospel message we proclaim.

The Kingdom of God

The kingdom of God is God's government. One of the best biblical clues to its meaning is the so-called Lord's Prayer in Matthew 6:9-13. The kingdom of God is the will of God being done on earth as in heaven (Matt. 6:10). It is the power and the glory of God (Matt. 6:13). The first article of the Apostles' Creed points to it: "I believe in God the Father Almighty, maker of heaven and earth." Isaac Rottenberg is right: "The kingdom of God is the power of the new age entering our world and transforming it according to God's plan for the fullness of time."[1]

69

The idea of God's reign is found in the Old Testament. However, only twice in the Psalms is the word *kingdom* used of God's kingdom (see Pss. 103:19; 145:10-13). "Life" and "eternal life" become euphemisms for the kingdom in John's Gospel. John did use the phrase a couple of times in John 3. The phrase "the kingdom of heaven" is preferred by Matthew because of the Jewish reluctance to pronounce the divine name. Therefore, A. B. Bruce is wrong when he takes "the kingdom of heaven" to mean a *spiritual* kingdom.[2] The three Synoptic Gospel writers were fond of the term.

Paul made a couple of references to it, particularly in 1 Corinthians 4:20 and Romans 14:17. So did Peter and the writer of Revelation. Perhaps we should also point out that the reference to the kingdom of God in Luke 17:21 can be either translated "within you" (KJV) or "in the midst of you" (RSV). Either is grammatically correct.

Martin Butzer noted that there are three biblical terms for kingdom: the kingdom of God, the kingdom of his beloved Son, and the kingdom of heaven.[3] H. Richard Niebuhr in 1937 documented how the idea of the kingdom of God has been the dominant idea in American Christianity. However, Niebuhr says that idea of the kingdom has not always meant the same thing:

> In the early period of American life, when foundations were laid on which we have all had to build, "kingdom of God" meant "sovereignty of God"; in the creative period of awakening and revival it meant "reign of Christ"; and only in the most recent period had it come to mean "kingdom on earth."[4]

Wolfhart Pannenberg tells us that in German theology "from Kant and Schleirmacher through Richard Rothe and Ritschl, there was no disputing the centrality of the kingdom to the Christian message."[5] There can be no doubt but that Herman Ridderbos is correct when he observes that the kingdom of God is the central theme of Jesus' message. We see this centrality of the kingdom even in the "recapitulatory" passages of the Synoptics, such as Mark 1:14-15, as well as in the narrative passages.[6] One can never hope to understand the miracles or the parables of Jesus apart from some comprehension of the kingdom of God. Most of the miracles of Jesus were signs pointing to the presence and reality of the kingdom of God in his own life and ministry. Most of the parables are stories about the kingdom of God.

Paul Minear outlines seven requisites for understanding the kingdom of God: (1) this reality is the kingdom *of God*. The King defines the kingdom; (2) it is to be understood through its continuing warfare with an enemy kingdom; (3) it is to be apprehended as a new age, a time of fulfillment which terminates a former age and imparts a new sense of duration; (4) it is a realm which a person enters by a new birth; (5) the kingdom of God is inseparable from his glory and power; (6) it will be realized only through the communion of saints, the fellowship of those who inherit it; (7) love is the key to understanding it. It is "the kingdom of the Son of his love" (ASV).[7]

Rottenberg finds five paradoxes of the kingdom and reminds us that the category of paradox is useful in understanding the dimensions of the kingdom of God. First, the kingdom of God is not of this world, yet it is very much related to this world (John 18:36; 17:15). Second, it comes as a gift, but it does not come cheaply (Luke 12:30-33; Mark 1:15; 2 Pet. 3:13-14). Third, the kingdom does not consist in talk, yet it is imperative that it be proclaimed (1 Cor. 4:20; Luke 4:43). Fourth, the kingdom doesn't mean food and drink, yet it can be compared to a wedding banquet (Rom 14:17; Matt. 22:1-14). Fifth, the kingdom is both hidden and manifested, both future and present (Mark 13:21; Luke 17:20).[8]

I shall let Paul Minear gather up much of what has been said about the kingdom of God in a paragraph which I treasure above all others on the subject outside the Bible:

. . . the term "kingdom" represents an analogy between

visible and invisible realities. Like human empires, God's Kingdom is a sphere for the operation of power, authority, and glory, a sphere where citizens obey and adore and fear their sovereign. Yet God's Kingdom is "other" than human empires. It cannot like them be touched or shaken or destroyed (Heb. 12:18-24). It cannot be located or dated by an external boundary: "Lo, here it is!" It represents none of the lines of time or space that men draw on their maps. It is the city of the invisible God, a city that can never grow old or corrupt. No census may be taken of its population, nor may its citizenry be purged by antisedition legislation. Knowledge of its walls and doors, its streets and its buildings may be gained only by knowing the purpose and character of its ruler. And this knowledge only the king can convey. Men who seek to enter may enter by the door which the king has opened, a door through visible historical experiences into the realm beyond the veil. Men are bound to misunderstand this reality so long as they construct diagrams of God's kingdom by projecting into infinity the arc of earthly measurements.[9]

Implications for Evangelism

If the message of evangelism is the gospel of the kingdom of God as I have sought to argue, then that has some weighty implications for evangelizing. Surely one implication is that the kingdom of God is the goal of evangelism. Our ultimate goal is not institutional church growth, as important as that is. Our goal is not to build *our* kingdom or *my* kingdom or *your* kingdom. Rather, our goal is to proclaim the gospel of the kingdom of God through word and deed, through our life-styles and our lips, in order that by the power of the Holy Spirit persons and structures may be converted to the lordship of Jesus Christ. Put more biblically, our goal is to disciple *panta ta ethnē* (all the nations) under the authority *(exousia)* of Jesus Christ (Matt. 28:16-20).

Our goal is to "declare the wonderful deeds of him who called" us "out of darkness into his marvelous light" (1 Pet.

2:9). Our goal is to open blind eyes, to turn persons "from darkness to light and from the power of Satan to God, that they may receive forgiveness of sins and a place among those who are sanctified by faith" in the risen Christ (Acts 26:18). In short, our goal is to be the body of Christ (Eph. 1:22-23). We are through the power of the Holy Spirit to seek to imitate Jesus Christ (John 20:21-23).

Another implication, which is closely related to and really grows out of this first one, is that we need to be careful not to reduce the kingdom of God to our brand of church or to any ecclesiology. Landmarkers are not the only Christians who confuse the church with the kingdom of God. Communal Christians, such as the Sojourners in Washington, D.C., tend to identify their society or coalition with the kingdom. A pastor of the Sojourners Fellowship and a tenant organizer, writes: "My growing understanding of the church is the foundation for my theology." Perkins continues, "When Jesus spoke of the kingdom of God being at hand, he was speaking of a new social reality that was manifesting itself in the world."[10]

When one begins theology with ecclesiology, one runs the risk of reducing God's kingdom to the "new social reality" of the church. That is just one step away from identifying the kingdom of God with our particular brand of church. Such theological reductionism can lead to a sect-type mentality. The task of evangelizing the world is so mammoth that no one group which thinks of itself as God's favorites can possibly succeed alone.

Pannenberg suggests that the kingdom of God reminds us of the *provisional* character of all ecclesiastical organizations. "The doctrine of the Church," says Pannenberg, "begins not with the Church but with the Kingdom of God."[11]

A third implication of the kingdom for evangelization is that God's rule is not only the goal of evangelism and of the church but it is also God's goal for human society and for the world. The existence and being of God cannot be conceived apart from his rule. Luther explained the first article of the Apostles' Creed by saying only that God is who can create heaven and earth. "Far from creation being at one end of the time spectrum and eschatology at the other," wrote Pannenberg, "creation and eschatology are partners in the creation of reality."[12] Perhaps those who hold to such a kingdom theology cannot be too hasty in pitting society against the kingdom.

Obviously God's goal has not yet been fully realized. There are some signs of the presence of his kingdom. But the "not yet" character of his rule is ever before our faces. Through the incarnation, crucifixion, resurrection, and ascension of the Christ, God has already won the war against the evil powers and principalities. Through the second coming, his victory will be manifested to all. Until then, we are engaged with him in the lesser battles which constitute a mopping-up operation.

A fourth implication has to do with conversion. I believe evangelism has an intentional aspect to it which seeks to convert persons and structures to the rule of God. Suppose Orlando Costas is right when he says: "Christian conversion is a journey into the mystery of the kingdom of God, which leads from one experience to another."[13] If conversion is a kingdom journey, an Abrahamic adventure, a process, then a *spiral* model may represent it more accurately than the traditional *concentric* model.[14] Conversion, seen from such a kingdom journey perspective, becomes not just one "Passover experience" but a whole long series of "Passover experiences." What we know about conversion experiences, communications theory, and the kingdom of God would seem to suggest that a spiral model of conversion makes better sense than a concentric model in our kind of world.

A fifth and final implication which I see is that ultimately the message of evangelism is *person* centered rather than *message* centered. Let me explain. Jesus preached the kingdom of God. But, more than that, Jesus embodied the kingdom. As Origen said, Jesus was *autobasileia,* the central expression of the kingdom of God. He was and is the King of the kingdom. Rottenberg expresses it this way: "He came not so much to preach the gospel, but that there might be a gospel to preach."[15]

Conclusion

The gospel message is, therefore, first and foremost a person—the person of Jesus Christ. The Christian does not represent Wall Street or the Kremlin, Karl Marx, or Carl Rogers. He represents Jesus Christ, the Lord of lords and the King of kings.

The gospel of the kingdom of God is not synonymous with the gospel of Madison Avenue. Membership in the kingdom of God isn't like membership in the health spa. You don't join up and get two or three for the price of one. Just because your mother is a Christian doesn't make you one. Unless one is born again one can't even see the kingdom of God, let alone become a citizen of it (see John 3:3,5).

Suggestions for Further Reading

Carl F. H. Henry, *The Uneasy Conscience of Modern Fundamentalism* (Grand Rapids: Wm. B. Eerdmans Publishing Co., 1947).

Isaac C. Rottenberg, *The Promise and the Presence: Toward a Theology of the Kingdom of God* (Grand Rapids: William B. Eerdmans Publishing Co., 1980).

"What Is the Kingdom of God?" in George Eldon Ladd, *The Gospel of the Kingdom* (Grand Rapids: William B. Eerdmans Publishing Co., 1959), pp. 13-23.

"Have the Problems about the Kingdom of God Been Solved?"

in George Eldon Ladd, *Crucial Questions about the Kingdom of God* (Grand Rapids: William B. Eerdmans Publishing Co., 1952), pp. 21-39.

J. Andrew Kirk, "The Kingdom of God and the Church in Contemporary Protestantism and Catholicism," in J. D. Douglas, ed., *Let the Earth Hear His Voice* (Minneapolis: World Wide Publications, 1975), pp. 1071-1080.

Notes

1. Isaac C. Rottenberg, *The Promise and the Presence: Toward a Theology of the Kingdom of God* (Grand Rapids, Mich.: Wm. B. Eerdmans Publishing Co., 1980), p. 22.
2. A. B. Bruce, *The Kingdom of God* (Edinburgh: T & T Clark, 1890), p. 58 *f*.
3. T. F. Torrance, *Kingdom and Church* (Edinburgh: Oliver and Boyd, 1956), p. 75. We have seen already, however, that Matthew uses "the kingdom of heaven" to refer to "the kingdom of God."
4. H. Richard Niebuhr, *The Kingdom of God in America* (New York: Harper & Brothers, 1959 Harper Torchbook ed.), p. xii.
5. Wolfhart Pannenberg, *Theology and the Kingdom of God* (Philadelphia: The Westminster Press, 1969), p. 51.
6. Herman Ridderbos, *The Coming of the Kingdom* (Philadelphia: The Presbyterian and Reformed Publishing Co., 1962), p. xi.
7. Paul S. Minear, *The Kingdom and the Power* (Philadelphia: The Westminster Press, 1950), pp. 219-227.
8. Rottenberg, pp. 16-19.
9. Minear, p. 219.
10. Perk Perkins, "Concrete Theology," *Sojourners*, Vol. 9, No. 9, Sept., 1980, p. 11.
11. Pannenberg, p. 78.
12. Ibid., p. 60. See also pp. 55 and 84.
13. Orlando E. Costas, "Conversion as a Complex Experience: A Personal Case Study" in John Stott and Robert T. Coote, eds., *Gospel & Culture* (Pasadena: Wm. Carey Library, 1979), p. 250.
14. The concentric model to which I refer may be represented by three concentric circles. The innermost circle would represent justification; the outer circle would represent glorification, and the middle sanctification.
15. Rottenberg, pp. 27-28.

Section III
The Models for Evangelism:
After Whom Should We Model?

6
Jesus as the Perfect Model

Deuteronomy 6:4-9; 1 Corinthians 10:31; 11:1

Introduction

We have looked at the *meaning* and *message* of evangelism. Now, let us consider the *models* for evangelism. We have sought to answer the questions: what is evangelism? and what should we share? Now, let us seek an answer to another very substantive question: after whom should we model?

Models and Modeling

Who are our models for evangelism? We all have one or more models, even if we are unconscious of them. I'll go a step farther and suggest that some of us have negative models, as well as positive ones. We may, at certain points in our Abrahamic journey, be more conscious of the models which we don't want to be like than we are of those whom we prefer to imitate. We are almost irresistibly drawn to certain models, but repelled by others.

We not only have models in our evangelism but we are also—like it or not—models to others. Robert Henderson, a Presbyterian pastor, relates an experience which brought that point home to him. Henderson went to visit a family one night in a home where there were several preschool children. The family was quite active in the congregation which he pastored. The four-year-old daughter opened the door, looked at him, and yelled over her shoulder: "Hey, Mommie! Jesus is here."[1]

Those who would evangelize are stuck with the necessity of having models and of being models. Probably it is

79

accurate to say that we equip others to evangelize more through modeling than almost any other way. One of the strengths of the Evangelism Explosion approach to evangelizing is that a trained evangelist models how to introduce an undiscipled person right before the eyes of two trainees. This modeling approach to training Christian witnesses is also one of the commendable features of that lay witness training program called Continuing Witness Training by Southern Baptists.

Modeling is of course not unique to evangelization. Edmund Burke said, "Example is the school of mankind, and they will learn by no other." Albert Camus once said that, if a thought is to change the world, it must first change the person who carries it; it must become an example. John H. Westerhoff III, in *Will Our Children Have Faith?* calls our attention to the importance of modeling in religious education.[2] I know, as I think back upon my boyhood Sunday School teachers, the thing I remember most about them is their personhood and character. For the life of me, I can't recall anything they said, but they did not fail to teach me some important truths.

Jesus the Perfect Model

Now, having said all of that, I want to go on to say that Jesus Christ is the only perfect model we have for our evangelizing. He is the perfect model evangelist.

We may not need specific Scriptures to lift up the role of Jesus as the perfect model for our evangelism. Because he is our Savior and Lord, he is our model. Nevertheless, let me point you to several biblical references. John 13:15-16 says, "For I have given you an example, that you also should do as I have done to you. Truly, truly, I say to you, a servant is not greater than his master; nor is he who is sent greater than he who sent him." Those words of Jesus specifically tell us that he is our servant example.

Another Scripture which lifts up Jesus as the model

evangelist is John 14:12, "Truly, truly, I say to you, he who believes in me will also do the works that I do; and greater works than these will he do, because I go to the Father." That verse is to be understood in light of the imitation of Christ by his disciples.

We will not do greater works than Christ in terms of more spectacular deeds. But we will do greater works than Christ in terms of quantity and time. We shall do the same kind of works he did; only we shall do more of them over a longer period of time.

The Great Commission of John's Gospel, more than any of the other forms of the evangelistic mandate, reveals Jesus as the perfect model evangelist. I think John 20:21-23 is probably the best clue we have to the meaning of those words at which we have just looked from John 14:12. One part of that Commission quotes Jesus, "As the Father has sent me, even so I send you" (John 20:21). His sending of us is modeled after the Father's sending of him.

We do say we abide in Christ if we claim to be Christians. And 1 John 2:6 says, "he who says he abides in him ought to walk in the same way in which he walked."

Luke 6:40 puts our imitation of Christ in terms of the disciple-teacher relationship, "A disciple is not above his teacher, but every one when he is fully taught will be like his teacher." Luke 10:16 puts our modeling of Jesus in terms of our mutual unity with Jesus and the Father, "He who hears you hears me, and he who rejects you rejects me, and he who rejects me rejects him who sent me."

Paul lifted up Jesus as the perfect model evangelist whom we are to imitate. Especially did he do that in 1 Corinthians 11:1, "Be imitators of me, as I am of Christ." Those words immediately follow, and actually conclude, what Paul said about his becoming all things to all persons that by all means he might save some.

Another passage where Paul clearly pointed to Jesus Christ as our model is the great self-emptying passage of

Philippians 2:5-11. Our perfect model emptied himself and became the Suffering Servant, even to the point of the cross death. We, too, are to have the mind of Christ.

The Imitation of Christ

This idea of modeling our evangelizing after Jesus Christ has much in common with the old idea of the imitation of Christ which Thomas a Kempis wrote about in *The Imitation of Christ*[3] or Charles Sheldon treated *In His Steps*.[4] Jonathan Edwards made a great deal of it in his great treatise on *Religious Affections*.[5]

We see it in Dostoyevsky's *The Brothers Karamazov*,[6] where Aloysha is a Christ figure. Aloysha is the character who knows the difference between loving people in his dreams and loving them in reality; between loving people at a distance and loving them close-up; between loving folk in words and loving them in deeds. Dostoyevsky wanted his readers to see Christ in Aloysha, so that they would desire to imitate Aloysha as he imitated the Christ.

We see it in Kazantzakis's *Zorba the Greek*.[7] On the beach, while watching dolphins, the boss suddenly notices that Zorba is missing almost half of the index finger on his left hand. He says to him: "What happened to your finger?"

Zorba replies to the effect: "Oh, it got in my way one day while I was at the potter's wheel; so I grabbed my hatchet and chopped it off."

Did not Jesus say: "if your right hand causes you to sin, cut if off and throw it away" (Matt. 5:30)? You can't get much more literal than that. Clearly Kazantzakis wanted us to see Zorba as a Christ figure. There is of course no such thing as a perfect Christ figure in literature.

We meet this idea of the imitation of Christ in some of the strangest places. It is even in Eldridge Cleaver's *Soul on Ice*.[8] I recall as a boy seeing some lovely violets growing in the midst of garbage dumps. There amid all of that ugliness and rubbish was one of the most beautiful purple violets I've ever seen. That's the way it is with Chris Lovdjieff, whom Cleaver calls "The Christ." Chris Lovdjieff was a teacher at San Quentin until he was fired. When I first read those eight pages where Cleaver describes "The Christ," I literally wept because Chris Lovdjieff reminded me of Jesus Christ.

When Cleaver was changed from a Black Panther into a professing Christian, my first thought was that this soul on ice had now become a *Soul on Fire*[9] because of Chris Lovdjieff. I saw Cleaver's model teacher as one of those goads against which he kept kicking. Now that he has joined a heretical Christian sect, I am not so sure. But I do believe that God usually chooses to use some Christ figure to bring persons into his kingdom.

Paul in one place even went so far as to say, "be imitators of God, as beloved children" (Eph. 5:1). Immediately following that admonition to imitate God, Paul pointed to Christ as our model for imitating God (see Eph. 5:2).

Implications

The writer of Hebrews referred to the Son as the one who "reflects the glory of God and bears the very stamp of his nature" (1:3). The meaning of that in the vernacular is that Jesus Christ was "the spitting image" of his Father. This emphasis upon the imitation of Christ teaches us that we ought to endeavor to become "the spitting image" of the Son.

One implication of lifting up Jesus as the perfect model for evangelizing is that God has given us a perfect model by which to evaluate all other models, including ourselves. The first Christian prayer Toyohiko Kagawa prayed was, "God make me like Jesus." Kagawa prayed like that after reading the Sermon on the Mount.[10] I believe the greatest compliment one can ever pay to another is to say: "You remind me of Jesus Christ."

If anyone should ever ask me, What kind of evangelist do you want to be? my reply will be: I want to be the kind of

evangelist Jesus was. I want to live as he lived, love as he
loved, labor as he labored, and laugh as he laughed. W. L.
Muncy, Jr., recognized that Jesus was the perfect model
evangelist. "The Church in Jerusalem won men day by day,"
wrote Muncy, "because the Church followed Christ. The
Church sought to continue, 'to do and to teach' what Jesus
'began both to do and to teach' during His earthly life."[11]

This idea of Jesus as the perfect model for our
evangelizing frees us from false bondage to lesser models,
without denying the validity of other models. We don't have
to choose Billy Graham or Billy Sunday or D. L. Moody or
any other human being as our evangelistic model. We don't
even have to choose Paul as our model. We can choose Jesus
as our model and judge these other lesser models by him.
On the other hand, insofar as these lesser models pattern
their evangelism after that of Jesus, we would be wise to
pattern after them. All models are good and true models to
the extent that they model after the only perfect Evangelist,
Jesus the Christ.

Another implication of choosing Jesus as our model is
that it requires us to take with absolute seriousness the reality
of Christ's incarnation. Jesus was the message he brought. So
are we. That's the reason Paul could say, "Be imitators of me,
as I am of Christ" (1 Cor. 11:1).

One of the most incisive statements I have read on the
imitation of Christ, as it relates to the incarnation of Jesus
and of us Christians, was made by the late Carlyle Marney:

> The heresy of the south is that for 200 years Jesus has been
> kept so godlike, so divine, that he has not been relevant.
> Technically the heresy is called docetic gnosticism. Religion
> in the south has kept Jesus in the heavens. Because if he
> ever gets in our alley, we'll have to be like him. And that'll
> make us clean it up. My whole ministry has been given to
> the proclamation that Jesus was human. This implies a real
> incarnation, because if he's really like us, we have the
> potential of being like him. But if we keep him God, we

don't have to be like him. A person who keeps Jesus too godlike doesn't have to be responsible as a human being.[12]

We should do nothing to belittle either our Lord's divinity or his humanity. But those evangelicals who are so strong on his divinity and so weak on his humanity should beware lest they also fall into heresy.

If we affirm Jesus as our perfect model for evangelizing and seek to pattern our evangelism after his, we shall have to flesh out the gospel through our life-styles. We shall have to combine the deed and the word in our very lives. A true story from the life and ministry of United Methodist Bishop Donald Tippett may illustrate the kind of life-style evangelism which is so sorely needed in our day.

Tippett, as a young man, was pastoring a church in New York City. Two men burst into his office one day demanding money. Tippett knew his secretary had a few dollars in her desk, so he picked up the phone to ask for it. The men panicked, thinking the pastor was trying to call the police. They beat him severely and stuffed him behind a radiator, leaving him for dead. During the struggle one of Tippett's eyes was gouged out.

He was found several hours afterwards by one of the church staff and taken to the hospital. For weeks his life hung in the balance between life and death. He was hospitalized for several months and only slowly made a recovery.

When Tippett was able to go back to work, he inquired about the two men who had beaten him. He asked that they be released into his custody. He and his wife took them into their home. They gave them an opportunity to start a new life.

One of them responded. The other went from bad to worse. He broke his custody conditions, was caught stealing; nothing seemed to work. Finally, he made off with Tippett's silver and was gone.

The one who responded was captured by Tippett's spirit. He found such love irresistible. He got a job. Later he went to college and on to medical school, specializing in eye surgery.

Years came and went. Tippett was elected a bishop in the Methodist Church. This man who had participated in the assault became one of the leading eye surgeons in San Francisco. As Bishop Tippett conversed with the eye surgeon one day, he told the bishop that it was he who had gouged out his eye.[13]

Conclusion

Perhaps there are other important implications to adopting the Jesus model in our evangelism. The idea, if logically followed, forces us to see ourselves as an extension of the incarnation. We are, indeed, the body of Christ in the world today. Such a substantive concept also points again to our dependency upon the Holy Spirit for power to imitate the Jesus model. We cannot be like Jesus in our own strength. A power greater than ourselves is required to implement the imitation of Christ. Again we are reminded that evangelism is spiritual work which requires spiritual persons who have spiritual power.

Did Jesus our model demand a hearing, or did he earn a right to be heard? *Agape* love always follows the servant model.

Finally, let us observe, concerning the only perfect Evangelist who ever practiced, that Jesus taught his disciples to make disciples through on-the-job training. We see that in the way he sent out the twelve and the seventy. We also see the disciples learning through the modeling of Jesus as they companied with him.

Suggestions for Further Reading

Robert E. Coleman, *They Meet the Master* (Huntingdon Valley, Pennsylvania: Christian Outreach, 1973).

"Jesus the Evangelist" in Rebecca Manley Pippert, *Out of the Salt-shaker & into the World* (Downers Grove, Ill.: Inter-Varsity Press, 1979), pp. 33-43.

"Jesus, Our Model" in David L. McKenna, *The Jesus Model* (Waco, Texas: Word Books, 1977), pp. 169-179.

"The Matchless Winner" in L. R. Scarborough, *With Christ After the Lost* (Nashville: Broadman Press, 1952), pp. 43-46.

Delos Miles, *Master Principles of Evangelism* (Nashville: Broadman Press, 1982).

Notes

1. Robert T. Henderson, *Joy to the World: An Introduction to Kingdom Evangelism* (Atlanta: John Knox Press, 1980), p. 58.

2. John H. Westerhoff, III, *Will Our Children Have Faith?* (New York: The Seabury Press, 1976), esp. pp. 84-86.

3. Thomas a Kempis, *The Imitation of Christ* (New York: Books, Inc., n.d.).

4. Charles M. Sheldon, *In His Steps* (Nashville: Broadman Press, 1979).

5. Jonathan Edwards, *Religious Affections*, Vol. 2 in *The Works of Jonathan Edwards*, edited by John E. Smith, gen. ed., Perry Miller (New Haven: Yale University Press, 1959). See esp. pp. 365-376.

6. Fyodor Dostoyevsky, *The Brothers Karamazov* (New York: The New American Library, 1957).

7. Nikos Kazantzakis, *Zorba the Greek* (New York: Simon and Schuster, 1966 ed.).

8. Eldridge Cleaver, *Soul on Ice* (New York: McGraw-Hill Book Co., 1968) esp. pp. 31-39.

9. Eldridge Cleaver, *Soul on Fire* (Waco, Texas: Word Books, 1978). Cleaver first joined the Church of Jesus Christ of the Latter Day Saints. He is now a member of the Unification Church.

10. William Axling, *Kagawa* (New York: Harper & Brothers Publishers, 1946 rev. ed.).

11. Cited by Daniel Wade Armstrong, *An Examination of Evangelism in America Beginning with the Eighteenth Century in the Light of New Testament Principles of Evangelism* (an unpublished doctoral thesis at The Southern Baptist Theological Seminary, Louisville, Ky., 1955), p. 50.

12. Bill Finger, "Preaching the Gospel, South of God: An Interview with Carlyle Marney," *The Christian Century*, Vol. XCI, No. 31, Oct. 4, 1978, p. 920. Reprinted by permission.

13. Related by Joe Hale, *God's Moment* (Nashville, Tenn.: Tidings, 1972), pp. 40-41.

7
Paul as a Model

Isaiah 54:1-3; 1 Corinthians 9:19-23

Introduction

Paul was "the master missionary who won more men for Christ than any other man" said William Barclay.[1] L. R. Scarborough called Paul "the topmost evangelist."[2] Certainly Paul is in a class almost alone, next to Jesus Christ the peerless Evangelist. The apostle Paul was a witness, a flaming torch, whose light continues to shine across the centuries.

Paul's evangelizing was characterized by inclusiveness, intentionality, and integrity. Please examine with me those three characteristics.

Inclusiveness

First, consider the inclusiveness of Paul's evangelism. He said, "I have become all things to all men, that I might by all means save some" (1 Cor. 9:22).

Paul's evangelism was inclusive in its *accommodation*. "I have become all things to all." Boswell spoke somewhere of "the art of accommodating oneself to others." Paul practiced the art of accommodation in his evangelism. To the Jews Paul said, "I became as a Jew." To the Gentiles, or those outside the Torah, Paul said, "I became as one outside the law." To the weak persons who had scruples about eating meat which had been sacrificed to idols, Paul said, "I became weak" (vv. 20-22).

Paul was careful never to sacrifice the liberty which he had in Christ. For example, he refused to require Titus to be circumcised when Titus accompanied him to Jerusalem and the circumcision party exerted great pressure upon him (Gal. 2:1-5).

Nevertheless, that same Paul circumcised Timothy "because of the Jews that were in those places" (Acts 16:3) where he was to visit in his missionary journeys. While Titus was a Greek, Timothy was the son of a Jewish woman, but his father was a Greek. This is an excellent example of Paul's accommodation to the Jews for the sake of winning them to Christ.

There are also two references in Acts to Paul's taking a vow and shaving his head in order to accommodate the Jews (Acts 18:18; 21:23-26). The first of these incidents occurred at Cenchreae before Paul went to Ephesus. The second incident occurred in Jerusalem and is much clearer than the first. James and the elders of the Jerusalem church said to Paul:

> You see, brother, how many thousands there are among the Jews of those who have believed; they are all zealous for the law, and they have been told about you that you teach all the Jews who are among the Gentiles to forsake Moses, telling them not to circumcise their children or observe the customs. What then is to be done? (Acts 21:20-22).

Paul knew what had to be done. He took a vow and shaved his head and thus accommodated himself to the Jewish customs for the sake of winning more Jews to Christ.

Paul also accommodated himself to the Gentiles, to those who were not under the law of Moses. The best illustration of his accommodation to Gentiles may be his public rebuke of Peter at Antioch (Gal. 2:11 *ff*.). Peter had been eating with Gentiles at Antioch until certain ones came from James. Then, he stopped eating with the Gentiles out of fear of the circumcision party. Even Barnabas and the other Jewish Christians were carried away by Peter's insincerity. So, Paul opposed them to their faces, saying to Peter:

"If you, though a Jew, live like a Gentile and not like a Jew, how can you compel the Gentiles to live like Jews?" (Gal. 2:14).

Furthermore, Paul in his evangelism also accommodated himself to the weak. The weak brethren were those who had bad consciences about eating meats which had been sacrificed to idols. Evidently much of the meat sold in the markets of Athens had been offered as sacrifice to many so-called gods and lords. Paul knew there was only one Lord, but he concluded that "if food is a cause of my brother's falling, I will never eat meat" (1 Cor. 8:13). Paul refused to use his liberty as a stumbling block to the weak.

We must, therefore, conclude that Paul's evangelism was inclusive in its accommodation to Jews, Gentiles, and the weak brethren of his day. Paul accommodated himself to the culture of his prospects. He was an expert in the art of getting alongside people.

Now, before you jump too quickly to the conclusion that Paul's accommodation meant a loss of his integrity, I remind you that his accommodation was also characterized by integrity. Therefore, I fully intend to address the question of integrity a bit later.

However, before we proceed, let me say again that Paul accommodated the message and the style of his evangelism to the cultural condition of his hearers and receivers. Others have sought to do the same. Whether they have succeeded, as did Paul, you can judge for yourselves.

Let me cite you three examples. Rudolph Bultmann of Marburg, Germany, who died in July 1976 at the age of ninety-one, was seeking to practice the principle of cultural accommodation in his theological process called "demythologization." Using certain ideas from Martin Heidegger's early philosophy, Bultmann sought to make the preaching of the apostolic church relevant and meaningful to modern people. In that sense, and to that extent, Bultmann was an evangelist.

The late theologian Paul Tillich illustrated this element of cultural accommodation in his three volumes of systematic "correlation" theology. Theology according to Tillich is always apologetic. That is to say, it is an attempt to answer humanity's deepest questions; it is evangelistic. First, Tillich contended that the theologian must find out what the questions are. That will demand a knowledge of humanity and of context—the inside and the outside of humanity. Then, the answer to those questions should be correlated from the Bible, church history, philosophy, art, literature, and the sciences.

What Tillich attempted in his systematic theology, Paul practiced in his evangelism. He sought to bring every thought (every area of knowledge) under captivity to Christ. Then, that thought was suited to the cultural condition of those whom he sought to win—whether Jews, Greeks, or the weaker brethren in the church.

The church growth movement of today teaches us that, in terms of cultural distance between the evangelist and those to be evangelized, there are at least four types of evangelism. These are E-0, evangelism of church members; E-1, evangelism of our own kin and kind outside the church; E-2, evangelism of cultural pockets of outsiders who live around or near us; and E-3, the evangelism of persons who live in a foreign place and culture. Paul instinctively, or by revelation and reason, knew that his evangelism must be accommodated to the persons whom he sought to reach.

Is there an element of cultural accommodation in your evangelism? Do you adapt yourself, your message, and your style to the cultural modes and mores of the persons whom you seek to convert?

Paul's evangelism was not only inclusive in its accommodation but it was also inclusive in its *object*. The object of Paul's evangelism was "all men." He aimed to include all and to exclude none. The references to "those under the law" and "outside the law" are all inclusive. To the Jews of the first century AD there were two major categories of humanity: Jews and Gentiles; those under the law and those outside the law; those who had been circumcised and the uncircumcised.

Paul also identified in 1 Corinthians a third category which he designated as the weak. They were characterized as the weak brethren. Apparently these were those people who believed it was sinful to eat meat which had been offered as sacrifice to some idol. They had weak consciences and incomplete knowledge of God. Nevertheless, Paul did not disdain the weak. Rather, he catered to them because he wanted to see them saved.

Hence, Paul's evangelism included Jews and Greeks, circumcised and uncircumcised, barbarians and Scythians, bond and free, wise and foolish, male and female (see also Rom. 1:14; Gal. 3:28; Col. 3:11).

Note the universality of those three *alls* in 1 Corinthians 9:22—all things, all men, all means. Though Paul was free from all men, he made himself a slave to all, that he might by all means win some.

Is there an element of universality in your evangelism? Are you concerned about the salvation of all people? The Communists as well as the capitalists? The poor as well as the rich? Those close by as well as those faraway? The blacks and reds and yellows and browns as well as the whites? The ignorant as well as the intellectuals? The senior adults as well as the young adults? The males as well as the females? The blue-collar workers as well as the white-collar? The church members as well as the outsiders? The unemployed as well as the employed? The mentally ill as well as the mentally healthy? The sick as well as the well? The criminals as well as the law abiding?

Paul's evangelism was characterized by inclusiveness in its accommodation, its object, and in its *means.* The phrase, "that I might by all means save some," shows us that Paul's evangelism was inclusive in its means as well as in its accommodation and in its object.

Paul used public preaching and teaching and singing to proclaim the gospel. He employed the means of missionary journeys for church planting. He used prayer meetings, prayers, and letters, substitutes and co-workers, a rented school, synagogues, house-to-house visitation, the out-of-doors, private homes, jails, and so forth. He made tents to support himself, shed tears, rejoiced, endured trials and hardships. He was a bivocational, itinerant evangelist and missionary.

If you want to see two radically different means employed in Paul's evangelizing, compare his encounter with the Gentile intellectuals in Athens (see Acts 17:16-34) with his encounter with his own people (Acts 22—23). The means which we use should be inclusive, eclectic, and flexible, depending upon our context. An autobiographical account of some of the means Paul used to save the lost may be found in 2 Corinthians 11:23-28.

Intentionality

So far I have spent considerable time saying that Paul's evangelism was characterized by the element of inclusiveness. It was inclusive in its accommodation, its object, and its means. Now, I should like to go on to say that the evangelism of this "topmost" evangelist was also characterized by the element of *intentionality*.

At least four times 1 Corinthians 9:19-23 lifts up the intentionality of Paul's evangelism:

> I have made myself a slave to all, that I might win the more (v. 19).
>
> To the Jews I became as a Jew, in order to win Jews . . . that I might win those under the law (v. 20).
>
> To those outside the law . . . that I might win those outside the law (v. 21).

To the weak . . . that I might win the weak . . . that I might
by all means save some (v. 22).

One gets the impression that Paul firmly intended to
win some. Five times the word *win* is used in these verses and
once the word *save*. The King James Version uses the word
gain. Paul knew that he might not win all, but he fully
intended to win some.

We have two clear illustrations in Romans and in Acts of
Paul's intention to save some. Romans 10:1 and 9:1-3 tell us
how much Paul longed for the salvation of the Jews, his
kinsmen. "Brethren, my heart's desire and prayer to God for
them is that they may be saved" (10:1). Paul wanted the Jews
saved so much that this was his heart's desire, and he made
intercessory prayer for their salvation.

Earlier in the Book of Romans Paul wrote:

I am speaking the truth in Christ, I am not lying; my
conscience bears me witness in the Holy Spirit, that I have
great sorrow and unceasing anguish in my heart. For I
could wish that I myself were accursed and cut off from
Christ for the sake of my brethren, my kinsmen by race
(9:1-3).

Here Paul was saying that his heart was so heavy for the
salvation of the Jews that if possible he would be willing to
lose his own salvation in order to accomplish their salvation.

Then, in Acts 26:28-29 there is a remarkable example
of Paul's intentionality in his evangelism. He was speaking to
King Agrippa, "And Agrippa said to Paul, 'In a short time
you think to make me a Christian!' And Paul said, 'Whether
short or long, I would to God that not only you but also all
who hear me this day might become such as I am—except
for these chains.'"

There can be no doubt about Paul's intention to make
Christians out of all persons. We might also note in this
connection that even the *style* which Paul adopted for his
evangelism was intended to win people. Note carefully what

he said in 1 Corinthians 9:19, "I have made myself a slave to all, that I might win the more." Paul had intentionally adopted the servant style which his Lord had commanded and exhibited.

Evidently there was a strong element of intentionality in Paul's evangelism. Paul confidently intended to save some Jews, Greeks, and weak brethren. He made himself a slave to all that he might win the more. His actions toward the Jews were that he, a Jew, might win those under the law. His actions toward those outside the Mosaic law were in order that he might win those outside the law. And so it was with the weak brethren. In fact, Paul summed up these three chapters on Christian freedom (1 Cor. 8—10) with the words: "So, whether you eat or drink, or whatever you do, do all to the glory of God. Give no offense to Jews or to Greeks or to the church of God, just as I try to please all men in everything I do, not seeking my own advantage, but that of many, that they may be saved" (10:31-33).

Is there a similar element of intentionality in your evangelism? If some twentieth-century King Agrippa should say to you, "In a short time you think to make me a Christian!" could you answer with Paul: "Whether short or long, I would to God that not only you but also all who hear me this day might become such as I am—except for these chains" (see Acts 26:28-29)? Do you want to see your own family and fellow countrymen saved as much as Paul wanted to see his fellow Jews saved? I believe an evangelism modeled after Paul's will intentionally seek to convert persons and structures to the lordship of Jesus Christ. Some of our evangelism is apathetic, anemic, and sickly because the element of intentionality is missing from it.

Integrity

A third element in Paul's evangelism was *integrity*. Add integrity to the elements of inclusiveness and intentionality. See this feature of integrity in 1 Corinthians 9:23 especially,

"I do it all for the sake of the gospel, that I may share in its blessings."

If you are prone to wonder about Paul's motivation in becoming all things to all people that he might by all means save some, I beg you to note that he did all of this for the sake of the gospel and not to feather his own nest. Paul was not sacrificing either his personal integrity or the integrity of the gospel by becoming all things to all men by all means. Quite the contrary.

Paul was not accommodating himself to all because he was an ethical chameleon. He was not so flexible in his evangelism because he subscribed to the philosophy, "When in Rome, do as the Romans." There was no hint of hypocrisy or of ethical compromise in Paul's practice of evangelism.

It is true, of course, that because of his flexibility in the use of means some of Paul's opponents accused him of compromise, duplicity, and hypocrisy. Paul specifically addressed himself to that charge in 2 Corinthians. "We have renounced disgraceful, underhanded ways;" said Paul, "we refuse to practice cunning or to tamper with God's word, but by the open statement of the truth we would commend ourselves to every man's conscience in the sight of God" (4:2). Again the great apostle said: "For we are not, like so many, peddlers of God's word; but as men of sincerity, as commissioned by God, in the sight of God we speak in Christ" (2 Cor. 2:17).

Although those who preach the gospel are entitled to live of the gospel, Paul had refused to accept money from the Corinthians for his labors. Instead he had worked with his own hands making tents and selling them to support himself. As someone said: "He refuses payment in money that he may make the greater gain in souls."

One pastor used the term "integrity evangelism" to describe the kind of evangelism he espoused. Certainly the apostle Paul believed in and practiced integrity evangelism. No cheap grace. No dilution of the gospel. No playing to the grandstands. No playing the numbers game. No preaching in order to "feather one's own nest" or to fatten one's own checking account! No personal empire building. No lies. No bribes. Abstaining from all appearances of evil. No progressive, locked-in invitations. No treatment of persons as though they were hearts without heads and bodies.

The master clue to understanding the integrity of Paul's evangelism may be found in the words in 1 Corinthians 9:21, "under the law of Christ." Someone has paraphrased that statement of Paul to read: "Not being an outlaw of God, but an inlaw of Christ."

What Paul did in his evangelism, and the way he did it, was to fulfill the law of Christ. And, what is the law of Christ? Is it not the law of love? "For the whole law is fulfilled in one word, 'You shall love your neighbor as yourself'" (Gal. 5:14). James called this "the royal law" (Jas. 2:8) because it comes from King Jesus! The law of love requires us to "bear one another's burdens" in order to fulfill the law of Christ.

Evangelism without the element of integrity can shipwreck a church and sabotage lives. Is your evangelism characterized by integrity—by fidelity to the apostolic gospel and by loyalty to the ethical demands of the God of the patriarchs, prophets and apostles? An Elmer-Gantry-Marjoe-Gortner approach to evangelism belongs to the church of Satan and has no place in the church of God.

Conclusion

Later, in 1 Corinthians, Paul admonished us: "Be imitators of me, as I am of Christ" (11:1). Clearly Paul wanted us to imitate him in his practice of evangelism. But he wanted us to imitate him only insofar as he imitated Christ.

The question, then, is: was Paul imitating Christ in these elements of inclusiveness, intentionality, and integrity? Paul's evangelism as we have seen was inclusive in its accommodation, its object, and its means. So was the evangelism of Jesus. Surely no greater example of accommodation in evangelism can be seen than that of Jesus Christ on our behalf in his incarnation and crucifixion. Jesus was the one who gave the command: "make disciples of all nations" (Matt. 28:19). Jesus also used all means at his disposal to make disciples.

Both sections of our Scripture lesson relate to freedom and evangelism. Paul quoted Isaiah 54:1 in connection with his discussion of Christian freedom in Galatians 4 (see vv. 21-31).

The church is not the barren one but the bearing one. She is not the desolate one but the covenant one because her womb is fruitful with the children of promise. Therefore, she is to enlarge the place of her tent, stretch out the curtains of her habitations, hold not back, lengthen her cords, strengthen her stakes, spread abroad to the right and to the left, possess the nations, and people the desolate cities.

If we apply the prophecy of Isaiah 54:1-3 to the church as did Paul, then we can better understand why Paul said in 1 Corinthians 9:22, "I have become all things to all men, that I might by all means save some."

Surely if our evangelism, like Paul's, were characterized by inclusiveness, intentionality, and integrity, we would not get hung up on any one method of evangelism or locked into any one technique of evangelism. Rather, our evangelism would include a wide variety of methods in order to reach a wide variety of persons. No one method of evangelism will appeal to all of the people all of the time. It never has and it never will. That is too much to expect. Methods change from generation to generation, from place to place, and from people to people. All one has to do to see that is to read the Bible and a little church history.

Suggestions for Further Reading

Roy J. Fish, "The Man with the Burning Heart" in James A. Ponder, compiler, *Evangelism Men: Motivating Laymen to Witness*

(Nashville: Broadman Press, 1974), pp. 33-44.

"The Topmost Evangelist," in L. R. Scarborough, *With Christ After the Lost* (Nashville: Broadman Press, 1952), pp. 55-58.

Roland Allen, *Missionary Methods: St. Paul's or Ours?* (Grand Rapids: William B. Eerdmans Publishing Co., 1962 ed.).

Notes

1. William Barclay, *The Daily Study Bible: The Letters to the Corinthians* (Edinburgh: The Saint Andrew Press, 1956 2nd ed.), pp. 93-94.
2. L. R. Scarborough, *With Christ After the Lost* (Nashville: Broadman Press, 1952), pp. 55-58.

8
Edward Kimball as a Model[1]

Proverbs 11:30; 2 Timothy 2:2

Introduction

On Saturday morning, April 21, 1855, Edward Kimball, a tall, thirty-year-old salesman in McGilvary's dry-goods store and a Sunday School teacher in the Mount Vernon Congregational Church of Boston, made his way to Holton's shoe store. He went to talk with an eighteen-year-old youth, who was a member of his Sunday School class, about surrendering his life to Jesus Christ.[2]

Kimball wondered whether he ought to go just then during business hours. He wondered if his visit would embarrass the young man. He thought to himself: "Suppose after I have gone, the other clerks begin to ask the boy who I am and taunt him because his Sunday School teacher came to see him to make him a good boy."

These negative thoughts so preoccupied Kimball's mind that he actually passed by the entrance to Holton's shoe store. When he came to himself and realized what had happened, Kimball turned around and made a dash for the store determined to have it over at once.

The youth was, to Kimball's surprise, all alone in the back of the store wrapping and stacking shoes. Kimball placed his hand on the young man's shoulder and said something like this: "I want you to give your life to Christ, who loves you and wants your love." Neither one of them could ever remember the exact words.

Then and there, Dwight Lyman Moody gave himself and his life to Jesus Christ!

Kimball urged Moody to make a public profession of his faith and to seek baptism and church membership. But when Moody professed his faith and sought membership, he was denied. The Mount Vernon Church, as did other churches in those days, required all new members to undergo an oral examination by pastor and deacons to test their spiritual sincerity. Moody didn't have much formal education. He was unable to give satisfactory answers to the questions. Two kindly deacons were assigned to tutor him. It took almost a year. But Moody finally made it and became a member of the Mount Vernon Church.

Shortly after joining the Mount Vernon Church, Moody moved to Chicago. There he continued to sell shoes. Immediately he aligned himself with another Congregational church. Moody rented four pews and filled them with young men from the streets to hear the gospel every Sunday.

Still Moody felt like he ought to do more for God. By that time he had taken a very profitable job as a traveling salesman and debt collector for the wholesale boot and shoe house of C. H. Henderson. After a brief period with the Wells Street mission, Moody started his own mission Sunday School, which came to be called the Illinois Street mission. That little mission Sunday School grew until one day it became the second largest Sunday School in the United States of America! We know it today as Moody Memorial Church, still holding forth the Word of life in the city of Chicago.

This inspiring story goes on and on. There is more—much more. But at this point let us stop and go back.

Examine with me some specific features of this true evangelistic model from church history of the nineteenth century.

A Layman

First, observe that it was a layman who introduced D. L. Moody to Jesus Christ—not a preacher, not someone specially trained in theology, but a lay person like most of the people in our churches.

I suppose if we knew church history as God knows it, we would see that the church has moved forward from generation to generation primarily through the faithful witness of men and women like Edward Kimball. Certainly this was true in the first century of the church's existence. Acts 8:4 says of the early Christians: "They that were scattered abroad went everywhere preaching the word" (KJV). We know that these were the rank-and-file members of the church because Acts 8:1 tells us that the apostles stayed in Jerusalem during this great persecution against the church.

What I want to say to you is that if Edward Kimball could do it so can today's lay Christians. Indeed, some of our lay persons have better jobs than he. Some of them have more money, more power, more time, more of almost everything. If he could do it, they can too.

Natural Point of Contact

Now notice a second feature of this evangelistic model from church history of the nineteenth century. Kimball had a natural point of contact with D. L. Moody. Moody was a member of Kimball's Sunday School class. What better point of contact would you want with a lost person than to have him enrolled and actively participating in a Sunday School class or department? God alone knows the number of lost Moodys enrolled in our Sunday Schools who are never visited, never witnessed to privately, and never introduced to the Savior of the world.

Kimball also had a second natural point of contact with Moody. Mr. Holton, who owned and operated Holton's shoe store, was Moody's uncle. He was an active member of the Mount Vernon Congregational Church and just as concerned for Moody's salvation as was Edward Kimball.

On one Thursday night in 1972, those of us enrolled in a lay evangelism school made about seventy witnessing visits in the homes of lost persons. That night in two hours, forty-four persons confessed their faith in Jesus Christ. Thirty-four of them were led to Christ by lay Christians, most of whom had never made a witnessing visit in their lives. All but three of these forty-four new converts have been baptized into the fellowship of that church. The one factor which made the most difference was the relationship which that church had with the prospects whom we visited. Most of them were active members of the Sunday School. They were cultivated prospects. The church had a natural point of contact with them.

I am suggesting that we ought to use the natural, normal contacts which we have with lost persons to lead them to Christ, as did Edward Kimball. We shall come closer to introducing those folk to Christ with whom we have natural relationships than we shall total strangers. To be sure, we can cultivate strangers, and we can at times reap where others have sown. Also, we must forever be sensitive to the leadership of the Holy Spirit.

God gives most lay Christians more opportunities to evangelize lost persons in the natural, normal course of their day-to-day lives than he gives ordained ministers. He expects us to utilize our relationships in a manner which will reflect our relationship with him.

The Initiative

The third feature of this evangelistic model shows how Kimball took the initiative in seeking out D. L. Moody. He did not wait for Moody to come to him and say: "Please, Mr. Kimball, tell me how to be saved." Most lost people do not take the initiative with us. We have to take the initiative with them.

That's the way it was with God in our salvation, was it not? Before we chose him, he had already chosen us: "Ye have not chosen me, but I have chosen you" (John 15:16, KJV).

Jesus said of himself: "For the Son of man is come to seek and to save that which was lost" (Luke 19:10, KJV). If we would learn from Edward Kimball and imitate the evangelism of Jesus, we shall seek out the lost wherever they may be found. There is no place in the Bible where lost people are commanded to go to church. But there are biblical commands for saved people to go into all the world and bring lost people to God.

The God who is like a shepherd, who leaves the ninety and nine safe in the fold and goes out after the one lost sheep until he finds it, expects us to do likewise. We should seek out the lost in their homes and in their places of business, whenever that may be appropriate. We should seek them in their clubs and organizations, their honky-tonks and nightclubs—wherever they may be found. We should seek them down all the labyrinthine ways of life just as God, the "Hound of Heaven"—in Francis Thompson's poem—sought us.

Tempted Not to Go

A fourth feature of this evangelistic model is one with which we are all well acquainted. Edward Kimball was tempted not to go. Some negative thoughts raced through his mind. He wondered if it were the best time and place.

The devil always tries to keep us from making witnessing visits. He suggests to us all kinds of negative thoughts, such as, he will be watching his favorite television program; he will be resting because he works on a swing shift; he has company; you're invading his privacy; you ought to wait until your own life is in better spiritual shape; who do you think you are anyhow?

The devil will even make one physically sick to prevent a witnessing visit. I recall one lady in a lay evangelism school who, upon hearing we would visit on Thursday night, told her pastor her ulcer was acting up. "In fact," she said, "I believe I'm getting an ulcer on my ulcer." In another lay evangelism school one of the finest deacons in the church got so sick on Thursday night with a tension headache that his wife had to call a doctor. The devil will do everything within his power to keep us from going to the lost with the gospel. But go we must because we have a divine mandate from God to go into all the world.

I remember hearing about an evangelist who made something like 10,000 witnessing visits into the homes of lost people. After making all of those visits, this evangelist said: "I never made one of those visits without being tempted not to go." Then, he went on to say: "I never made one of those visits without finding that God was there before I arrived; and I never made one of those visits and was sorry I went after I had gone." It will be the same way with us.

Call to Break with Old Life

Kimball asked Moody to make a clear break with his old life of sin and to commit himself unconditionally to Jesus Christ. That's a fifth feature of this evangelistic model. Sooner or later all evangelism must come to that point. If not on the first visit, then on the second. If not on the second, then on the third. Somewhere along the way, the evangelist must name the name of Jesus and call for repentance from sin and faith in Jesus Christ.

We do not go on a witnessing visit to talk about ourselves, our ideas, or opinions. We go to communicate what Christ has done for us and what he can do for the persons we visit. We do not go to talk about the church. We go to bear witness to Jesus Christ. It is the gospel which is the dynamite of God unto salvation. Therefore, it is the gospel which we must share.

Sought to Lead into Church

Edward Kimball sought to lead D. L. Moody into the church. He urged Moody to confess publicly his faith and to become a member of the church. Evangelism which stops with the initial conversion experience stops short of biblical evangelism.

We cannot be content with getting persons just to say yes to Christ. We must get them to say yes to baptism, to a local church, to a life of discipleship. We are not playing the "numbers game." We are building up the body of Christ both quantitatively and qualitatively. The decision which we seek is a free and voluntary one—a decision for life, not just a verbal agreement which will get them rid of us.

Evangelism is never complete until the evangelized become evangelists. The evangelism which we prize and practice must labor mightily to fit new converts into those grooves of grace which will enable them to grow until they reach after the maturity which Christ exhibits.

Chain Reaction

Edward Kimball started a chain reaction when he introduced D. L. Moody to Jesus Christ, a chain reaction which has not ended and will not end until Jesus returns and all the accounts are settled by God in the judgment. That is the seventh feature of this evangelistic model.

Kimball had no way of knowing that Moody would rent four pews and pack them with people to hear the gospel every Sunday. If Moody had never done anything else, that would have been something worthwhile. I surely would like to lead someone to Christ who would fill up even one pew every Sunday with prospects. Wouldn't you?

Kimball had no way of knowing that Moody would start a mission Sunday School which would grow into the second largest in this country. He didn't know he was starting that kind of chain reaction.

Nor did Kimball know that Moody would become a leader of the YMCA, back in those early years when that organization was a powerful evangelical force in the world. He surely didn't realize that Moody would become a chaplain with the United States Christian Commission and minister so faithfully and effectively to the Union Army soldiers and their families during the American Civil War.

We know how Moody went on to launch his brilliant career as an itinerant evangelist, how he preached the gospel to thousands on two continents, how he started Northfield Schools and Moody Bible Institute. When Moody Bible Institute opened, it was an innovation in evangelistic methodology. Never before in the history of the church in this country had a school been founded just to train lay Christians to share their faith.

It was on Moody's farm in Northfield, Massachusetts, that the Student Volunteers got their powerful impetus. From the Student Volunteers came the Student Christian Movement and in its time the Inter-Varsity Christian Fellowship. This was one of the streams which flowed into the International Missionary Conference at Edinburgh in 1910 under John R. Mott. Not in his wildest dreams could Edward Kimball have foreseen this kind of chain reaction!

Some students of evangelism have called attention to the direct chain of witnesses from Edward Kimball to Billy Graham. The greatest mass evangelist in the history of the church can trace his ministry back through Mordecai Ham to Billy Sunday to J. Wilbur Chapman to F. B. Meyer to D. L. Moody to Edward Kimball.

One never knows how much good he is doing when he introduces just one person to Jesus Christ. But he can be sure that he is doing a lot of good—and perhaps the best thing in all the world. You may introduce one person to Jesus Christ who will in turn introduce one thousand or one million to Christ. And the chain goes on and on. It will not end until time is no more and all the records are before God in the consummation of all things.

Conclusion

The quickest and surest way I know for you to duplicate this model in your own life is for you to surrender your life completely to Jesus Christ and participate in witness training through a local church. The quickest and surest way I know for your church to duplicate this model is for your church to conduct well-planned lay witness training which is open to all the members.

Perhaps up to now, we have been holding back in the area of witnessing. But let us from this day forth resolve to become living links in that great chain of witnesses reaching from the beginning of time until the end of time.

That seems to be something of what Paul had in mind when he wrote to Timothy: "And the things that thou hast heard of me among many witnesses, the same commit thou to faithful men, who shall be able to teach others also" (2 Tim. 2:2, KJV). Four generations of witnesses are included in that one verse: Paul, Timothy, "faithful men," and "others."

Where do you fit into that ever lengthening chain? Or, do you? It is entirely possible that you might introduce one person to Christ who will in turn introduce one hundred or one thousand or one hundred thousand to him.

Suggestions for Further Reading

"The Little Lancashire Lad" in J. C. Pollock, *Moody: A Biographical Portrait of the Pacesetter in Modern Mass Evangelism* (New York: The Macmillan Co., 1963), pp. 64-75.

James A. Ponder, compiler, *Evangelism Men: Motivating Laymen to Witness* (Nashville: Broadman Press, 1974).

Maurice A. P. Wood, "Lay Training for Evangelism" in Sherwood Eliot Wirt, *Evangelism the Next Ten Years* (Waco, Texas: Word Books, 1978), pp. 79-92.

Notes

1. This chapter is from the book *Evangelism Men: Motivating Laymen to Witness,* compiled by James A. Ponder. Copyright 1974 by Broadman Press assigned to the compiler, 1980, and used by permission. It has been slightly revised.

2. The facts about D. L. Moody in this chapter are based on J. C. Pollock's *Moody: A Biographical Portrait of the Pacesetter in Modern Evangelism* (New York: The Macmillan Company, 1963).

Section IV
The Motives for Evangelism:
Why Should We Evangelize?

9
The Love of God

Jeremiah 31:3*b*; John 3:16

Introduction

We come now to consider the motives for evangelization. Why should we evangelize? What is our theological rationale for making Christian disciples?

We evangelize because "the love of Christ controls us" (2 Cor. 5:14). The King James Version translates that verb *sunechei* as "constraineth." *The New English Bible* translates the whole clause, "For the love of Christ leaves us no choice." Phillips more freely translates, "The very spring of our actions is the love of Christ."

The Love of Christ

Precisely what is this love of Christ which leaves us no choice but to engage in the ministry of reconciliation? Let us be clear that this is Christ's love for us and not in the first place our love for him. It is not so much our love for Christ, as it is his love for us and for the world which moves us to share the message of reconciliation.

First John 4:19 says, "We love, because he first loved us." Both 2 Corinthians 5:14 and 1 John 4:19 are referring to *agape* love. *Agape* love originates with God, never with humankind. God is the source and the resource for this kind of love. Therefore, we love God (the Son, ourselves, others) because he first loved us. To put it another way, "We love period because he first loved us." There is no *agape* love which does not come from the Heavenly Father.

Nor should we make the mistake of separating the love

113

of Christ from the love of God. Paul put the two together in no uncertain terms in Romans 5:8, "But God shows his love for us in that while we were yet sinners Christ died for us."

This compulsion which motivates us to be ambassadors for Christ is not our love for the unreconciled. Rather it is the love of God which is seen in the death of Christ and has been poured out upon us by the Holy Spirit. "God's love has been poured into our hearts through the Holy Spirit" (Rom. 5:5b).

When Sam James was serving as a missionary in Vietnam, someone broke into his house and stole some toys. Later that day, James got into a taxi and struck up a conversation with the driver. The cab driver, realizing James spoke his language, asked him how long he had been in Vietnam. Then, he said: "You must really love the Vietnamese very much. What do you love about them?" That question kept gnawing at James all day and into the night: "What do you love about them?" James couldn't sleep. He went to his study and began to pray. As he talked with God, he realized that he really didn't love the Vietnamese and confessed it to him. Then, it seemed as though God spoke to James, saying: "Sam, I didn't send you here because you love the Vietnamese. I sent you here because I love them, and I want to love them through you."[1]

Eros and *Philos* Love

It is not my intention to imply that God will only accept *agape* love. Nor do I wish to suggest that our motivation is always on that high a plane. On the contrary, I think our motives are often mixed with *eros* and *philos* love.

Gaines S. Dobbins reminds us that, while *agape* love is Christian love, it is possible for Christians to be motivated by *eros* love or *philos* love. Peter was recommissioned on the basis of *philos* love.[2] When Jesus asked, "Simon, son of John, do you love me?" (John 21:15-17), the first two times he used the Greek verb form of *agape*. Only on the third repeat did Jesus

change to the Greek verb form of *philos*. However, each time
when Peter answered, "I love you," he used the Greek verb
form of *philos*. Jesus began on the plane of *agape* love; only to
accommodate Peter did he come down to the plane of *philos*
love. Our Lord, we may be sure, will meet us at our points of
weakness as well as at our points of strength. Nevertheless,
we are called to *agape* love.

John Merrick, the Elephant Man, had one of the most
grotesque bodies of all human beings. His disfigurement
resulted from a severe form of neurofibromatosis. When he
was eleven or twelve years old, his mother died. Anthropolo-
gist, Ashly Montagu, concluded that his mother's love forti-
fied the Elephant Man throughout his life. While I do not
question that conclusion, I should like to suggest that love of
God may have also accounted for Merrick's lack of cynicism.
The building of the church model of Saint Phillip's Church,
we should recall, became the central metaphor in Bernard
Pomerance's play, *The Elephant Man*.

Agape Love

There is no higher motive for evangelization than the
love of God. It was *agape* love which moved God to send his
only begotten and beloved Son into the world, "For God sent
the Son into the world, not to condemn the world, but that
the world might be saved through him" (John 3:17).

The Bible is a book of love. There is much about the
love of God in the Old Testament as well as in the New.
Twenty-six times in Psalm 136 the psalmist wrote, "his
steadfast love endures forever" (vv. 1-26). But the whole
Bible is capsuled in John 3:16, "For God so loved the world
that he gave his only Son, that whoever believes in him
should not perish but have eternal life."

John 3:16 has been called the "little gospel." There we
have the gospel in microcosm. God exists in a love relationship with the world. He sent his Son to be the Savior of the
world.

That text, which may be thought of as the golden text of the golden Book, says "For God so loved the world." The world is the object of his love, not merely Israel or the church. That is the nexus of the Christian faith.

God's love for us and for the world compels us. That is the source of the divine compulsion to tell the whole world about the love of God, which is in Christ Jesus our Lord.

This world which God so loved is a world in rebellion against him. It is a world of villains. The faculty of the Catholic University of America prepared in 1981 a list of the ten worst villains of all time. Their list included Idi Amin (1925-), Mao Tse-tung (1893-1976), Joseph Stalin (1879-1953), and Adolf Hitler (1889-1945). They gave dishonorable mention to Jack the Ripper and Ayatollah Ruhollah Khomeini. Those who made the choices considered the villains' impact on history, their brutality, and whether their villainy was deliberate.[3] God loves all of these and those who did not make the list too.

Agape love is a no-strings-attached love. It is unmerited love. God's love is not conditioned by the nature of the loved object. Rather, it is conditioned by the nature of the lover. It is God's nature to love unconditionally.

If the incarnation tells us anything, it is that God loves our world. He loves our whole world, all of it and everybody in it. God really does care about us. The central message of the New Testament may well be God's grace toward the unworthy.

God does love the world. But let us not forget that means he loves us too. He loves me. He loves you. This wonderful love is personal. It includes me. It includes you. You and I are loved. Robert McAfee Brown said, "The Bible is a special delivery letter with your name on it."

God so loved the world that he gave his only Son. Those two verbs, "loved" and "gave," belong together. You can't have one without the other. Love always gives. It is the nature of love to give.

God's love is not some beautiful detached emotion. It is love which pays the supreme price. We see God's love for the world in the cross of his Son. One would have to have a heart of stone in order to contemplate the cross and not see the great love of God for lost humanity.

"The crucifixion of Jesus was not the execution of a criminal, the death of a martyr, or a divine example," said Herschel H. Hobbs.[4] It was the expression of divine love (1 John 4:8-10).

I read of two strangers, each oblivious to the other, who stood gazing at a painting of the crucifixion of Jesus. Finally, one of them whispered, "I love him!" Unconsciously, the other added, "I love him too!" The love of Christ does, indeed, control us. We evangelize because love demands it.

Things may be even worse than they seem in our world. Only the light of Christ can deliver us from the "black holes" of our universe. Were it not for the love of Christ, all of us would have been dead a long time ago.

Telling God's Love

Such matchless love motivates us to tell others about it. This is good news too good to keep to ourselves. We are moved to go and tell it everywhere. While you may not personally respond positively to the words: "God loves you, and I love you too," those very words or similar statements have begun to turn some persons around and draw them to the Savior.

George W. Truett, himself a babe in Christ, won his first convert while he was principal of Hiawassee Academy. The new convert said to Truett: "Teacher, I have found the Saviour, and that time that you told me you loved me started me toward Him."

Pastor A. C. Archibald tells about a church visitor who called on a prospect family. No one in that family attended church. The visitor found a father, mother, and three children. She was wise enough to get the ages and even the birth dates of the children. They were ages eight, twelve, and fourteen. One happened to have a birthday at the end of that very week. She purchased a small picture book of Bible stories and mailed it to the child on her birthday. The gift was sent from her personally, but she signed the card, "with love from the First Baptist Church."

That was the first touch of church interest and concern which that home had experienced. Two Sundays later those three children were in Sunday School. Within six months the father, mother, and one child had been baptized.[5]

David Wilkerson, whose book *The Cross and the Switchblade* has sold over five million copies since its publication in 1958, told Nickie Cruz, "God loves you." Cruz was a leader of the Mau Maus, one of the meanest gangs in New York City. Cruz spat on Wilkerson and told him to go to hell. Soon, however, Cruz was converted and became an evangelist.[6] God's love is powerful enough to change a hardened gang leader into a flaming evangelist.

It is God's love which motivates him to tell us about his love for us through the Bible, through nature, through his servants, and through His Son. If God's love has captured us alive and transformed our lives, we have a story which must be told to the world.

> Get you up to a high mountain.
>   O Zion, herald of good tidings;
> lift up your voice with strength,
>   O Jerusalem, herald of good tidings,
>   lift it up, fear not;
> say to the cities of Judah,
>   "Behold your God!" (Isa. 40:9).

Doing God's Love

This wonderful love of God for us and for the world motivates us to love the world with deeds of love, justice, and mercy. Love is meeting the needs of persons. We cannot love adequately with only words.

The word *love* does not appear in the Book of Acts. Acts is not so much the words of the apostles as it is their deeds. "And with great power the apostles gave their testimony to the resurrection of the Lord Jesus, and great grace was upon them all" (Acts 4:33).

Bishop Fulton Sheen told what happened when he visited a hospital for lepers in Nigeria. His purpose was to give a small silver crucifix to each of the patients. The first patient to which the bishop came had a great ulcer on the side of his leg. That sight so unnerved bishop Sheen that he dropped the silver crucifix which he was preparing to give to the leper into the giant, red, running sore. He started to leave but could not tear himself away. Instead Sheen plunged his hand down into the great, angry ulcer and retrieved the shining crucifix.

"When I touched his hurt," said the bishop, "I loved him."[7] We do not have to see any special power in a crucifix in order to believe in the power of the cross. There are millions of dirty, running hurts that drain the joy and very life from us, our society, and our world. The key to evangelistic success is our willingness to plunge our hands into those hurts and love those neighbors with the *agape* love which comes from the God who is love.

Mother Teresa, who was awarded the Nobel Peace Prize in 1980, was surely right when she said, "True love *hurts*."[8] It hurt God when he gave his only Son to the world. It hurt Jesus when he died on the cross. It hurt his mother, Mary, to see him suffer so. Everyone who has loved deeply knows that love hurts. Doing God's love may hurt, but it also heals.

Being God's Love

The love of God motivates us to tell the world about his love, to do deeds of love which will authenticate that love, and to be a living demonstration of that love. One of the ways God makes his love known for others is through incarnating *agape* love in his sons and daughters. His love takes on flesh and blood through those of us who are citizens of his kingdom.

Mother Teresa of India gave a speech in Bangalore in 1980, which addressed the questions: How do we love God? Where is God for us to love him? Her answer was:

> I will love him in the hungry person. Not only hungry for a piece of bread, but hungry for understanding love. I will love him in the naked person who is not only naked for a piece of cloth, but naked for that human dignity and respect that has been taken away. I will love him in the homeless person who longs not just for a home of bricks, but for a home of understanding love.[9]

D. L. Moody majored on the love of God in his preaching. Love was his main theme. He once commented that the reason a seemingly powerful sermon did not move persons to trust Christ was that it lacked love. Moody firmly believed that evangelistic sermons devoid of love would bear little or no evangelistic fruit. He suggested that we "pepper our discourse with love, salt it with love, and we will walk into the affections of the people and turn them toward God. If we don't," said Moody, "our words will be as sounding brass and tinkling cymbals." He believed that there is no power where there is no love.[10]

Conclusion

Before the Africans returned the body of David Livingstone to England, they cut out his heart and buried it in that land to which he had devoted his life. Do you love your community, your city, your country, your state, whatever turf God has given you, so much that when you die they will want to keep your heart there forever? Have you so given your very heart to a people and to a task that everybody knows your love for them and for that task? "For where your treasure is, there will your heart be also" (Matt. 6:21).

Suggestions for Further Reading

William E. Hull, *Love in Four Dimensions* (Nashville: Broadman Press, 1982), especially chapter I, "What Wondrous Love Is This?" pp. 13-27.

Leon Morris, *Testaments of Love: a Study of Love in the Bible* (Grand Rapids: Wm. B. Eerdmans Publishing Co., 1981), especially chapter 7, "The God of Love and the Love of God," pp. 129-164.

Michael Green, *Evangelism in the Early Church* (Grand Rapids: Wm. B. Eerdmans Publishing Co., 1970), esp. pp. 236-243 of chapter 9, "Evangelistic Motives."

Notes

1. Related by Robert Culpepper in a chapel message at Southeastern Baptist Theological Seminary on July 15, 1981. Taken from my personal notes.
2. Gaines S. Dobbins, *Evangelism According to Christ* (Nashville: Broadman Press, 1949), pp. 188-190.
3. Associated Press report, "Hitler, Stalin Lead Top 10 List of Villains," *The Kansas City Times,* June 30, 1981, p. A-5.
4. Herschel H. Hobbs, *New Testament Evangelism* (Nashville: Convention Press, 1960), p. 22.
5. Arthur C. Archibald, *New Testament Evangelism: How It Works Today* (Philadelphia: The Judson Press, 1946), p. 78.
6. Edmund K. Gravely, Jr., "Wilkerson Returns Cross to Switchblade Territory," *Christianity Today,* vol. XXV, No. 15, Sept. 4, 1981, pp. 51-52.
7. Related by Porter Routh in an unpublished paper titled, "Evangelism and Southern Baptists," pp. 14-15.
8. Mother Teresa, "God's Understanding Love," *Seeds,* vol. 4, no. 2, February, 1981, p. 7.
9. Ibid, pp. 7-8.
10. Daniel Wade Armstrong, *An Examination of Evangelism in America Beginning with the Eighteenth Century in the Light of New Testament Principles of Evangelism* (an unpublished doctoral thesis at The Southern Baptist Theological Seminary, Louisville, Ky., 1955), p. 131.

10
The Imperative to Make Disciples

Daniel 7:13-14; Matthew 28:16-20

Introduction

We should make disciples because Christ's love demands it and he himself commands it. "Go therefore and make disciples of all nations" (Matt. 28:19). That is the heart of the Great Commission in Matthew's Gospel. Each of the four canonical Gospels has a version of the Great Commission (see Matt. 28:18-20; Mark 16:15-17; Luke 24:46-49; John 20:21-23).

We sometimes forget that Acts 1:8 is another form of the Great Commission. That verse is the leitmotiv of the Book of Acts. It lifts up five basic truths which dominate the book:

- The Holy Spirit is the divine Agent to initiate, supervise, energize, and accomplish the purpose of God in the church-building program referred to in Matthew 16:18.
- The apostles of Jesus Christ are the representatives of the church of Jesus Christ and the initial agents of the Holy Spirit through whom the divine purpose is to be initiated and directed.
- Witnessing is to be the major means of accomplishing the divine purpose.
- Jesus Christ himself is the content of the Christian message.
- The total inhabited world is to become the sphere of God's gracious operations and gospel witnessing.[1]

While the words and phrases may differ, whichever

Gospel version you choose has at its heart the making of disciples. I should like for us to concentrate primarily upon Matthew 28:18-20.

The Authority of Christ

The first part of the Great Commission in Matthew's account deals with the *authority* of the risen Christ. "All authority in heaven and on earth has been given to me," said Jesus.

That word "authority" is *exousia* in the Greek. Literally it means "out of being." Therefore, the resurrected Lord, out of the very nature of his being, commands us to disciple all nations. "Power," as used in some versions, is too weak a word to convey the idea of *exousia*. *The New English Bible* gets closer by translating the phrase *pasa exousia* (literally "all authority") as "full authority."

There are several factors preceding and surrounding this great claim which may help us to understand it. Jesus could claim all authority on heaven and earth because he had been raised from the grave. He was the One who had triumphed over death and the tomb. He has, as Paul said, been "designated Son of God in power according to the Spirit of holiness by his resurrection from the dead" (Rom. 1:4).

If you will back up to the two verses immediately preceding this stupendous claim to all authority, you may see several other fingers pointing to its utterance. One of these fingers is "the mountain to which Jesus had directed them" (Matt. 28:16).

Jesus had ordered his disciples to meet him on a certain mountain in Galilee. The mountains have a theological significance in Matthew's Gospel. Seven mountains are mentioned in Matthew in connection with the life and ministry of Jesus. One of the temptations occurs on "a very high mountain" (Matt. 4:8). The Sermon on the Mount was given on a mountain. The transfiguration of Jesus occurred on "a high mountain" (Matt. 17:1). We might conjecture that the Great Commission was given from one of those same mountains—perhaps that very mountain where the Sermon on the Mount was given.

The mountain of Matthew 28:16 is number seven in Matthew's list. I need not remind you that seven is the number which symbolized perfection. Matthew apparently wanted readers to see the resurrected Christ as a kind of second Moses appearing on a new kind of Mount Sinai to give a new commandment to the new people of God. Jesus is a new Joshua who leads his people forward in world conquest. This closing mountain scene accentuates his authority.

Another of these other fingers which points to authority is the worship of the risen Jesus by the eleven disciples, "And when they saw him they worshiped him" (Matt. 28:17). This is the kind of full-blown worship which the early church rendered to her resurrected Lord.

Still a further finger which points to the authority of Jesus is encompassed in the phrase, "but some doubted" (Matt. 28:17). That appears at first glance to be a wrinkle in the Great Commission. It sounds like a sour note on an otherwise sweet ending. Mind you, that is a statement of fact, made matter-of-factly, about eleven of the twelve apostles. What shall we make of such an unexpected word about doubt? The fact that some doubted accentuates Jesus' authority.

Chaucer in his *The Canterbury Tales* has one of his characters say, "If gold rusts, what shall iron do?" Surely, these eleven apostles represented the gold of the early church. For them to doubt was for the gold of the church to rust. And if such pillars of the church doubted, what could be expected of the rank-and-file members of the church who represented the iron?

Yes, even some of the apostles doubted at that time. One of the reasons I believe the Bible is inspired is that it doesn't gloss over the weaknesses and warts of the leaders among the people of God. Why didn't some astute editor doctor up that passage? The Bible speaks the truth and squares with reality.

This word about doubt is all the more remarkable by being couched in a passage which reeks with authority. How could any one doubt Jesus at such a time as that?

Does not such a word regarding doubt reveal something about both the ways of God and the weakness of persons? Was Bonhoeffer correct when he said the only true God is the God who is always "allowing himself to be edged out of the world"? God does not knock us down with sheer power. His ways are often invisible and imperceptible. Some may prefer to call this "the weakness of God."

Then, notice how worship and doubt are coupled in the text, "they worshiped him, but some doubted" (Matt. 28:17). I take it that they all worshiped him, although some of them doubted. Is it possible to both worship and doubt God simultaneously? Evidently so. Tennyson said, "There lives more faith in honest doubt,/Believe me, than in half the creeds."

Therefore, when Jesus claimed all authority in heaven and earth, that may have been the greatest claim ever made. He who made it is the resurrected One, the firstborn from the dead. He is the second Moses who is greater than Moses, the new Joshua. He was the one whom the apostles worshiped. He was the one so great and who did such miraculous deeds that even some of the twelve apostles doubted. He uttered his imperative to evangelize from the appointed mountain. That command to make disciples is as authoritative and binding as the Ten Commandments. Indeed, if anything this new commandment is even more authoritative and more binding upon the new people of God.

The Command of Christ

Let us now look at the *command* of Christ which constitutes the second and largest part of the Great Commission. The full command may be seen in Matthew 28:19-20*a*, but the actual imperative to evangelize are the words translated in the Revised Standard Version as "make disciples" (v. 19*a*). That phrase is a translation of the Greek verb *mathēteusate*.

It is the imperative mood and is, therefore, a forthright command which probably lays upon the church the greatest task in the world. Roland Q. Leavell could appropriately title one of his books *Evangelism: Christ's Imperative Commission* and call the Great Commission "the Magna Charta of evangelism"[2] because of that imperative.

The "therefore" of verse 19 points us back to the claim made in verse 18. The Commander in Chief of heaven and earth issues the church her marching orders. The imperative to make disciples arises out of the authority of the risen Lord Jesus Christ.

However, this may be an appropriate place to observe that even if we did not have an explicit imperative to make disciples, such as is found in Matthew 28:19, evangelization would still be an imperative because in the Christian faith the imperative always arises out of the indicative. God acts and people respond. We love because he first loved us. God's authority is such that his slightest wish is our immediate imperative.

We are not here commanded to go. It is assumed that we shall go. One might even translate: "as you go disciple the nations." Hence, the impact may be not so much that we go and then make disciples, but that we make disciples as we go. That would fit what some say about life-style evangelism.

I like what George Worrell says about there being two kinds of witnessing strategies. One he calls the "going to witness" strategy, and the other he labels the "witness-as-you-go" strategy. Worrell believes the first strategy is followed in organized house-to-house visitation, such as some churches do weekly, perhaps on Thursdays. That kind of witnessing sets the stage for the "witness-as-you-go" strategy. The "witness-as-you-go" strategy, however, will enable you to witness to more persons.[3]

We would do well not to set either of those two strategies over against the other. Centrifugalism as over against centripetalism is the important point to note here. Mission in the Old Testament was centripetal; whereas in the New Testament it is centrifugal. The nations in the Old Testament were to *come* to Jerusalem; whereas in the New Testament the church went to the nations. "Evangelism must go on to the ends of the earth until the end of the age," said George W. Peters.[4]

The evangelist has a "go" mentality, as over against a "come" mentality. Instead of saying "Come to church," he or she says, "Go and reach persons where they are." Some of our failure to catch persons for Christ may be traced to our failure to go on fishing trips. My experience has been that I catch more fish when I go where the fish are.

We are commanded to disciple all nations. The Greek phrase is *panta ta ethnē,* or literally "all the nations." This is probably a reference to the Gentile mission by the Jewish Christians. The Great Commission of Acts 1:8 would interpret Matthew 28:19 in geographic terms. All the nations begins at Jerusalem, reaches out to Judea and into Samaria and to the uttermost parts of the earth.

Another way of analyzing those whom we are commanded to disciple in our time is to look at the statistics for religious commitment. Those worldwide figures look something like this:

Christians	1,000,000,000
Muslims	720,000,000
Hindus	600,000,000
Secular religions	
(Marxism, Communism)	800,000,000

Chinese traditionalists (usually including elements of Buddhism, Confucianism, and Taoism)	500,000,000
Buddhists	250,000,000
Local traditional religions	275,000,000
Others	175,000,000[5]

Several facts stand out about the nearly three billion non-Christians in the world. First, multitudes of them are already adherents of non-Christian religions. That means we shall have to learn how to communicate with these persons in accordance with their particular world view. Much greater clarity and compassion will be needed than we have thus far exhibited.

Second, it is urgent that we seek to convert tribal people and animists to Christ before they are converted to one of the non-Christian faiths. Evangelization is much easier then than afterwards.

Third, only approximately one billion of the three billion non-Christians can be evangelized by near-neighbor Christians. The other two billion will require that we cross geographical, cultural, linguistic, or other boundaries in order to evangelize them. These two billion, among whom there are not Christians or Christian churches, constitutes for us the most difficult evangelistic challenge of the next two decades.[6]

Add to the above the fact that many of the one billion Christians are only nominal believers in Christ, and you begin to see the urgency of evangelization. Perhaps half or more of the one billion Christians need what church growth theoreticians call E-O evangelism.[7]

The Greek text for Matthew 28:19-20a has only one imperative. However, there are three participles. The first one is translated as "Go." Actually it is more literally "having gone." The other two are "baptizing" and "teaching."

Those three clauses in verses 19-20a, each of which

begins with a participle in the Greek text, are not sequential, temporal clauses, each one equal with the other and building upon the preceding one. Rather, the key phrase is, "disciple the nations" in the first clause. The other two clauses about baptizing and teaching specify two ways to make disciples.

We are to baptize all nations into the name of the Trinity. Note that this is one name, not three. Most likely that way of stating it emphasizes the unity of Father, Son, and Holy Spirit. Baptism is the initiation of believers into the kingdom.

We are also to teach all nations to observe what Jesus has commanded. You will note the emphasis on doing and keeping Christ's commandments. The Christian life is a life of obedient action. This kind of teaching can be an evangelistic function. C. H. Dodd in 1936 challenged the idea that teaching is evangelistic. He separated the *kerygma* from the *didache*.[8]

I believe Dodd was mistaken. The Great Commission ties the imperative to make disciples with teaching the nations to keep what Christ has commanded us. It is precisely at this point that the great commandments of Matthew 22:37-40 interface with the Great Commission.

The Promise of Christ

The third and final part of the Great Commission in Matthew deals with the promise of Christ's presence, "and lo, I am with you always, to the close of the age" (Matt. 28:20b). If the first part of the Great Commission represents the greatest claim ever made and the second part of it represents the greatest command ever given, then we may be in order to call the third part the greatest promise ever made.

Jesus did not make claims without backing them up. He did not lie. All authority belongs to him. Nor did he give a command to do the impossible deed. He made it possible for his disciples to disciple the nations through his presence with them.

This "I" is emphatic in the Greek text, and it is in the present tense. The One who promised to be with us is none other than the great "I am" (see Ex. 3:14). He is the one who was before Abraham.

There is no recorded ascension in Matthew's Gospel. Although the Holy Spirit is referred to in the baptismal formula of Matthew 28:19, we learn from John's Gospel about the sending of the Holy Spirit as our Counselor and advocate (see John 14:15-17; 15:26; 16:7 *ff.;* 20:22-23).

Humanly speaking the Great Commission would be impossible. But he who is the great I Am makes it possible through his outpoured and empowering Holy Spirit.

Subverting the Great Commission

Let me close by suggesting several ways through which the Great Commission may be subverted. If we professionalize this evangelistic mandate, we subvert it. If we make it apply only to ordained preachers and missionaries, we shall utterly overthrow it.

To whom was the Great Commission given? To the mission boards? To the parachurch organizations? To individual Christians? Was it not given to the church both in macrocosm and in microcosm? Are we not all sent ones? The apostolic succession which I prize seeks to reproduce the faith-response experience of the twelve apostles. The call to be a Christian is a call to mission and ministry. There is a real sense in which every Christian is ordained to the ministry of body building in his or her baptism (Eph. 4:12).

Charles G. Finney taught that each Christian ought to have a sense of personal responsibility for the salvation of the world. Apparently referring to the Great Commission, Finney said: "No man ever begins to obey this command who does not feel a personal responsibility in this thing which brings it home to his soul as *his own work.*"[9]

A second way to subvert the Great Commission is by prioritizing *baptizing* over *teaching.* The text will not allow us to chop the Commission up into two parts with one called *discipling* and the other labeled *perfecting*. Matthew 28:19 is not the only reference to discipling in the Great Commission. Nor does Matthew 28:20 refer to perfecting only. That is false exegesis. Both the baptizing and the teaching clauses are coequal and coterminous. They modify the primary clause, "make disciples of all nations."

We make disciples through baptizing them and teaching them. That baptizing is circumscribed by the formula, "in the name of the Father and of the Son and of the Holy Spirit." That teaching is circumscribed by both its purpose and its content, "to observe all that I have commanded you."

It will not do to dichotomize the Great Commission. That is a source of all kinds of errors in evangelism and mission. Ethical errors arise in our converts when we do not teach them to do the commandments of Christ. One of his commands, for example, is to love God supremely and neighbor as self. Another of his commandments is that we love each other. Then, too, is not this very command to make disciples one of those commandments of Christ which we should teach our converts to obey?

Such false dichotomizing contributes to the polarization between: evangelism and Christian social action; the Great Commission and the great commandment; the *kerygma* and the *didache;* preaching and teaching; evangelism and ethics; etc. About the only thing worse than cutting up the Great Commission into two parts is dividing it into three or even four *sequential* activities. I have known some interpreters who organize it into the four points of (1) go, (2) *then* make disciples, (3) *then* baptize them, and (4) *then* teach them. The biggest problem with that is that there is no *then* in the text.

If we wonder why so many of our converts are eternal children, part of our answer may be that we are not fulfilling the Great Commission of our Lord. Making disciples is far more than mere enlistment. So long as we major on the first five seconds of the initial conversion experience and minor on or make an elective out of the next five decades of the Christian life, we can't expect to produce much fruit which abides forever.

There are at least two aspects to making disciples which ought to concern us: making *new* disciples and making *true* disciples. When we make new disciples the church grows numerically. When we make true disciples the church grows in the depth of its discipleship. New disciples equal quantitative church growth. True disciples equal qualitative church growth.

Still a third way to subvert the Great Commission is to limit Christ's authority only to the spiritual realm of life. Do the words, "All authority," imply anything about the separation of life into compartments, such as religion, politics, economics, physical, spiritual? Does his authority stop at the front door of our church houses?

If ever we are tempted to believe in the old doctrine that there are two absolutely separated realms, the secular and the spiritual, each having nothing to do with the other, we need to remember what happened to Nazi Germany under Adolph Hitler. When we relegate making disciples only to the spiritual aspects of our existence, we strengthen the diabolical rulers of wickedness and make more room for the powers of darkness in our world.

I am quick to say that the Great Commission commands us Christians to make way for a new kingdom, a new government, which is operational right here and now. All other kingdoms will ultimately and utterly fail, but our Lord's kingdom is an everlasting one. We serve the one who has all authority in heaven and on earth.

Conclusion

Baptists in America split early in the nineteenth century over the question of missions. One group held that God had elected some to be saved and others to be lost. These were known as the antimissionary and antievangelistic Baptists.

The others believed that "God had elected a plan of salvation and a people to proclaim it." They were known as missionary or evangelistic Baptists. Today, those Baptists are the largest non-Catholic denomination in America.[10]

I thank God that my personal heritage has been with the evangelistic Baptists. On the old cornerstone of my home church building in South Carolina were the words, "Bethel Missionary Baptist Church." That word *Missionary* did not refer to a denomination; it referred to a theological conviction of an evangelistic church.

Suggested Study Questions

1. Exactly what does God command his disciples to do in the Great Commission of Matthew 28:16-20?
2. What does God promise to do for his disciples in the Great Commission of Matthew 28:16-20?
3. Is there any reference to the Holy Spirit in Matthew 28:16-20?
4. List, summarize, and critique the three ways suggested in this chapter for subverting the Great Commission. Also, briefly add other ways in which you believe the Great Commission may be subverted.

Notes

1. This is an adaptation from George W. Peters, *A Theology of Church Growth* (Grand Rapids, Michigan: Zondervan Publishing House, 1981), pp. 16-19.
2. Roland Q. Leavell, *Evangelism: Christ's Imperative Commission* (Nashville: Broadman Press, 1979 rev. ed.), esp. p. 15.
3. George Worrell, "Spiritual Foundations," in a larger discussion of "Spiritual Preparations for Your Missions," *World Mission Journal*, Vol. 52, No. 12, December, 1981, p. 9.
4. Peters, p. 216. See also pp. 210-211.
5. David J. Hesselgrave, "Non-Christian Faiths and the Twentieth Century Challenge,"

Voices, Vol. VIII, No. 1, Fall, 1981, p. 7. This is a quarterly publication of Trinity Evangelical Divinity School, Deerfield, Ill. See also Edward R. Dayton, *That Everyone May Hear* (Monrovia, Calif.: MARC, 1980, 2nd ed.), pp. 21-23.

6. Hesselgrave, pp. 7-8.

7. Delos Miles, *Church Growth—A Mighty River* (Nashville: Broadman, 1981), pp. 124-125.

8. C. H. Dodd, *The Apostolic Preaching and Its Development* (London: Hodder and Stoughton, 1936), p. 7.

9. Cited from Charles G. Finney's *Gospel Themes* (New York: Fleming H. Revell Co., 1876), p. 322, by Daniel Wade Armstrong, *An Examination of Evangelism in America Beginning with the Eighteenth Century in the Light of New Testament Principles of Evangelism* (an unpublished doctoral thesis at The Southern Baptist Theological Seminary, Louisville, Ky., 1955), p. 110.

10. Herschel H. Hobbs, *New Testament Evangelism* (Nashville: Convention Press, 1960), pp. 26-27.

11
The Lostness of Persons

Jeremiah 50:6-7; Luke 19:1-10

Introduction

A third motive for evangelizing is the lostness of persons apart from faith in Jesus Christ. We cannot evangelize aright until we believe that persons outside of Christ are lost and undone, without hope in this world or the one to come. J. Wilbur Chapman said, "That man is evangelistic who realizes that men are without Christ and that the gospel is the only way of salvation."[1]

George W. Truett, a great pastor-evangelist, in a sermon on "The Salt of the Earth," expressed his desire to live a thousand years in order to serve Christ. Said Truett:

I would like to live a thousand years and then ten thousand more, if that would please Christ, because the world needs Christ, and is doomed and lost without Christ and His gospel. Without yonder cross on which the Lord of Glory died, the world is lost, and for all its little perfumed philosophies, as a means of salvation from sin, I have nothing but unmeasured contempt.[2]

Charles H. Spurgeon was once asked if the heathen would be saved if Christian people did not preach the gospel to them. His answer was, "The question is, are we saved if we do not preach the gospel to them."[3]

The lost persons of the world are increasing ten times faster than the churches are growing. This fourth world of the lost is rapidly increasing. There are now more than three billion lost persons on our planet.

God's Eternal Purpose

"The eternal purpose" (Eph. 3:11) of God was, and is, to redeem lost persons. Hence, evangelism is not an isolated sideshow of history. On the contrary, it is the main event!

Scripture teaches that the Lamb of God was slain before the foundation of the world (see, for example, Rev. 13:8; Eph. 1:4; Heb. 4:3). Revelation 5 tells of a scroll, or book, sealed with the seven seals (v. 1). Herschel H. Hobbs prefers to call this scroll, "the roll of history from eternity to eternity." That scroll symbolizes God's dealings with all peoples and nations. Only the "Lion of the tribe of Judah, the Root of David" could open the scroll (v. 5). That Lion was also the Lamb who was slain and did ransom "men for God from every tribe and tongue and people and nation" (v. 9). Apparently, only in the redemptive purpose of God in Christ may be found the true interpretation of history.[4]

Jesus believed that unregenerate persons are lost. He said, "For the Son of man came to seek and to save the lost" (Luke 19:10). Jesus told the parables of the lost sheep (Luke 15:3-7), the lost coin (Luke 15:8-10), and the lost prodigal (Luke 15:11-32).

The apostolic church recognized that all persons were lost and needed the Savior. That was true of the Jews gathered in Jerusalem on the day of Pentecost (Acts 2:5 *ff.*); of Samaritans, or half-Jews (Acts 8:5); of an Ethiopian God-fearer (Acts 8:26 *ff.*); of a Roman centurion (Acts 10:1-48); and of pagan intellectuals (Acts 17:16 *ff.*). Paul believed that his Jewish kinsmen were lost and his heart's desire was that they might be saved (see Rom. 9:1-3; 10:1).

Moreover, salvation was to be found only in Christ. "And there is salvation in no one else, for there is no other name under heaven given among men by which we must be saved" (Acts 4:12). The context makes it clear that the name referred to is Jesus Christ of Nazareth. Paul said it this way, "For there is one God, and there is one mediator between God and men, the man Christ Jesus" (1 Tim. 2:5).

A Word from the Lord

Is there any word from the Lord for our day? Yes, that word is "Jesus is Lord." Jesus saves, and he alone saves because he is Lord (Heb. 1:1-3).

Romans 3:23 says, "all have sinned and fall short of the glory of God." That verse does not say that *some* have sinned but that *all* have done so. As Herschel H. Hobbs says, "Outside of Christ the Junior child is lost. The cultured lady is lost. The wealthy banker is lost. The scholar is lost."[5]

D. L. Moody once said, "I see every person as though he had a large L in the midst of his forehead. I consider him lost until I know he is saved."

It is said that as Peter Cartwright, a Methodist evangelist, once preached of man's condemnation in sin, General Andrew Jackson entered the church. Someone in the congregation whispered a little loudly, "General Jackson has come in." Fixing his eyes on General Jackson, the preacher declared, "Who is General Jackson? If he doesn't get his soul converted, God will damn him as quickly as he would a Guinea Negro."[6]

Each person, in order to be saved and to do God's will, should repent for himself or herself, believe for himself or herself, be baptized for himself or herself, and answer to God for himself or herself, both in time and eternity.

Not even Bible study will save a person. "You search the scriptures, because you think that in them you have eternal life, and it is they that bear witness to me; yet you refuse to come to me that you may have life" (John 5:39-40). Only when we come to Christ himself can we receive eternal life. When Paul said, "work out your own salvation with fear and trembling" (Phil. 2:12), he was saying, "work out what God has already worked in you."

Meaning of Lostness

The word *lost,* according to Professor William B. Coble, means someone out of touch with eternal reality. It is the

Greek word *apollumi,* which describes a thing not used or claimed. It means no longer visible, known, possessed, or attainable. A lost person is one who is unable to find the way, confused, helpless, ruined, or destroyed physically, mentally, or morally.[7]

One of the best ways to get at the meaning of lostness may be to examine its meaning in the three parables of Luke 15. Something is lost in each of the parables. In the first parable, it is a sheep that is lost. In the second parable, it is a silver coin that is lost. In the third parable, it is a son who is lost.

Something valuble is lost in each of the parables. In the first parable, it is a sheep valuable for wool, food, and sacrifice. Wool has always been valuable; but in the days of Jesus, it was exceedingly valuable. Moreover, the sheep could be eaten on festival occasions or offered as a sacrifice to God in religious ceremonies.

In the second parable, the valuable thing is a silver coin. That coin was worth more than one day's wages for the average working man. It might have been part of a woman's life savings. It could have spelled the difference between food and hunger. Probably the lost coin was one of ten held together by a silver chain and worn on a head piece to signify a married woman. Such was the custom in those days. In other words, that coin was one of ten which would be the equivalent of a wedding ring today. Therefore, the lost coin had symbolical and sentimental value, as well as monetary value.

In the third parable, the thing of value was a lost son. He was a person created in the image of God, the son of a loving father, a young man who laid claim to his third of a great estate. Here was a human being who belonged to a father and a family.

Note the ascending value of the lost objects. The sheep was valuable for wool, food, and sacrifice. The coin was valuable as money, memory, symbol, and sentiment. Surely no sheep could equal the value of a wedding ring! The son was valuble as a unique creation of God and as the fruit of conjugal love. Jesus used the most precious and costly objects to illustrate God's love for the disinherited and despised outcasts of his day. To the Pharisees and scribes, the tax collectors and outcasts were fuel for the fires of hell. To Jesus these poor, forgotten, and unloved sinners were as precious as a lost sheep, a lost wedding ring, and a lost son.

What did it mean for the sheep, the coin, and the son to be lost? In each case, it meant something different. In the case of the sheep, it meant subjection to the perils of being eaten by some wild beast, stolen by wandering thieves, or perishing in the darkness, dust, or drought. In the case of the lost coin, it meant failure to fulfill its purpose in creation and missing the mark for which it was intended. In the case of the lost son, it meant squandering his inheritance, living in a country far away, wasting his money in reckless living, spending everything he had on fair-weather friends, a severe famine, and grave poverty. It meant not being himself, hunger, and working at the degrading occupation of feeding hogs. No good Jew would eat, feed, or raise pork. So this fellow had gotten about as low as a man can get and still be called a man. I believe Jesus wanted us to understand that the prodigal son had broken God's commandments, became a moral profligate, an alcoholic, a beggar, and had descended almost to the level of the pigs he fed. He got so hungry he wanted to feed himself with the slop which he gave the pigs but "no one gave him any."

Note the progressive nature of the son's lostness. First, he rebelled against his father and sold his birthright for money. Second, he left home and went to a faraway country. Third, he wasted his money in reckless living. Fourth, a severe famine befell him. Fifth, he became almost like the hogs he fed. Doesn't that sound more like a modern biography than a parable of the first century?

What did it mean for the sheep, the coin, and the son to

be lost? In each case it meant something similar. It meant separation. In the case of the sheep, it meant separation from the fold, the pasture, the ninety-and-nine, and from the shepherd. In the case of the coin, it meant separation from the rest of the wedding band and from the wife to whom it belonged. In the case of the son, it meant separation from his father, his home, his inheritance, and his country.

Lostness always means separation, isolation, and alienation. To be lost means to be separated from one's owner, to fail in one's purpose, to be cut off from true existence. Every lost person is as lost as the lost sheep, the lost coin, and the lost son.

Models of Lostness Today

The world as we know it is lost. A part of it is preoccupied with strewing beer cans and whiskey bottles along the highway of life. Richard Burton spoke for this age when he said, "I've been in trouble all my life; I've done the most unutterable rubbish, all because of money. I didn't need it . . . the lure of the zeroes was simply too great."[8]

What does it mean to be lost in our society? Three different models come to mind: Jean Harris, who was convicted of killing her unfaithful lover, Dr. Herman Tarnower; Rita and John Jenrette; and Gary Gilmore.

Look first at Dr. Tarnower and Ms. Harris. Some of us have been blessed with weight loss and better health through the famous Scarsdale Diet of Dr. Tarnower. Apparently the doctor felt that his wealth and celebrity status freed him from the need to be committed in relationships with women. He carried on many affairs with a variety of women, promising to marry them and then dropping them when he tired of them, buying them off with money, jewelry, and even drugs.

One of Tarnower's mistresses was Jean Harris. Harris seemed to have everything our society could offer. She was a professional success, headmistress of a posh girls' school. Her job afforded her entry into an elite social circle on Capitol Hill in Washington, D. C. She was highly regarded as smart, witty, and charming. What more could any person want?

Harris wanted Dr. Tarnower for herself alone. This time Dr. Tarnower's offer of money and drugs didn't work. He had discarded Harris for a younger woman. Almost insane with jealousy, grief, pride, and drug dependency, Harris ended up shooting the doctor four times. Today she is serving a long jail term, alone, her career shattered, her lover dead. The sentence is being appealed.

Next, look at Rita and John Jenrette. John Jenrette was a powerful, popular congressman from South Carolina. He was caught in the Abscam investigation, convicted for taking a bribe, and defeated for reelection. On top of all that his wife, Rita Jenrette, filed for divorce. She charged the former congressman with numerous adulteries, drunken binges, and other related shenanigans.

Rita Jenrette, however, didn't stop there. She posed in the buff for *Playboy*; signed a fat book contract in which she told all and then some; and was catapulted to instant stardom on television and in the press. She was asked on one TV show if she felt any responsibility to her embattled husband or to the constituents they had served. She sighed, managed a coy smile, and said, "I've paid my dues." Is that what it means to pay ones dues in our society?

Now, consider Gary Gilmore. Norman Mailer's book, *The Executioner's Song,* may have made Gilmore an unforgettable character of the twentieth century. Mailer describes how after Gilmore's release from prison he was jumping in and out of bed with girls who had been doing the same thing since they were eleven years old. Gilmore's hedonistic joy ride, complete with drugs, six-packs, and eroticism was utterly senseless. It ended with two senseless murders for which he was convicted and executed.

Instead of coming to know God, Gilmore came to know what Augustine said: "The punishment of sin is sin."⁹ His death was a media event. But "what will it profit a man, if he gains the whole world and forfeits his life? Or what shall a man give in return for his life?" (Matt. 16:26).

Lostness in our society is the celebration of sin. It is bondage to the god Mammon. It is searching for satisfaction in professional success, sex, drugs, booze, crime, publicity, power, and hedonism. It is breaking the laws of God and of society.

Our Response to the Lost

If we would know what God's love for the lost is like and how we should respond to them, let us ponder the stories of the lost sheep, the lost coin, and the lost son in Luke 15. *Agape* love grieves over the lost. It values every person even as the shepherd valued the lost sheep, the woman valued the lost coin, and the father valued the prodigal and his elder brother.

Moreover, *agape* love searches for the lost and seeks to restore that which is found. We do need to pray for persons to be saved. But, more than that, we need to pray that the Lord will send us out after the lost (see Luke 10:2). A humorous story may illustrate this for us. A man stood before a judge charged with stealing a turkey. The man said that his crime was in answer to prayer. When asked to explain, he said: "I prayed for the Lord to send me a turkey. When nothing happened, I prayed for the Lord to send me after a turkey." While we may not agree with the man's theology; we can learn from his philosophy.

Jesus, the Great and Good Shepherd, exhibits the same kind of love which the shepherd, the woman, and the father revealed. That same love has been poured into our hearts through the Holy Spirit (see Rom. 5:5).

We too are to love the lost and straying with a love that grieves over them, values them as crown jewels of God's creation, searches after them down all the labryinthine ways of life, and restores them to the flock of him who is the Good Shepherd. To be sure, we cannot generate such love. It is the gift of God. "We love, because he first loved us" (1 John 4:19).

If our love for the lost grieves over them, we shall weep over their plight. God's mood over rebellion, ingratitude, and insensitivity to others is one of grief—not disgust or anger.

A hardened criminal was awaiting execution. Many pastors tried to reach him for Christ without success. They told him what a great sinner he was and how he needed salvation. They only succeeded in hardening his heart further. Finally, a humble layman asked to see the notorious criminal. He said, "You and I are in a terrible fix, aren't we?" Soon the man was in tears, as he repented of his sins and trusted the Savior.[10]

C. E. Matthews and a pastor sat in a car one night during a revival meeting trying to win a lost man to Christ. Every kind of approach failed to reach him. Finally the pastor began to weep over this lost soul. His compassionate tears melted the heart of the man, and soon he was saved.[11]

If our love for the lost values them highly enough, we shall love them without restrictions, recommendations, or reciprocations. God's love is not an *if* love. Nor is it a *because* love. It is an *anyhow* love.

If our love for the lost searches after them as did the shepherd after the sheep, the woman after the coin, and the father after the prodigal, it will be a sacrificial love as seen in the search of Jesus Christ for us. We too shall be willing to lay down our very lives in that search for lost persons.

If our love restores, as modeled in the shepherd, the woman, and the father, we shall be as gracious to wandering persons as was Jesus to tax collectors, adulterers, and other outcasts of his day. Jesus found us and restored us to his fold. We are to find the lost of our place and time and restore them to his fold. *Agape* love is like that.[12]

Conclusion

Do we love the lost as God does? Do we hate sin as does God? Boldness does not mean brashness. It is always sensitive to persons. Charles G. Finney, the lawyer-turned-evangelist, in his *Memoirs* said of his call to preach: "I had no longer any desire to practice law . . . no labor, I thought, could be so sweet, and no employment so exalted as that of holding up Christ to a dying world."[13]

Suggested Study Questions

1. In one-half page or less, state the rationale which some Christians give for shying away from the use of the word *lost* in referring to non-Christians.
2. What role has the belief in theological universalism and double-edged or two-way predestination played in eroding the belief that all persons apart from Christ as their Savior are lost?
3. Using the biblical meaning of the word *lost,* as cited by Professor Coble in this chapter, write a one-page description of one contemporary person (other than those described above) whom you consider to be a model of what it means to be lost today.

Notes

1. Quoted by Daniel Wade Armstrong, *An Examination of Evangelism in America Beginning with the Eighteenth Century in the Light of New Testament Principles of Evangelism* (an unpublished doctoral thesis at The Southern Baptist Theological Seminary, Louisville, Ky., 1955), p. 138.
2. George W. Truett, *The Salt of the Earth,* edited by Powhatan W. James (Grand Rapids: Wm. B. Eerdmans Publishing Co., 1953), p. 25.
3. Herschel H. Hobbs, *New Testament Evangelism* (Nashville: Convention Press, 1960), pp. 10-11.
4. Ibid., pp. 16-17.

5. Ibid., p. 63.

6. Related in a slightly different form by Hobbs. See ibid, p. 65.

7. William B. Coble, "Lost: Someone Out of Touch with Eternal Reality," *Word and Way,*
Vol. 118, No. 17, April 23, 1981, p. 12.

8. Quoted by Foy Valentine, "Doing the Word," *Light,* September, 1981, p. 2. A
publication of The Christian Life Commission of the Southern Baptist Convention.

9. These three models are based upon Charles Colson, "A Society that Celebrates Sin,"
Christianity Today, Vol. XXV, No. 17, Oct. 2, 1981, p. 17.

10. This story is related by Hobbs, p. 114.

11. Ibid., p. 116.

12. I acknowledge indebtedness to Professor Harold Bryson of New Orleans Baptist
Theological Seminary for some of the ideas encompassed in this section on our
response to the lost. See "Bryson Stresses God's Eternal Love," *Word and Way,* Vol. 118,
No. 44, Nov. 5, 1981, p. 14.

13. Cited by Armstrong, pp. 106-107.

12
The Wrath of God

Exodus 32:7-14; John 3:35-36

Introduction

David Wilkerson, whose Teen Challenge center in Brooklyn was said to have a better cure rate than any drug treatment center in the nation, said he heard a new term from the drug culture in 1981. It is the "80-year-bang," meaning "God gives you 80 years to turn on."[1]

The psalmist addressed himself to the length of a person's days in Psalm 90.

> The years of our life are threescore and ten,
> or even by reason of strength fourscore;
> yet their span is but toil and trouble;
> they are soon gone, and we fly away (v. 10).

Have you noticed that those words are preceded and succeeded by statements about the wrath of God? All of our days "pass away under" God's wrath (v. 9). And if the Lord should give us eighty years, apparently the psalmist believed God gives us those years to turn off from his wrath and to turn on to his steadfast love (vv. 11-17).

Contrary to what the drug culture says, God does not give us eighty years to turn on to drugs or any other escape mechanism. He does not grant us longevity in order to find god substitutes or to waste our energies in riotous and unholy living. All of our days, be they ever so long or brief, are lived out under the wrath and the mercy of God. Time is a precious gift from God to build our character and to gain "a heart of wisdom" (Ps. 90:12).

Novelist Taylor Caldwell wrote of a person who died at fifteen but was not buried until he was seventy-five! The author of Psalm 90 seemed to have been acquainted with such persons.

A Great Chasm Fixed

A very sobering point made by the New Testament is that however long we live on this earth, physical death fixes forever our status in heaven or in hell. Let us ponder long and hard the words of Father Abraham to the rich man in Hades, "between us and you a great chasm has been fixed, in order that those who would pass from here to you may not be able, and none may cross from there to us" (Luke 16:26).

We need not suppose that the death of the wicked will change their character. "The rich man in the Lord's story," said J. A. Motyer, "bore in hell the same personal marks as he did in life: desire for sensual gratification, subjection of the welfare of others to his personal whim, absence of any regard for the law of God."[2]

I agree with Motyer that "every sensitive person, facing the question of human destiny, must surely long to be a universalist."[3] Nevertheless, we dare not give that much weight to what sinners think about the seriousness of sin.

The postconversion Bob Dylan uttered the unadulterated truth when he said: "I was blinded . . . I was gone. . . . How weak was the foundation I was standing upon."[4] Jonathan Edwards was right: we are all sinners in the hands of an angry God. God is angry with sin. "The Bible speaks more frequently of the anger of God than it does of the anger of man," said H. Michaud.[5]

God's Attitude Toward Sin

God hates sin. His anger is always a revelation of his righteousness. "For the wrath of God is revealed from heaven against all ungodliness and wickedness of men who by their wickedness suppress the truth" (Rom. 1:18).

Even sinners like ourselves find certain sins repulsive. "We cannot tolerate child abuse, cruelty, egotism, or gluttony," says Leon Morris. "Such sins repel us."[6]

God's hatred for all sin is such that he is "of purer eyes than to behold evil and canst not look on wrong" (Hab. 1:13). He can never condone sin even though it be in a David, one after his own heart. To put it in the vernacular, God has no pets when it comes to sin. His face is forever set against sin and evil of all sorts.

After Adlai Stevenson had been the United States ambassador to the United Nations for sometime, he said: "I have learned a new word, yo. It can mean either yes or no." God thunders an eternal no to sin. His holy nature will not permit him to use the word *yo*. A yo-yo God regarding sin would be a strange contradiction.

God without exception hates all sin whether expressed personally or corporately, whether committed by individuals or by groupings of individuals. His face is as dead set against social sins as it is personal sins. The wages of all sin is death (Rom. 6:23).

If we are to be imitators of God, then we too shall have to think and feel about sin as does he. Insofar as our nature conforms to his nature, we are not at liberty to use the word *yo* regarding sin.

The Nature of God's Wrath

We have been speaking of the wrath and anger of God. Those are some words which the Bible uses to describe a fourth motive for world evangelization. One reason persons need salvation, according to Paul, is that they have sinned and are under the condemnation of God's wrath (see Rom. 1:18 to 3:20). Following a reference to "the judgment seat of Christ" (2 Cor. 5:10), Paul said: "Therefore, knowing the fear of the Lord, we persuade men" (2 Cor. 5:11).

The wrath of God is his anger and indignation against sin. It is that rational and responsible action of God which expresses his aversion to sin. This passion against sin arises out of the nature of God.

God's wrath is after the analogy of human wrath, and yet it is other than human anger. It is holy wrath, freely directed against sin without partiality. His wrath is motivated by his love.

Some of us may be accustomed to think that the Old Testament emphasizes the wrath of God, whereas the New Testament lifts up the love of God. N. H. Snaith says, "such a sharp distinction is unwarranted." Both God's steady anger against sin in every form and his forebearance to execute the fierceness of his anger may be seen throughout the Old Testament story. An extreme example is that of the golden calf in Exodus 32:7-14. It was a saying of the rabbis that in every sin there is something of the golden calf.[7]

According to John's Gospel, God's wrath is a present reality in the world. It is even now being poured out upon those who do not obey the Son of God. As a matter of fact, the same Scripture which tells us such good news about the love of God also tells us the bad news about the wrath of God.

John 3:16 speaks of the incomparable love of God for the whole world. But John 3:18 speaks of the fearful condemnation of unbelievers: "He who believes in him is not condemned; he who does not believe is condemned already, because he has not believed in the name of the only Son of God." John 3 closes with the words: "the Father loves the Son, and has given all things into his hand. He who believes in the Son has eternal life; he who does not obey the Son shall not see life, but the wrath of God rests upon him" (vv. 35-36).

The wrath of God rests upon all who do not believe in Jesus Christ as their Lord and Savior. "A person can go to hell behind a mahogany desk as quickly as behind a lathe," said Herschel H. Hobbs, "from the cloistered halls of a university as from the raucous atmosphere of a brothel."[8]

Can you agree with this statement by David Wilkerson? "Drinking won't send you to hell. Drugs won't send you to hell. Sleeping with women won't send you to hell. Cheating on your income tax won't send you to hell. Only one sin can send you to hell—rejecting the love of God."[9]

We may need to preach hell more to Christians than to non-Christians. C. S. Lewis suggested that the doors to hell are locked from the inside. Persons say something like, "Hey, God, I don't need you; I never wanted to be friends with you anyhow."

God's wrath is tied up with condemnation, judgment, darkness, evil deeds, disobedience, and unbelief. The light of Christ brought judgment upon the lovers of darkness and the doers of evil deeds. God has given all authority to the Son. Either we acknowledge and accept his authority over us and over all or we suffer the consequences of our rebellion against him and his kingdom.

Heaven begins right here on earth. So does hell. Eternal life is a present possession. Even so the wrath of God is a present reality. Much as salvation is past, present, and future; so is God's wrath past, present, and future. God does not wait until the righteous get to heaven to reward them. Nor does he always wait until the unrighteous get to hell to reward them.

God's wrath is poured out in the hereafter, as well as in the here and now. There is such a thing as "the wrath to come" (1 Thess. 1:10). Some persons may go through this world robbing widows and cheating orphans. They may do it legally. They may now enjoy great prosperity, live high, and even receive respect and honor from others. Their evil deeds toward the poor and lowly may never come to light in this world. But the blood of their victims cries out against them from their cheap coffins in some pauper's cemetery. And someday beyond this world's sunsets will be designated payday for them. We can be sure that there is a payday someday. God's wrath will fall one day; great will be the cries of the unjust, the unmerciful, and the unprepared.

The Bible speaks of "the day of wrath" which seems to be in the future and connected with the judgment (see Rom. 2:5; Matt. 16:27). Paul said, "for those who are factious and do not obey the truth, but obey wickedness, there will be wrath and fury. There will be tribulation and distress for every human being who does evil" (Rom. 2:8-9).

Evangelist Sam P. Jones went to hold a revival meeting in West Point, Georgia. Only four persons showed up at the first morning service. That afternoon he and the pastor went throughout the town saying to all the men just one thing, "You are going to hell." Two of the women who were present went from door-to-door, telling the women the same thing, "You are going to hell." That created much anger and a lot of curiosity. There was a crowd present that night and every service thereafter. A great revival came to West Point.[10] I do not recommend that we follow that pattern today. But, in some clear and concise way, we need to warn persons to flee the wrath of God.

Accountability goes along with responsibility and stewardship. God will hold us accountable for responding to the light he has given us. Furthermore, he will hold us accountable for sharing that light with the human race.

Someone asked Sir Winston Churchill on his seventy-fifth birthday if he feared death. "I am ready to meet my Maker," he replied. "Whether my Maker is prepared for the great ordeal of meeting me is another matter."[11]

The Cross of Christ

The love of God and the wrath of God are woven together in his character as constituents of his righteousness. Both come together in the cross of Jesus Christ, God's beloved Son. "In this is love," wrote John, "not that we loved God but that he loved us and sent his Son to be the expiation for our sins" (1 John 4:10).

The cross brought a new dimension to religion. The

cross was the means which God used to deal with humanity's sin. That word "expiation" is also translated "propitiation" by some versions. It is a word which means "that which averts wrath." Therefore, we see in the cross of Christ just how seriously God takes sin and how radical is *agape* love's solution to the problem of the wrath of God. Leon Morris puts it like this: "When we see man for what he is, the wrath of God for what it is, and the cross for what it is, then and only then do we see love for what it is."[12]

God has created a moral universe. He cannot deny himself. He must punish sin. But the radically new thing is that "God shows his love for us in that while we were yet sinners Christ died for us" (Rom. 5:8). We were "weak" (a word probably meaning sick), "ungodly" and "enemies" (see vv. 6,10). We were condemned and perishing in our sins, but "by this we know love, that he laid down his life for us" (1 John 3:16). The death of Jesus makes our justification possible and saves us from the wrath of God (see Rom. 5:9).

Conclusion

You and I, who once were by nature children of wrath, know what a terrible thing it is to fall into the hands of an angry God. Now that we are children of God through faith in Jesus Christ, we also know what a blessed experience it is to be supported by God's everlasting arms of love. Therefore, we can say with the apostle Paul to those who are children of wrath:

So we are ambassadors for Christ, God making his appeal through us. We beseech you on behalf of Christ, be reconciled to God. For our sake he made him to be sin who knew no sin, so that in him we might become the righteousness of God (2 Cor. 5:20-21).

Finally, consider this one example: "What if it's true after all, and Jesus is coming back?" Those words in a tract, wrapped in a roll of toilet tissue, helped turn Iris Urrey toward God. Urrey had done everything wrong. She had sold out to the devil. But that tract, which was also wrapped up in the life of a man of God, led Iris Urrey to sell out her whole life to Jesus Christ. Today, she is a twentieth-century Mary Magdalene.

Our God can turn a tramp into a saint! He is in the business of making persons into new creations. He can save you no matter who you are or what you may have done. Those who believe in Jesus Christ not only escape the wrath of God; they become apostles of his love.

Suggested Study Questions

1. Why should we not make too sharp a distinction between the Old and New Testaments in considering the wrath of God as over against his love?
2. How do you see the wrath of God and the love of God relating to each other?
3. Cite one or more biblical examples and/or texts which illustrate that the wrath of God is past, present, and future.

Notes

1. Edmund K. Gravely, Jr., "Wilkerson Returns Cross to Switchblade Territory," *Christianity Today*, Vol. XXV, No. 15, Sept. 4, 1981, p. 52.
2. J. A. Motyer, "The Final State: Heaven and Hell" in Carl F. H. Henry, ed., *Basic Christian Doctrines* (New York: Holt, Rinehart and Winston, 1962), p. 293.
3. Ibid, p. 290.
4. Quoted by Martin Sarvis in a letter to the editor, published in *Christianity Today*, Vol. XXV, No. 15, Sept. 4, 1981, p. 10.
5. H. Michaud, "Anger" in J.-J. Von Allmen, gen. ed., *A Companion to the Bible* (New York: Oxford University Press, 1958), p. 19.
6. Leon Morris, *Testaments of Love: A Study of Love in the Bible* (Grand Rapids: Wm. B. Eerdmans Publishing Co., 1981), p. 133.
7. N. H. Snaith, "Wrath, Anger, Indignation," Alan Richardson, ed., *A Theological Word Book of the Bible* (New York: The Macmillan Co., 1956), p. 289.

8. Herschel H. Hobbs, *New Testament Evangelism* (Nashville: Convention Press, 1960), p. 63.

9. Quoted by Gravely, p. 51.

10. Mrs. Sam P. Jones and Walt Holcomb, *The Life and Sayings of Sam P. Jones* (Atlanta, Ga.: The Franklin-Turner Co., 1907, 2nd rev. ed.), p. 89.

11. Quoted in an editorial in *Christianity Today*, Vol. XXV, No. 17, Oct. 2, 1981, p. 16.

12. See Morris, pp. 130-131.

Section V
The Messenger in Evangelism:
What Means Are Available
to Every Witness?

13
The Spiritual Autobiography[1]

Jeremiah 9:23-24; 1 Corinthians 1:26-31

Introduction

We have examined the meaning, message, models, and motives of evangelism. Now, I would like to introduce a new section dealing specifically with the messenger who is moved to share the gospel with the unreconciled. This section will seek to answer the question: what means are available to every Christian witness? Those means are the spiritual autobiography, the personal testimony, an evangelistic life-style, the work of the Holy Spirit, and the prayer life of the witness.

This chapter concentrates on the spiritual autobiography. One might even call it the evangelistic autobiography insofar as it becomes an instrument for evangelizing the lost.

The spiritual autobiography is your firsthand religious experience as it relates to the gospel story. It has much in common with what William James calls the "twice-born" religious experience in his famous book on *The Varieties of Religious Experience*.[2] Such autobiography may at some points be identified with what Abraham Maslow called "peak experiences" and with what Herbert A. Otto labeled "Minerva experiences." It even has some kinship with what Andrew Greeley calls "ecstasy as a way of knowing."

Franklin Littell contends that there is such a thing as "alpine events" in the life of persons. The spiritual autobiography is an attempt to identify and interpret those "alpine events" in one's life.

Think of your life story as one bolt of cloth. Like a cloth

161

bolt, it has a beginning and an ending. Yet, all that is in-
between is still the same cloth. It may wind and twist, flow
and cling, but it's still the same cloth. So it is with one's life
story. The entire life is but one bolt of cloth even if it is
refashioned, recycled, and colored anew.

Then, too, follow the threads in that bolt of cloth. See
how intricately they are woven. Our lives have many threads
running through them. As our story interfaces and inter-
sects with God's story, all of these threads are pulled together
into an harmonious whole.

Analogues

We are beginning to hear more and more about the use
of story and biography in the service of theology. All of what
I have to say about evangelistic autobiography should be
placed in this larger context and related specifically to
evangelism.

This is not to say that the use of autobiography in the
service of evangelism is a new thought. Far from it. We know
from the history of the formation of the New Testament
canon that a major criterion for including the twenty-seven
books was the belief that these books were authentically
apostolic. And no one could be an apostle on a par with the
twelve unless he was an eyewitness to the resurrection of
Jesus Christ (see Acts 1:22). There is a sense, then, in which
the whole New Testament may be considered as an evangelistic autobiography of the twelve and of Paul.

Surely the four canonical Gospels may be seen as
evangelistic autobiographies. We do refer to the four authors as the four evangelists. The evangelistic intention of
John's Gospel is clearly spelled out for us in John 20:30-31.
C. H. Dodd and others have pointed out the kerygmatic
nature of the four Gospels. The Christ of faith and the Jesus
of history are so commingled in the four Gospels that they
are inseparable. Those strange "we" sections of Acts (see
Acts 16:10; 20:5), the second volume of the Luke-Acts

narrative, lend credence to the supposition that at least these are more evangelistic autobiographies than they are lives, or historical biographies, of Jesus Christ.

James S. Stewart in *A Faith to Proclaim* says something to the effect that the early messengers of Jesus Christ became themselves a part of the gospel message.[3] This was certainly true in the Book of Acts (see Acts 2:32; 4:20).

Paul's witness to Jesus Christ was both objective and subjective. On the one hand Paul said: "For what we preach is not ourselves, but Jesus Christ as Lord" (2 Cor. 4:5). You can't get much more objective than that. While on the other hand, Paul also said: "I have been crucified with Christ; it is no longer I who live, but Christ who lives in me; and the life I now live in the flesh I live by faith in the Son of God, who loved me and gave himself for me" (Gal. 2:20). You can't get much more subjective than that kind of Christ mysticism.

Therefore, autobiography has been enlisted in the service of evangelism from the earliest days of Christian history. There has always been, and will always be, a prominent place for autobiography in the witness of the church.

It is an effective way to tell the gospel story because it communicates with authority, variety, and interest from an incarnational stance. You are more believable than someone from the distant past.

Guidelines

But how shall we escape from drowning in the sea of our own subjectivity when using our spiritual autobiographies? It seems to me that four guidelines may be laid out to govern the use of autobiography in the service of evangelism. The first and most important of these guidelines is that such autobiography should exalt God above all else and glorify him above all others. As Gabriel Fackre puts it, "Autobiography in evangelism does its work when it points beyond itself to the biography of God."[4]

The purpose of autobiography is not personal glory,

but the glory of God. Jeremiah 9:23-24 was so firmly riveted
in the mind of Paul that he quoted and commented on it in
1 Corinthians 1:31 and in 2 Corinthians 10:17; he referred to
it again in Galatians 6:14, and almost certainly in Philippians
3:2-11. And what does Jeremiah 9:23-24 say?

> Thus says the Lord: "Let not the wise man glory in his
> wisdom, let not the mighty man glory in his might, let not
> the rich man glory in his riches; but let him who glories
> glory in this, that he understands and knows me, that I am
> the Lord who practice steadfast love; justice and righteous-
> ness in the earth; for in these things I delight, says the
> Lord."

In other words, Jeremiah's injunction is: "Don't glory in
anything or anyone except God and your knowledge of
him." So the apostle Paul could say over against those who
glory in the circumcision of the flesh:

> But far be it from me to glory except in the cross of our
> Lord Jesus Christ, by which the world has been crucified to
> me, and I to the world. For neither circumcision counts for
> anything, nor uncircumcision, but a new creation (Gal.
> 6:14-15).

A second guideline for using autobiography in the
service of evangelism is that it should be intimate knowledge
of God, religious experience which is firsthand, knowledge
of God which is mediated through one's own sensorium.
Such knowledge should be as personal as that which a
husband and wife experience in the intimacy of marriage.
First John 1:1-3 may be a good biblical model for us to follow.

A third guideline for using autobiography in the service
of evangelism is that it should be capable of being communi-
cated through varied forms of media. It would be a gross
mistake to suppose that one can communicate his or her
experience of God only through one medium, such as pen
and ink, or spoken words in narrative form.

The apostle Paul used the medium of spoken words in prose form to share his story in Acts 22 and 26. Francis Thompson used poetry to tell his story in "The Hound of Heaven." Charles Wesley used poetry set to music to share his story in "O for a Thousand Tongues to Sing." The great Augustine created a new genre which we call *The Confessions of St. Augustine.* John Bunyan used fiction. Surely much of *The Pilgrim's Progress* is autobiographical. Frank Buchman even created a movement which majored on sharing personal data at house parties. This movement was known as the Oxford Group and later called Moral Rearmament. The outstanding evangelical Episcopalian, Samuel Shoemaker, was closely connected with Buchman at one time. Shoemaker's split with the Oxford Group led to the formation of Faith at Work, a group which still makes a great deal out of sharing. Ben Johnson's Institute for Church Renewal is a spiritual grandchild of Frank Buchman's Oxford Group.

Many Christians have used their journals and diaries to tell of their experiences with God. In John Wesley's journals, we read about his heartwarming experience on Aldersgate Street. In George Whitefield's journals, we read of his conversion experience. Whitefield's journals were published during his lifetime. In Dag Hammarskjold's *Markings,* we learn he was a twice-born man.

A host of Christian witnesses have chosen to communicate their testimony to God's transforming grace in full-scaled autobiographies. Examples are C. S. Lewis' *Surprised by Joy,* Oral Roberts's *The Call,* and Elton Trueblood's *While It Is Day.*

Mike Parker tells his story through the use of magic. As a 1980 student summer missionary, Parker moved every week to a different resort entertaining and ministering with magic. Calling himself "Mike the Magnificent," he emphasizes that he does not have magic power.[5]

One of my former students created a simple, three-character drama to tell his story. If you are gifted with paint, brush, and canvas, you may be able to use that medium to help tell your story.

A fourth guideline for using autobiography in the service of evangelism is to remember that such data will be more effective when used with those who come out of one's own cultural context. Each time that Paul shared his story in Acts, it was with those who understood his cultural background. Luke recorded Paul's testimony in Acts 22:2: "When they heard that he addressed them in the Hebrew language, they were the more quiet." Paul used his listeners' mother tongue. Then, in Acts 26:2-3, Paul said to King Agrippa: "I think myself fortunate that it is before you . . . I am to make my defense . . . because you are especially familiar with all customs and controversies of the Jews."

However, that same Paul used a very different approach and style when he witnessed to the intellectuals standing in the middle of the Areopagus at Athens (see Acts 17:16-34). That time he quoted an inscription on one of their idols and a line from one of their poets.

The Church Growth Movement teaches us that there are four cultural categories in which we share our witness to others. All have to do with the degree of cultural distance between the evangelists and those to be evangelized. The E-0 category is evangelism to those of our own culture who are already affiliated with a church but who have no valid Christian experience. The E-1 category crosses the "stained-glass barrier" and moves out into its own culture. The E-2 category crosses a barrier of culture. The E-3 category is at the end of the spectrum crossing the most difficult culture barrier of people from other countries. Evangelistic auto-biography is most effective in E-0 witnessing and least effective in E-3 witnessing.[6]

My Autobiography as a Paradigm

Now, in order to clarify further what I mean by evangelistic autobiography, I shall share with you some excerpts from my own life story. Imagine you are in a church house, let us say a typical congregation to which I might speak on a Sunday morning.

Many hundreds of years ago the psalmist said: "Come and hear, all you who fear God, and I will declare what he has done for me" (66:16). You respect God, or else you would not be here today. Perhaps you have come to this house of prayer for all people to hear what God has done, is doing, and will do for humankind. Therefore, as did the psalmist long, long ago, I invite you to hear some of the things which God has done for me.

I was born and reared on a tobacco farm in Florence County, South Carolina, where my father was a day laborer who could neither read nor write. He had to sign an X for his name. My mother did go to the third grade in school.

There on the farm I grew up in an atmosphere of both spiritual and physical poverty—spiritual poverty because my parents were not practicing members of any religious group, physical poverty because of my family's social and economic standing in the community. We were on the bottom rung of the social and economic ladder, if indeed on the ladder at all. I recall how my older sister and I would at times steal chickens from the people on whose farms we lived.

The first pair of shoes which I remember owning was a second-hand pair of brogans given to me by my first-grade schoolteacher. I was very proud of those shoes.

The first real crisis in my life came when I was seven. It was on the day of the big Easter egg hunt at school, supposedly a very happy day. Yet, it turned out to be one of the saddest days of my life. At that time my father was working away from home during the week. When my older sister, younger brother, and I returned home on the school bus that afternoon, our first cousin met us. He told us that our mother had left home, taking our baby sister with her, and that she intended never to return. I can't describe to you how deeply that hurt me. At that time I couldn't understand any of my mother's reasons for doing a thing like that. It hurt me so much that I couldn't even cry about it. A root of bitterness sprang up in my heart toward my mother which required many years to remove.

My father got the three of us children together and tried to make a home for us. Then, shortly after my eighth birthday another tragedy befell us. Daddy left home early on Saturday afternoon, the day before Pearl Harbor was bombed, with his brother and a friend with whom he had grown up—a big, husky man.

He told me and my sister and brother to go to our uncle's house and to wait for him until he returned home that Saturday night. But he never came home. The three men went to a little beer joint near Florence on U.S. 301 and got to drinking and having a "good time." As the evening wore on, my dad's friend got into a fight with another man. My father tried to break up the fight, but was knocked down to the floor. His friend got on top of him, pulled out his big pocket knife, and in his drunken stupor stabbed and cut my father to death.

My whole world caved in because when I lost my father I thought I had lost the only adult person in the world who deeply cared for me. And because of some things which my dad's friend had said about my mother when he came by our house on Saturday to pick up my father, I got it into my head that my mother had hired him to kill my father. You can imagine how twisted I was with hatred and hurt.

After a few months with relatives, moving from place to place, not really being wanted by any of them, something very good happened to me. I was invited to live with some folk whom I knew, but who were in no way related to me. For the first time in my life I had a bed of my own, three good meals to eat every day, and decent clothes and shoes to wear. Yet, more important than these material blessings, these folk were believers in Jesus Christ and members of the Baptist church in that rural community. They took me to church with them every Sunday morning, every Sunday night, every Wednesday night, and even once a quarter on Saturdays to attend the business conferences.

There in that little country church I discovered the Bible, a Book to which I was a total stranger, although I had been reared in what is called the Bible Belt. And I learned some things about God. When I was eleven years old, I felt separated from God. I had a miserable feeling inside of me. I was so unhappy that I felt like I was going to die unless something was done soon. I talked this over with my Sunday School teacher and with my foster parents. They all told me that I ought to confess my sins to God, ask him to help me, and place my life into his hands. As best I knew how, I followed their advice. That unhappy feeling left me. Peace and joy came into my life. Later, I went before the whole congregation and publicly confessed my faith in Jesus Christ as the Son of God and as my Lord and Savior and was baptized into the body of Christ by that congregation in Lynches River.

I grew in grace and in favor with God and men until my fourteenth birthday. Then, shortly before my fourteenth birthday, I was reconciled to my mother. I became convinced that she had nothing to do with my father's death and that she did, in fact, love me very much. So, on my fourteenth birthday I ran away from my foster home in the middle of the night, borrowed five dollars from a friend, walked eleven miles, caught a bus, and went to live with my mother and stepfather in Charleston, South Carolina.

Shortly after arriving in Charleston, I discovered that my stepfather drank a great deal. Life was unpleasant in that environment. So at the age of fourteen years and three months, I quit school prior to finishing the ninth grade and joined the United States Army. Of course, I lied about my age and persuaded my mother to sign for me.

I was just a kid thrust overnight into a completely adult world at Fort Jackson. And for some reason, I wanted very much to be accepted by the men in my company as one of them. I started doing the things which most of them did. I stopped going to church, ceased to read my Bible, and discontinued praying. I started drinking, smoking, cursing, gambling, and fighting. In short, I became a moral reprobate, broke God's covenant with me, and forsook my baptismal vows. I continued that wayward life for a little more than two and one-half years.

Then a great shaking of the foundations of my whole being came during the Korean War. I was a platoon sergeant of a rifle platoon in an infantry company. We had made our way deep into North Korea through the Changin Reservoir within about five miles of the Yalu River, the boundary between Manchuria and North Korea. Snow was many inches deep on the ground. Sometimes at night the temperature would drop down to twenty or thirty degrees below zero.

On the night of November 26, 1950, about midnight, we heard bugles blowing and rifles firing. My platoon was not under attack. But for the first time in the Korean War the Chinese Communists had entered the war in our section of the front.

Soon we got an order on the telephone to move our platoon out of position and to try to plug one of the holes where the Chinese had broken through our lines. We moved as rapidly as possible across the snow, engaged the enemy until about mid-morning on November 27. Then they broke off the battle.

We discovered that during the night the Chinese had completely encircled our position and cut us off from the First Marine Division some twelve to fifteen miles behind us. There was no way to get our dead or wounded out, and no way to get food and ammunition supplies in—both of which were running low. On that particular day the overcast was too heavy for an airdrop.

So we regrouped, placed our men two to the hole, and dug in a few feet apart on the forward slope of the mountain for the attack which we felt would certainly come when darkness fell. I was in the platoon command post with our lieutenant and our platoon medic and messenger. Our command post was a large bunker which the North Koreans had dug into the side of the mountain. It consisted of two parts. Each part was about six by six feet and was covered with poles and dirt; and the parts were connected with a trench about four feet deep.

About dusk the Chinese began to probe our lines. They shot flares into the air and charged our position in successive waves at the sound of a bugle. The lieutenant and I were in the trench which connected the two parts of our bunker, firing at the Chinese and giving orders to our men, trying to encourage them to hold fast. To our right in one part of the bunker were our medic and messenger passing ammunition to us and taking care of our telephone contact with the company command post.

Bullets were flying all around us. There were so many of the Chinese that we couldn't stop them. When I saw they were going to overrun us, I turned to the lieutenant and said: "Sir, what are we going to do?"

He said: "Sergeant, you know what the orders are." We had orders not to withdraw under any circumstances. In a matter of moments the lieutenant was shot. He fell over in the trench and groaned for a while before he died.

I didn't know what to do. But the thought came to me to throw down my M-1 rifle in the snow and to jump back into the vacant end of our bunker and to play dead. I lay down on my back, sort of on my right side, facing the entrance to the hole.

Almost immediately a Chinese soldier came into the bunker firing his rifle. He didn't see me at first because of the darkness. However, one of his bullets hit me in my right little finger, entering at the end joint and going out at the knuckle. It scared me. I thought I was going to die. I had not prayed for a long time. But I began to pray silently in my mind to God.

As the soldier came on into the hole and found me, he shook me with his hand and shouted something in Chinese. Then, I guess he wanted to make sure I was dead. So he placed his rifle on my forehead. When I felt that cold steel, I thought it was the end. I don't remember everything I said to God, but as best I recall, my thoughts went something like this: *Lord, if you are all powerful like I've always heard you are, you can bring me out of here alive. If you will save my life, I'll do anything you want me to do.* I was so desperate I was trying to bargain with God for my life. And, God is my witness, when the soldier pulled the trigger, instead of going through my head, the bullet went down past my right ear. It did not knock me out. In my memory, as I reflect back upon it, it seems like a red hot iron had been placed against my head and left there. There was that burning sensation.

He went on out. After an hour and a half or maybe two hours, the firing ceased. Two Chinese came into the hole with me. They slept and rested a couple of hours. Then two more would come in. All night long there were two in the hole with me. The next morning two of them came in and searched me. They removed my gloves from my hands, took everything from my pockets, ran their bayonets up my arm and took my military watch. They pushed several layers of clothing up on my stomach and felt around, and pulled my pants out of the top of my combat boots where I had them bloused. This was another difficult time for me.

To make a long story short, I lay there in that hole for more than eighteen hours slowly bleeding and freezing to death, without consciously moving a muscle in my body, reliving my past life in my memory and imagination. I confessed all of my sins to God and made the most solemn promises I knew how to utter. If God would just get me out of there alive, I would serve him the rest of my life; I would do anything he wanted me to do.

God did bring me out with a strong hand. After three days and three nights and more sorrows and horrors, I finally got back to the First Marine Division, where I was flown out to a hospital. Seven men came out alive from my entire company. I spent almost nine months in various hospitals, undergoing treatment and surgery. During the first few weeks of those months, I thought I might never walk again. My feet had frozen and turned black all the way up to the ankles. I had a long time to reflect upon those experiences and the vows which I had made to God.

Finally I was discharged. I was still only seventeen, though I had spent three years, five months, and nineteen days in the Army. I knew that I had to try to follow through on the promises which I had made to God. So, before getting my discharge, I took the GED tests, a series of five competitive tests, and was able to get the equivalent of a high school diploma. But even with that, Furman University wasn't anxious to have me as a student because of my poor academic background. I can appreciate that much more now than I could then. Nevertheless, my pastor interceded for me, and Furman agreed to let me in on a trial basis for one semester. That was the most difficult semester of my life. Some nights I studied until two or three o'clock in the morning. Occasionally, I studied all night long. Seldom did I go to take a test or an examination without preparing to do my best and asking God to help me. Because of this strong sense of mission, I graduated along with the top of my class, magna cum laude.

For ten years I served as a pastor in South Carolina and Virginia. Since 1963 I have worked full time in the field of evangelism for Southern Baptists, three of those years in

Virginia, twelve in my native state of South Carolina, and the rest teaching evangelism at Midwestern and Southeastern seminaries.

Conclusion

I share these experiences with you in order to bear witness to the reality of God. God is real. I know he is real because he has made himself known to me. I did not come to believe in God through any of the classical arguments for his existence. I came to believe that God is through a personal encounter with him. I believe Francis Thompson was right in his great autobiographical poem when he referred to God as the Hound of Heaven and said he is on the trail of every person. Sooner or later every person must meet God, if not here, then hereafter.

Second, I share these experiences with you in order to bear witness to the greatness of God. God is great. He is omnipotent, almighty, all-powerful, a God who can do anything he wills to do. I know God is great because his great power has changed my whole life. Only a truly great God could have changed me from what I was into what I am now in the process of becoming. And I am convinced that God in answer to my prayers literally turned the course of that bullet, or else my body would have long since turned to dust on a Korean mountain. The God in whom I believe is a miracle-working God.

Third, I share these experiences with you in order to bear witness to the goodness of God. God is good. I know he is good because his goodness has literally led me to repentance time and time again. And especially can I never forget his exceeding goodness to me in Korea. When there was no other human being to help me, I called upon God in my distress. As far as I can tell, God was under no obligation to hear my prayer. If I had received what I deserved at that point in my life, it would have been wrath, judgment, death, and perhaps even hell. But God did not give me what I deserved. He heard my prayer, brought me out safely, and delivered me from my enemies. God does not always deal with us according to his wrath and after our sins. Most of the time he deals with us according to his great love and with an infinite patience.

Now, what does all of this have to do with you? Well, for one thing, I hope you can see in these excerpts from my own life story a microcosm of needs which we Christians should seek to meet through Jesus Christ. Poverty, illiteracy, a broken home, crime, alcoholism, war, physical suffering, loneliness, lostness, and the struggle of the human soul for acceptance, dignity, and meaning—each of these needs you may see in my own pilgrimage. And each of these needs, along with a thousand more, we Christians should seek to meet day by day in the name and through the strength of him who is the Lord of life. God did not save us that we might become more Dead Seas. One Dead Sea in the world is enough. He has saved us that we might become a channel of blessing to humanity.

What does all of this have to do with you? What God has done for me and for others, he can do for you. And he will, if you will let him. But God will not force himself upon you. God is not like some cosmic policeman who walks the beat of the world with a blackjack in his hand, knocking persons over their heads and dragging them against their will into his kingdom. Rather, God is like the Hound of Heaven who pursues us relentlessly down all the labyrinthine ways of life and who pays us the supreme compliment of letting us choose between life and death.

The writer of Proverbs best summed up what I have been trying to say when he wrote: "Trust in the Lord with all your heart, and do not rely on your own insight./In all your ways acknowledge him, and he will make straight your paths" (3:5-6).

Suggestions for Further Reading

Frederick Buechner, *The Sacred Journey* (San Francisco: Harper & Row, Publishers, 1982).

Joyce Neville, *How to Share Your Faith Without Being Offensive* (New York: The Seabury Press, 1979), esp. pp. 22-28.

William G. McLoughlin, ed., *The Diary of Isaac Backus,* Vols. I-III (Providence: Brown University Press, 1979), pp. 1523-1526. These pages (1523-1526) are an autobiographical account of Backus's conversion.

Notes

1. This chapter was originally given as a lecture entitled "Autobiography in the Service of Evangelism" to Golden Gate Baptist Theological Seminary on March 5, 1975. It was published in a supplement to *Home Missions,* Vol. 46, No. 10, Nov.—Dec., 1975, under the title, "Autobiography Serves as Witness." The present version has been revised.
2. William James, *The Varieties of Religious Experience* (New York: University Books, 1963).
3. James S. Stewart, *A Faith to Proclaim* (New York: Charles Scribner's Sons, 1953), p. 41 *ff*.
4. Gabriel Fackre, *Word in Deed* (Grand Rapids: Wm. B. Eerdmans Publishing Co., 1975), p. 11.
5. Reported in the *Baptist Courier,* Vol. 112, No. 33, Aug. 21, 1980, p. 3.
6. Delos Miles, *Church Growth—A Mighty River* (Nashville: Broadman Press, 1981), pp. 56-57, 124-125.

14
The Personal Testimony

Psalm 71:15; 1 John 1:1-3

Introduction

Every Christian has a spiritual autobiography. Even brand-new Christians who were not reared in Christian homes have autobiographies which may be used in the service of evangelism. They may not be lengthy. You may not have thought through it. But if you are a citizen of the kingdom of God, you do have a life story which has interfaced with the gospel story. "Our theological task," wrote theologian Robert McAfee Brown, "is to find ways to 'tell the old, old story' so that the listener says, 'Aha! That's *my* story too.' In hearing about Abraham or Sarah or Jeremiah or Judas I am learning about myself."[1]

The personal testimony is another means available to every Christian for faith sharing. How then does the personal testimony differ from the spiritual autobiography?

Differences Between Autobiography and Testimony

The testimony deals with just one or two clips out of one's spiritual lifescript. It might take fifteen to twenty-five minutes to share one's story as it relates to the gospel story. But it only takes up to ninety seconds or so to share one's personal testimony. One's testimony can be condensed into two hundred words or less, whereas one's life story might take six to ten pages typewritten and double-spaced.

If you will go back to my autobiography in the previous chapter, you will find one long paragraph which contains the essence of my testimony. I shall add only two sentences, one at the beginning and the other at the end. Now, look at it.

I have not always been a Christian; nor did I grow up in a Christian home. When I was eleven years old, I felt separated from God. I had a miserable feeling inside. I was so unhappy that I felt like I was going to die unless something was done soon. I talked this over with my Sunday School teacher and with my foster parents. They all told me that I ought to confess my sins to God, ask him to help me, and place my life into his hands. As best I knew how, I followed their advice. That unhappy feeling left me. Peace and joy came into my life. Later, I went before the whole congregation and publicly confessed my faith in Jesus Christ as the Son of God and as my Lord and Savior and was baptized into the body of Christ by that congregation in Lynches River. Has anything like that ever happened to you?

You can see from that example how the testimony is just a few picture frames or a few feet of film taken from the whole picture of one's life in Christ.

The testimony can be used to capsule what God has done for you. It may also be used as a bridge into the sharing of the gospel. Consider, for example, this recast version of my testimony.

Before I received eternal life I was very lonely. My mother and father had separated when I was seven. My father was killed in a fight when I was eight. I was separated from my brother and sisters. My relatives already had too many children of their own to take me in. But God gave me some foster parents who took me into their home, loved me, and provided for my needs.

Then I received eternal life. Now that I have eternal life I am a permanent member of the family of God and no longer feel so alone and rejected. Now, instead of having just one brother I have many brothers. Instead of having just two sisters, I have many sisters. Instead of having just one mother I have many mothers.

Nothing can separate me from my new family. Not even death. I know that when I die I am going to heaven and will always be with them. May I ask you a question?

I like to think of the personal testimony in terms of BC and AD, before Christ and after Christ. Every Christian has a BC and an AD. In the testimony you tell how you moved from your BC to your AD. The essence of the personal testimony is your move from BC to AD. The quintessence of the testimony is the words of the man born blind in John 9: "One thing I know, that though I was blind, now I see" (v. 25).

First Corinthians 6:9-11 present us with a biblical model of the BC and the AD. Verses 9-10 of that passage lay out our BC. Verse 11 tells us what the AD is. Other biblical passages which may instruct us on the testimony are Psalm 66:16; John 9:1-41; Acts 22:1-21; 26:1-32; 1 John 1:1-3; 1 Peter 3:15.

An Outline for the Testimony

There is a popular hamburger chain which has a slogan, "We Fix Hamburgers 256 Ways." If you don't believe they can do it, read their brochure. There must be at least 256 ways to share your personal testimony. I have shown you a couple of ways already. However, I would suggest the following two outlines as possibilities for beginners.

Outline 1:
- My Life Before Receiving Christ
- How I Realized I Needed Christ
- How I Became a Christian
- How Christ Helps Me in My Daily Life

Outline 2:
- I Have Not Always Been a Christian
- God Showed Me My Need of Christ

- I Committed My Life to Christ as Lord and Savior
- My Life in Christ Is Different

Now, look at this testimony which was organized and written by outline 2.

Even though I am a pastor, I have not always been a Christian, although I cannot remember when the church was not a vital part of my life. You might say that I didn't realize that I was not a Christian until I was told that I was not!

But, God showed me my need of Christ through a faithful Sunday School teacher who believed the Bible.

One Sunday morning as she taught God's Word, I realized:

 —that I was not a Christian,

 —that I could be, and I knew in my heart

 —that I wanted to be.

I became a Christian that very morning, simply by believing Jesus and asking him to come into my heart. My life in Christ is different today because I have found a friend who really cares for me.

 —He lifts me up when I am down.

 —He listens to me when I need to talk.

 —He guides me when I need direction.

This friend is Jesus. Will you let him be your friend too?[2]

If you don't like either of those outlines, then create your own. The important thing is to write out the testimony so that it will have some self-conscious and intentional structure to it.

You may wish to consider prefacing your testimony with this kind of question: "May I share with you the most meaningful experience of my life?" Also, you may want to close your testimony with a question like: "Has anything like that ever happened to you?" I am a strong believer in bracketing the testimony with appropriate questions, especially if you intend to use it as a bridge into the sharing of the gospel.

Why Is Testimony So Useful?

The testimony is an ideal witnessing tool. It is the most useful tool we have for sharing our faith for several reasons.

Every Christian has a testimony. If you have come to know God through Jesus Christ, you have an experience to share. That can be a beginning point in evangelizing which each believer has in common. Our personal religious experience with God in Christ is one characteristic which distinguishes us from the rest of humanity.

The testimony is always relevant and forever up-to-date. You incarnate it before persons' eyes. You give flesh and blood and reality to the good news of the kingdom of God. You are more believable than someone or something from the distant past. Some persons will believe you quicker than they will believe the Bible. Those who have a prepared and fresh testimony will always be prepared to make a defense to any who calls them to account for the hope that is in them (see 1 Pet. 3:15).

Your testimony is authoritative because it is unique. You may not be an authority on anything else. Nevertheless, you are the only authority there is when it comes to your experience with God. You know more about your personal relationship with God than any other person. It is authoritative because you are speaking out of firsthand knowledge of God. You don't have to be an authority on the Bible in order to be an authority on your knowledge of God.

God comes into every life through a private door so to speak. No one has had an experience with God quite like yours. Therefore, if you do not share that experience, no one else can. It is also unlikely that many will seek to refute your firsthand experience with God.

Another factor which makes the testimony such a powerful tool is that it really communicates. It is interesting because it is the stuff out of which real life is molded. You don't try to impress others with your theological vocabulary. You simply tell another beggar that you know where one can find bread which will satisfy hunger. You tell him or her as one beggar to another beggar that you have found in Jesus Christ the Bread of life. You are speaking as a satisfied customer. Your message is: "Jesus Christ satisfies all the deepest hungers of my life." To change the metaphor, when you share your testimony, you are telling another blind person that Jesus Christ has cured you of your blindness and that you believe what he has done for you he can do for him or her.

Finally, the testimony is such a useful witnessing tool because it holds up a mirror to the unreconciled person. The lost may see themselves in your testimony. They may also see that, since Christ could change your life, he can make a difference in their lives. You become a model with which they can identify. Sometime their appetite is so whetted by what you are and say that they gain renewed hope and dare to believe that God can help them too.

The Less Dramatic Testimony

What do you say to those who wonder if they have anything to share because they think their testimony is not very dramatic? First, all you can share is what God has given to you. We dare not add to, or subtract from, that which God has done for us. Second, what do you mean by dramatic? Is there anything more dramatic than raising the dead? If you are a Christian, you were dead. Jesus Christ has raised you from the death of sin. You were dead in trespasses and in sins (Eph. 2:1).

Furthermore, is there anything more dramatic than opening blind eyes? If you are a Christian, you can say: "Once I was blind, now I see." Jesus Christ has delivered you from blindness.

Third, just because you have not had a Damascus road-like experience, doesn't mean you don't have a story to tell. Your's may be more like the experience of Timothy who had a godly mother and grandmother. If you used to be a tadpole, now you are a bullfrog; however imperceptible your transformation, you do have a story to tell to the nations.

A lady who grew up in church gave her testimony to a medical doctor from Canada while they were traveling on an airplane to Switzerland. She told how she started to church when she was ten days old, grew up in a pastor's home, how she became a Christian as a young girl, how thankful she was that God had become so personal and real to her, and how grateful she was that God had spared her from being exposed to many forms of sin and evil through his grace. The doctor's eyes welled up with tears. He said, "I too grew up in a Christian home. The difference between you and me is that God became personal to you, but that never happened to me."

I am thankful to report to you that several weeks later, that doctor was led to Christ by another medical doctor in Canada. God did become personal to him. But that beautiful and humble testimony apparently opened the door of his heart to hear the word of the Lord.

Some Don'ts and Dos

When you share your testimony, you may wish to take notice of the following don'ts:

1. Don't confuse your testimony with your spiritual autobiography.
2. Don't tell more about your BC than your AD.
3. Don't share too much at once.
4. Don't be trigger-happy in sharing your testimony.
5. Don't expect your testimony to be as powerful when you are culturally distanced from your receiver.

Conversely, I would suggest this list of dos:

1. Do dwell more on what God has done for you than what you have done for him.

2. Do keep revising and reworking your testimony. It will help you to write and rewrite it many times and to tape and retape it from time to time.

3. Do use those parts of your testimony which are most relevant to your prospect.

4. Do learn how to begin it and end it with appropriate questions. One way to begin it is with the question: "May I share with you the most meaningful experience of my life?" Another way to get into it is to ask: "May I share with you how I came to know for certain I will go to heaven when I die?" One way to end the testimony is with the question: "Have you experienced this?" Another way is the question: "Has anything like that happened to you?"

5. Do use language and vocabulary which your prospect understands.

6. Do seek the leadership of the Holy Spirit in writing your testimony.

7. Do speak distinctly and in a natural tone of voice.

8. Do memorize your testimony until it becomes a natural part of you.

9. Do relive your testimony as you tell it.

10. Do undergird your testimony with a disciplined prayer life.

Guidelines for Writing Your Testimony

Let me suggest in closing several guidelines which I have found useful in actually writing one's testimony:

- Don't write anything which you would be embarrassed for anyone to read, including those significant others in your life.

- Don't share so much or so deeply that you may later feel you have undressed yourself in public.

- Don't build yourself up by tearing anyone else down.

- Be honest; tell the truth. But don't be *brutally* honest. Speak the truth in love. Exhibit kindness.

- Write your testimony as though you were preparing it to share with unbelievers. Prepare it very much as though you were going to speak it.

Suggested Study Questions

1. What does it mean to liken the spiritual autobiography to a microcosm of the personal testimony and the personal testimony to a microcosm of the spiritual autobiography?
2. Among the five senses of sight, sound, smell, taste, and touch, which ones are specifically mentioned in 1 John 1:1-3? Which senses are mentioned more than once? What, if anything, does this Scripture say about the use of our sensorium in sharing our personal testimony with others?
3. If you were asked to write out in your own words the personal testimony of the man who had been blind from birth in John 9:1-41, based on what is said in the text, what would you say in two hundred words or less?
4. Write out your personal testimony based on one of the two outlines given in this chapter.

Notes

1. Robert McAfee Brown, "Starting Over: New Beginning Points for Theology," *The Christian Century,* Vol. XCVII, No. 18, May 14, 1980, p. 548.
2. This is the testimony of the Reverend Don Purvis, pastor of Lakeview Baptist Church, Hartsville, South Carolina. It is used by permission of Mr. Purvis.

15
Life-Style Evangelism

Psalm 69:6; Colossians 4:5-6

Introduction

Another means which every Christian has at his or her disposal for witnessing is life-style evangelism. Alfred Adler was the psychologist who coined the word *life-style*. He saw it as a clue to helping persons understand why life was directed in certain ways. It is a twentieth-century term. By life-style we mean

> the way a life is oriented, based on expressed or unexpressed values and beliefs which manifest themselves in such things as the clothes we wear, the food we eat, the way we comb our hair, the friends we associate with, the very furniture we have in our houses.[1]

Lyle E. Schaller credits C. B. Hogue with "a remarkedly lucid introduction to the concept of life-style evangelism."[2] Hogue in one place defined life-style evangelism as "a life-sharing, life-giving evangelism which includes a verbal life-sharing of what Christ means in a person's life."[3] Earlier he said life-style evangelism is "that life-giving, life-sharing expression of one's faith that begins with the new birth experience and ends with the last breath."[4] Hogue in *Love Leaves No Choice* makes an even more comprehensive and remarkable statement about life-style evangelism:

> It is a commitment.
> A person has to make a total commitment to Christ. Once he does, he commits himself to everything Christ is and stands for. He acts with sensitivity and understanding.

That means giving a cup of cold water when someone needs it, but doing so "in Jesus' name."

Evangelism that becomes a person's life-style may be giving someone in need bread to eat, a house to live in, clothes to wear, because Christ said, "If you do it for the least of these, you do it for me."[5]

While the term is not biblical, the concept is. Colossians 4:5 in the King James Version says, "Walk in wisdom toward them that are without." That phrase, "them that are without," is a technical phrase in the Greek meaning "outsiders" (as in RSV) or those who are not members of the family of God through faith in Jesus Christ. Therefore, Paul was saying something like this: "Watch your life-style around unbelievers because they are watching you"; or, "Be careful how you live in relating to non-Christians, because they are looking at you."

Every Christian would do well to pray with the psalmist: "let not those who seek thee be brought to dishonor through me, O God of Israel" (69:6). When our life-style is so shoddy that it brings those who seek God to dishonor, we bring shame upon God and the body of Christ.

Every-Member Evangelism

In 1922 J. E. Conant wrote a book entitled *Every Member Evangelism*.[6] Life-style evangelism is every member evangelism.

There is no such person as the omni-competent clergyperson able to operate as an effective one-person-band. The clergypersons are not omni-competent, nor can they be omnipresent. There are too few of them to be everywhere and to do all of the evangelizing.

Every Christian may not be an evangelist in the sense of one who is specially gifted to introduce lost persons to the Savior. But every Christian is a witness. He or she may be a winning and willing witness or a reluctant witness. Nevertheless, a Christian who is not a witness to Jesus Christ is a contradiction.

Where did we ever get the idea that we could witness by proxy, that we could pay somebody else to do our witnessing for us? No Christian can ever be let off the hook in witnessing.

We need to democratize the idea of witnessing. Witnessing is something for the whole people of God, for the rank-and-file members of the church as well as for the leaders. Two church papers which come to my desk each week have on their mastheads the words, "Ministers—Every Member." Then the pastor and other staff members are listed.

Howard Snyder is right when he says, "Believers need to know by experience that the Most High God is also the Most Nigh God." Isaiah 57:15b says: "I dwell in the high and holy place, and also with him who is of a contrite and humble spirit."

Those of you who may not feel any call to publicly preach or teach need to know that God is with you too. Those of you who may hold no office whatever in the church can be assured that God is in you if you are of a contrite and humble spirit.

Life-style evangelism is every Christian being a witness to Jesus Christ. It is democratic evangelism which involves the members, as well as the ordained preachers and missionaries and church staff members.

A. C. Archibald cites an example of life-style evangelism by a lady in one of his New England pastorates. She won to Christ no less than twenty-one young women in eight weeks and repeated that with varying success for several years. She was very unprepossessing and very humble in life's station but had an illuminated countenance that came from much talking with her Lord.

When Archibald first saw her, he wondered if she could be used at all as an evangelistic visitor. She was so apparently withdrawn and almost self-depreciating. Her work was with a textile mill in that community.

The pastor assigned her the names of two young women who worked in the mill. At prayer meeting the following week, the lady startled her pastor by appearing with both young women who made simple confessions of faith. He gave her two more names. On the second week, she appeared with one more convert. For eight weeks she took her assignments and each week she appeared with at least one convert. However, she broke out of the bounds of her assignments and made some additional assignments on her own initiative.

What was the secret of her success? She called at the homes of those assigned to her and invited the girls to her home for dinner. She lived alone. Once each week she had a "prospect" dinner. After dinner it was her custom to talk to these girls in her quiet manner, leading up to the thing dearest to her heart. One of the new converts told the pastor, "When she got on that love of God in Christ, we just could not resist her."[7]

Everyday Evangelism

Life-style evangelism is the rank-and-file Christians witnessing every day in their natural, normal, daily contacts and relationships. It is not something a Christian does just on Thursday night from 7:00-9:00. We do it all the time seven days a week, twenty-four hours a day. There are no breaks and no vacations from life-style evangelism.

Paul spoke the most direct word to this timing factor in evangelism. Colossians 4:5 says: "Conduct yourselves wisely toward outsiders, making the most of the time." The parallel passage in Ephesians 5:15-16 says: "Look carefully then how you walk, not as unwise men but as wise, making the most of the time, because the days are evil."

Paul may have been saying that we are to conduct ourselves wisely toward outsiders at all times. However, the word for time which he used is *kairos* instead of *chronos*. And *kairos* is a special kind of time. It is the time of divine appointment. It is the time of opportunity, the opportune time. So, Paul was probably saying something like this: "As you relate to outsiders watch for the opportune time to share with them. Watch for the seasons of the soul when they will be most receptive to your witness."

We know from observation and experience that persons are more receptive to conversion when they have undergone some change or been uprooted from familiar surroundings. This is what Paul would refer to as *kairos* time in their lives. The great Indonesian revival in the 1960s which swept more than 100,000 Moslems into the Christian churches is an example which has been widely studied. That had not happened in more than a thousand years of church history. Yet, during sociopolitical upheavals it did happen. A more personal example would be the death of a spouse or simply a major change in one's residence.

I think the conversion of William Cozad is an example of this kind of life-style evangelism. Cozad was a compulsive gambler. He gambled away everything he made as a cook in San Francisco. He borrowed everything he could through hook or crook and gambled that. He hocked every item of value in his possession and lost that gambling. He lied to his own father and secured a loan of $5,000 under false pretenses. That, too, was gambled and lost. He lost everything gambling. His wife left him and secured a divorce.

Cozad ended up on the Golden Gate Bridge thinking suicide would be his answer. A Christian police officer talked him into coming down from his suicide perch. That officer befriended him, helped meet his immediate physical and mental needs, kept working with him, and finally was able to introduce him to Jesus Christ.

Now William Cozad has been forgiven of his sins. God has liberated him from his gambling. He and his wife are reconciled. Says he, "I'm living proof that Christ can change a person. . . . I'm free now of the passion to gamble when disappointments happen in life."[8] But who knows what might have happened to Cozad if that Christian police officer had not been engaged in life-style evangelism?

Everywhere Evangelism

Evangelism is wherever you want to find it. Jesus found an evangelistic opportunity as he passed by the tax collector's seat and called Matthew, the publican, to follow him. Jesus found an evangelistic opportunity as he passed through Jericho and saw Zacchaeus up that sycamore tree. Jesus also found an evangelistic opportunity as he was being crucified between two thieves and said to the one who repented at the eleventh hour: "Today you will be with me in Paradise" (Luke 23:43*b*).

Life-style evangelism has no special place where it is practiced. It can be done anywhere, anytime, and by any Christian. Jesus was doing life-style evangelism when he introduced the woman of Samaria to living water beside Jacob's well (see John 4). Andrew was doing life-style evangelism when he found his brother, Simon Peter, and brought him to Jesus (see John 1:40-42). Philip was doing life-style evangelism when he found Nathanael under the fig tree and introduced him to Jesus (John 1:43-51).

Even bad ham can lead to good witnessing! A total of 310 persons were stricken with food poisoning at a Christian conference center. A good ham was apparently contaminated when it touched a burn on an employee's arm. It caused vomiting, diarrhea, and other more frightening symptoms. The incident, in fact, resulted in a medical emergency for the entire county. Nevertheless, one man who was hospitalized thanked God that he had the opportunity to witness to three men who were in the hospital room with him.[9]

Life-style evangelism can be done by Sunday School teachers outside the formal setting of their classrooms. "In one friendship hour alone," said Archibald, "a teacher often will do more effective evangelistic work than in fifty Sunday School class sessions." Archibald advised teachers to invite pupils into their homes one by one. He felt that was better than asking a child to become a Christian in his or her own home in a hostile environment before non-Christian parents. Moreover, he wanted teachers to invite their pupils to accompany them on social outings and special trips where they were more likely to get a friendly hearing.[10]

One teacher who had a class of rather boisterous boys was deeply concerned for their salvation. He prepared his lessons well but seemed to get no response to his appeals. It seemed that he would lose his class without winning one to Christ. He brought his problem to the pastor. His pastor suggested that, since he was a single man and ate out at restaurants a good bit, he consider inviting his class one by one to have a meal with him and get to know them. The teacher followed his pastor's suggestion. In one year he had won six of his eight boys to Christ through life-style evangelism.[11]

At-Home Evangelism

Life-style evangelism is every Christian evangelism, every day and everywhere. It is evangelism where we are at the moment. It is also at-home evangelism.

The best person to win your relatives and friends and business associates to Christ may be you. When Jesus had healed the Gerasene demoniac, the man who had been demon possessed begged to go with Jesus. But Jesus refused and said to him: "Go home to your friends, and tell them how much the Lord has done for you, and how he has had mercy on you" (Mark 5:19). The amazing sequel to that story is that "he went away and began to proclaim in the Decapolis how much Jesus had done for him; and all men marveled" (Mark 5:20).

The best way for most of us to follow Jesus is to

proclaim him through our natural webs of friendship and kinship. If Jesus Christ has really made a difference in our lives, that difference will be more apparent to those who know us and love us than it will be to total strangers.

God used my witness to help lead my younger brother to Christ when he got out of the army and started to college. My stepfather who is now deceased said to me one day: "Son, I'd give anything in the world to have what you have." I saw him confess his faith publicly shortly after that in a revival meeting following one of my sermons. If I had been more conscientious about my life-style and more loving toward other members of my own family, more of them may have also come to Christ. I am absolutely convinced that the most logical person to lead your lost loved ones and friends and neighbors and business associates to Christ may be you—and not someone who is a stranger to them.

It pleases God to move into the lives of others across the natural bridges of kinship and friendship and association. One who is a brand-new Christian can be used of God to bring his or her relatives and friends to Christ. The Gerasene demoniac who proclaimed what Jesus had done for him to his fellow citizens in the Decapolis had never attended a witnessing clinic. Yet, our Lord sent him to witness to those who knew him. The first person whom Andrew brought to Jesus was his brother, Simon Peter. The first person whom Philip brought to Jesus was his friend, Nathanael.

One fact which we sometimes forget is that the new convert probably knows more lost persons than the Christian who has served Christ for many years. For example, when James Eaves was pastor of First Baptist Church, Albuquerque, New Mexico, a cocktail waitress was converted. She sent out invitations to her friends to attend her baptism and afterwards a party at a friend's home. She also invited her pastor to the party and gave him an opportunity to say a few words. More than seventeen of that waitress's friends were converted to Christ as a result of her conversion and her witness.

A Mennonite pastor by the name of Arthur G. McPhee has a little book entitled *Friendship Evangelism* in which he says: "Your greatest witness is your deepest relationship."[12] Do you believe that? If so, then you are well on your way to understanding what life-style evangelism is all about.

Demonstration Evangelism

Love is not just something you say; it's something you do. Life-style evangelism is total communication, not just verbal communication. The *New American Standard Bible* translation of Hebrews 1:1-2 makes this clear: "God, after He spoke long ago to the fathers in the prophets in many portions and in many ways, in these last days has spoken to us in His Son, whom He appointed heir of all things, through whom also He made the world." Both the King James Version and the Revised Standard Version might seem to indicate verbal communication.

God spoke *in* the prophets and *in* the Son. He spoke through their life-styles and through their incarnation. For example, Hosea's marriage to Gomer and the names given to their children were living parables which said something about God's love for the nation Israel (see Hos. chs. 1—3). Another prophetic example of life-style evangelism is Isaiah naming his son Maher-shalal-hash-baz. Every time Isaiah spoke the name of his son, he was reminding those around him that God's judgment was going to fall.

Life-style evangelism is living in such a way that what we are speaks as loudly as what we say. Life-style evangelism is show-and-tell evangelism. It is witnessing in such a way that one's very life endeavors to be a living example of God's intention for humanity.

One example of what is meant by demonstration evangelism comes from Fernando Vangioni of Argentina, an associate evangelist with the Billy Graham team. Following

one of Vangioni's evangelistic services, some persons stayed
for counseling and were guided to a smaller room. The
evangelist began counseling with a young woman who said,
"I shouldn't be here at all. I don't know what made me
respond. You can't do anything for me." The young woman
told him something of the debauchery of her life and then
stood up to leave. Vangioni said, "Before you go, may I pray
for you? Then I will not try to keep you."

Courteously, but reluctantly, the woman sat down and
the evangelist began to pray. His concern for the woman was
so great that the sadness of her life spilled over on him and
he could not help but weep for her. Finally, pulling himself
together, the evangelist finished his prayer. Somewhat embarrassed, he said, "You have kept your part of the bargain.
You have allowed me to pray for you. You may go now." But
the woman made no move to go. She said quietly, "You have
wept for me. Now you may talk to me."[13]

Sometime we demonstrate our love for others by weep-
ing with them and over them. At other times we demonstrate our love more concretely by refusing to let them live in
a hell here on earth when we have the means to deliver
them. Whatever else life-style evangelism may be, it is
meeting the potential Christian at his or her point of need
and interest. It is evangelism "warts and all." The life of the
witness becomes transparent in life-style evangelism.

Body Evangelism

Life-style evangelism is body evangelism. It is concerned with building up the body of the Christ, the church.
Life-style evangelism seeks to relate the convert to the
church. It seeks to help persons find their places in that
mystical body of Christ and in a local body of believers.

Life-style evangelism is body evangelism in the sense
that it involves every member of the body of Christ. Life-style
evangelism sees the church as a body gifted by the Holy
Trinity with the necessary spiritual gifts to build up the body

of Christ in the world. As such, it is dependent upon the Holy Spirit for its power and its qualifications. The essential qualifications for witnessing are charismatic rather than academic. We tend to identify the supernatural with the sensational, and thus underplay this fact.

Life-style evangelism is not only body evangelism in the sense of body building and spiritual gifts but also body evangelism in the sense that we are to offer our very bodies as a living sacrifice to Christ. Have you ever thought it strange that Paul referred to our "spiritual worship" in terms of the presentation of our bodies as a living sacrifice to God (see Rom. 12:1)? Really, life-style evangelism begins with death to self and the offering of our very bodies to Christ in his service. Whatever else life-style evangelism may be, it is certainly body evangelism.

Conclusion

The best evangelism is life-style evangelism. I agree with Archibald, that outstanding pastor-evangelist, who cautions us against instruction in evangelism which stereotypes Christian workers. We should guard against methods which stifle and stiffen Christian witnesses. Archibald's opinion is that if one is denaturalized, artificialized, and devitalized beyond a certain degree, that witness may as well stay at home. "The best way to succeed is to be natural," says he. "The best training is in doing."[14]

Suggested Study Questions

1. *The Living Bible* translates 1 Corinthians 9:22*b*, "Yes, whatever a person is like, I try to find common ground with him so that he will let me tell him about Christ and let Christ save him." What is the "common ground" which we should seek in life-style evangelism?

2. Based on the quotations from C. B. Hogue, do you agree or disagree with his understanding of life-style evangelism? Share in two or three brief paragraphs why you agree or disagree.

3. Describe what the author means by his characterization of life-style evangelism as "at-home evangelism."

4. How is the term "body evangelism" used in the text?

Notes

1. William P. Clemmons, *Discovering the Depths* (Nashville: Broadman Press, 1976), p. 11.

2. Lyle E. Schaller, *Assimilating New Members* (Nashville: Abingdon, 1978), p. 16.

3. Jan Trusty, "The World and the (New) Way," *Home Missions*, Vol. 51, No. 5, Sept.-Oct., 1980, p. 35.

4. C. B. Hogue, *Love Leaves No Choice: Life-Style Evangelism* (Waco, Texas: Word Books, Publisher, 1976), p. 151.

5. Ibid., p. 150.

6. Roy J. Fish and J. E. Conant, *Every Member Evangelism for Today* (New York: Harper & Row, Publishers, 1976).

7. Related by Arthur C. Archibald, *New Testament Evangelism: How It Works Today* (Philadelphia: The Judson Press, 1946), pp. 141-142.

8. William Cozad, "I Gambled and Lost," *Decision*, Vol. 23, No. 2, Feb., 1982, p. 3.

9. "Bad Ham Leads to Good Witnessing," *Baptist Courier*, Vol. 113, No. 32, Aug. 13, 1981, p. 15.

10. Archibald, p. 126.

11. Ibid., pp. 125-126.

12. Arthur G. McPhee, *Friendship Evangelism* (Grand Rapids: Zondervan Publishing House, 1978), p. 101.

13. Related by W. Stanley Mooneyham, "Evangelism and Social Action" in Sherwood Eliot Wirt, ed., *Evangelism the Next Ten Years* (Waco, Texas: Word Books, 1978), pp. 50-51.

14. Archibald, p. 90.

16
The Role of the Holy Spirit[1]
Joel 2:28-32; Acts 2:1-21

Introduction

Evangelism without the Holy Spirit is like a body without a soul. There is no evangelism worthy of the name apart from the enabling and energizing power of God's Spirit.

The Holy Spirit filled a role in the creation (see Gen. 1:2,26). He inspired the sacred Scriptures which we call the Bible (see 2 Tim. 3:16). He helps us with our prayer life (see Rom. 8:26-27). He has a role in satisfying the deepest thirst of persons' souls (see John 7:37-39). He is our Comforter to help us with our loneliness and desolation (see John 14:18). He is like the "second self" of Christ our Savior. We are never alone (see Matt. 28:20).

That same Holy Spirit fills many functions in evangelism. He is an inexhaustible resource upon which every Christian may draw. What a tragedy that some Christians today are like those disciples at Ephesus whom Paul encountered. "We have never even heard that there is a Holy Spirit," (Acts 19:2) said they. One of the positive contributions of the modern charismatic movement is a renewed emphasis upon the Holy Spirit in almost every branch of the church.

I should like to lift up several functions of the Holy Spirit in evangelization.

Empowers

The Holy Spirit empowers us to bear witness to Jesus Christ. Acts 1:8 says, "But you shall receive power when the

199

Holy Spirit has come upon you; and you shall be my witnesses." We do not have to witness in our own strength. Because the Holy Spirit empowers us, witnessing is not a drudgery which we do with dread but a task which we gladly perform with joy.

The Holy Spirit is the wind of God which turns the windmill of witnessing. He is the fire of God which stokes the boiler of witnessing in the church.

The power of the Holy Spirit in Luke-Acts is connected with witnessing to Jesus Christ. When the Spirit was poured out at Pentecost in Acts 2, the Scripture says, "And they were all filled with the Holy Spirit and began to speak in other tongues, as the Spirit gave them utterance" (2:4). And what did they speak in the power of the Holy Spirit? They spoke about "the mighty works of God" (Acts 2:11). Peter preached his great Pentecostal sermon in the power of the Holy Spirit and "those who received his word were baptized, and there were added that day about three thousand souls" (Acts 2:41).

We hear a great deal about demons in our day. The word *exorcism,* meaning the casting out of demons, has returned to our vocabulary. Especially has this been true since the appearance of the film called *The Exorcist.*

Jesus was an exorcist. His enemies accused him of casting out demons by the power of Beelzebub, the prince of the devils. But Jesus refuted their charge and claimed to cast out demons by the power of the Spirit of God. "But if it is by the Spirit of God that I cast out demons, then the kingdom of God has come upon you" (Matt. 12:28). Jesus claimed, in other words, that his exorcisms were signs of the presence of the government of God in his ministry.

The really interesting point to note is that, according to Luke's Gospel, when both the twelve and the seventy were sent out two by two to preach the kingdom of God they found that even the demons were subject to them (see Luke 9:1-6; 10:1-24). We can be bold to believe that those of us who go out in the name of Jesus to bear witness to him have power over the demonic forces of evil which oppose us. "For he who is in you is greater than he who is in the world" (1 John 4:4).

How does the Holy Spirit empower us? Does God make a deposit of power in us? No, the Holy Spirit through his constant presence gives us strength to overcome fear. The Holy Spirit fills us with love. He gives us love power and the power of purity. So many hymns on the Holy Spirit speak of this.

We can be sure that a supernatural power is available to ordinary Christians who conscientiously seek to share their faith. Consider the example of Sin Soum. He and his wife became Christians in 1973 in an evangelistic campaign. Sin Soum was a Cambodian schoolteacher. God called them to move into a large refugee settlement outside Phnom Penh where there were no Christians.

That meant personal hardships. It was a difficult decision. Shopping was a half-day's journey. The nearest water was a fifteen-minute walk. Their first shelter was a tiny thatched hut which they built with their own hands.

After a short while, that little hut was overflowing with persons coming to study the Bible. Thirty persons had believed by the time six months had passed. Within two years, this couple was shepherding a congregation of over one thousand persons. Almost all were their spiritual children or grandchildren. They were untrained in evangelistic techniques. But such is the power of the Holy Spirit working through a nonprofessional.[2]

Convinces

A second function of the Holy Spirit in evangelism is to convince the world of sin, of righteousness, and of judgment.

"And when he comes, he will convince the world concerning sin and righteousness and judgment; concerning sin, because they do not believe in me; concerning righteousness, because I go to the Father, and you will see me no more; concerning judgment, because the ruler of this world is judged" (John 16:8-11).

The Holy Spirit convinces the world on the three counts of sin, righteousness, and judgment. "World" here means the realm of darkness over which Satan rules. The Holy Spirit convinces of sin because it is the world which is on trial and not Christ. When a tourist remarked in the Bargello that he did not think much of what he was being shown, the custodian answered crushingly: "Sir, these pictures are not on trial; you are." So for the world to be offered Jesus Christ and to crucify him and find no beauty in him is the world's condemnation.

The Holy Spirit convinces the world of righteousness because of the resurrection and the ascension. If Jesus had stayed in the grave, evil would have won. But death and the grave could not hold him. He arose and ascended to the Father where he ever lives to make intercession for us.

The Holy Spirit convinces the world of judgment because in the cross of Christ a great confrontation between the Prince of peace and the ruler of this world occurred, and Christ won the decisive victory. Instead of evil judging good at the cross, it was the other way around. We don't have to judge the devil. God has already done that.

You and I, however clever we are, cannot convince anyone of sin, righteousness, and judgment. That is the work of the Holy Spirit. I think we make a mistake if we seek to argue persons into the kingdom. "An ounce of honest testimony," said Ralph Sockman, "is worth a ton of argument." Persons are not argued into the kingdom. We dare not think we can overpower persons with our clever arguments.

Jesus said, "No one can come to me unless the Father who sent me draws him" (John 6:44). One of the ways that the Father draws persons to the Son is through the convincing power of the Spirit. Our role is to bear witness to the

Son. The Spirit's role is to convince and convict. When persons are cut to the heart through Holy Spirit powered witnessing, then they will cry out as did the outsiders at Pentecost: "What shall we do?" (Acts 2:37).

Regenerates

The Holy Spirit regenerates. He effects the new birth. That same Spirit who was active in the first creation is also active in the second creation, which Paul called the new creation (see 2 Cor. 5:17). Jesus said,

> "Truly, truly, I say to you, unless one is born of water and the Spirit, he cannot enter the kingdom of God. That which is born of the flesh is flesh, and that which is born of the Spirit is spirit. Do not marvel that I said to you, 'You must be born anew'" (John 3:5-7).

Jesus used an interesting analogy in John 3 while conversing with Nicodemus: "The wind blows where it wills, and you hear the sound of it, but you do not know whence it comes or whither it goes; so it is with every one who is born of the Spirit" (v. 8). This is probably a reference to Ezekiel 37 where the prophet was told to prophesy to the valley of dry bones. Ezekiel said to the dry bones: "Thus says the Lord God to these bones: Behold, I will cause breath to enter you, and you shall live" (v. 5). The breath of God is the wind of God's Holy Spirit.

Only God's Spirit can raise from the dead those who are dead in trespasses and sins. It is his work to regenerate the dead. I have been helped to liken the new birth to the first creation and to the virgin birth of our Lord. The same Spirit who brooded over the primeval chaos of darkness broods over every person who is dead in the darkness of sin. That same Spirit who brought order out of chaos in the birth of the world brings order out of chaos in the birth of a Christian. Also, just as that which was conceived in the womb of the virgin Mary was the work of God's Spirit, so when one is conceived and born into the family of God, it is the work of the Holy Spirit.

Every new birth is a miracle wrought by God through his Spirit. Only the wind of God's Spirit can blow with enough power to bring eternal life. Dried bones can be brought back together again. Hope need not be lost. The dead can live again (see Ezek. 37:11-12). God still says today as of old, "I will put my Spirit within you, and you shall live" (Ezek. 37:14).

Equips

The church is a charismatic people. She is a gifted community equipped by God's Spirit with the necessary spiritual gifts for building up the body of Christ in the world. Those gifts are many (see Eph. 4:11; Rom. 12:6-8; 1 Cor. 12:4-30). Among them is mentioned the gift of evangelists.

Please note that it is not the gift of evangelism which the Holy Spirit bestows upon the church. Rather, it is that some are gifted to be evangelists.

There are some who use the reference to evangelists in Ephesians 4:11 to excuse themselves from involvement in evangelism. The argument is that because they do not have the gift of an evangelist they need not bother with evangelism.

I think we should readily acknowledge that some Christians seem to be gifted in evangelism above other Christians. Nevertheless, it should be remembered that in Ephesians 4, all of the gifts are intended to equip the saints for the work of ministry, for building up the one body of Christ. So body building, and in this case the body is the whole church, is the purpose of every spiritual gift.

Furthermore, one spiritual gift does not exclude all other gifts. There are Christians who have more than one spiritual gift. Certainly Jesus was himself an apostle, a prophet, an evangelist, a pastor, and a teacher. Paul was a

many-gifted person. So are some of you. And the word of
Christ which says, "Every one to whom much is given, of him
will much be required" (Luke 12:48), applies to us all.
Therefore, whatever your gift or gifts, you must use them as
faithful stewards of God to build up the church of God.

Perhaps we should not automatically identify those who
are called evangelists today with those called evangelists in
New Testament days. So far as I can determine, an evangelist in the apostolic age was more akin to what we know today
as a pioneer missionary. He was one who broke new ground
for God—a kind of itinerant missionary who went about
planting churches. That was a part of the work which Philip
did (Acts 21:8). And it seems to be the work that Paul
exhorted Timothy to do (2 Tim. 4:5).

Whatever you may make of the spiritual gift of an
evangelist, make no mistake about this: the Holy Spirit is the
great Benefactor and Teacher who equips the people of God
with spiritual gifts for building up the body of Christ.
Evangelism is the work of God before it is the work of
people. God has not commissioned us to do the impossible.
He equips us through his Spirit in order that we might equip
the rest of the people of God to do the work of ministry.

Inspires

The next observation I want to make about the role of
the Holy Spirit in evangelism is that he inspires us with what
we are to say. The Spirit helps us with what we are to say in
three ways. First, the Holy Spirit helps us with what we are to
say by inspiring the Scriptures. Second, the Holy Spirit
inspires what we are to say by, at times, giving us the very
words and thoughts which we are to utter. Third, the Holy
Spirit inspires us with what we are to say in preaching. Take
a closer look with me at these three ideas.

Paul wrote to Timothy: "All scripture is inspired by
God" (2 Tim. 3:16). That is to say, all Scripture is God
inbreathed. By what breath? The breath of God's Spirit.

Jesus said in John's Gospel: "You search the scriptures, because you think that in them you have eternal life; and it is they that bear witness to me" (5:39). Remember how Jesus said to the two downcast disciples on the road to Emmaus: "O foolish men, and slow of heart to believe all that the prophets have spoken!" (Luke 24:25). Then, Luke went on to say: "And beginning with Moses and all the prophets, he interpreted to them in all the scriptures the things concerning himself" (v. 27).

The Bible is full of Christ. It is inspired truth which points us to him who is the way, the truth, and the life. The Holy Spirit helps us with what we are to say in our evangelizing by giving us an inspired Bible. This is the reason we use the Bible in seeking to convert lost persons to Jesus Christ.

Not only does the Holy Spirit give us inspired Scripture to use in our witnessing, he at times gives us the very words and thoughts we are to use. Listen to what Christ said about this in Matthew 10:17-20:

> "Beware of men; for they will deliver you up to councils, and flog you in their synagogues, and you will be dragged before governors and kings for my sake, to bear testimony before them and the Gentiles. When they deliver you up, do not be anxious how you are to speak or what you are to say; for what you are to say will be given to you in that hour; for it is not you who speak, but the Spirit of your Father speaking through you."

Sometimes we get uptight about what we will say if we are put on the spot. And may I remind you that many Christians in Marxist lands and even in Korea and El Salvador and elsewhere today find themselves in exceedingly tight straits. But I believe those who do their best to learn how to share their faith and who try diligently to be prepared with what they will say can always claim this promise. "In that hour" it "will be given to you" by the Holy Spirit.

There is also a third way that the Holy Spirit inspires us with what we are to say in our evangelism. He helps us with our preaching. True preaching is what the Bible calls prophecy. And prophecy in the Bible—especially in the New Testament—is not so much foretelling the future as forthtelling God's will for the present.

Joel listed one sign of the outpoured Holy Spirit as:

"your sons and your daughters shall prophesy,

. . . .

I will pour out my Spirit; and they shall prophesy"
(Acts 2:17-18).

The Holy Spirit is the Spirit of prophecy.

The prophecy uttered at Pentecost was the 120 speaking about "the mighty works of God" (Acts 2:11) and Peter's great sermon which resulted in the conversion of about 3,000 persons. It was the Holy Spirit who inspired and emboldened the 120 and the apostle Peter to call their hearers to repentance.

Later in Acts we read of Stephen preaching and saying: "You stiff-necked people, uncircumcised in heart and ears, you always resist the Holy Spirit. As your fathers did, so do you" (Acts 7:51).

Paul was very clear on this point. "So faith comes from what is heard, and what is heard comes by the preaching of Christ" (Rom. 10:17). Elsewhere he said: "It pleased God through the folly of what we preach to save those who believe" (1 Cor. 1:21). That public proclamation of Jesus Christ which we call preaching is, at its best, inspired utterance which the Holy Spirit gives to the church through today's apostles, prophets, evangelists, pastors, and teachers (see Eph. 4:11).

Seven times in Revelation 2 and 3, once to each of the seven churches, we are told: "He who has an ear, let him hear what the Spirit says to the churches" (2:7,11,17,29; 3:6,13,22). And to each of the seven churches the Spirit speaks through "the angel of the church," that is, through the messenger who is the pastor. The Holy Spirit inspires us in our evangelism by helping us with what we are to say in our preaching.

Guides

The Holy Spirit often guides us in our evangelism. He frequently guides us to those to whom we are to witness. An excellent New Testament example of this is the way Philip was led to the Ethiopian eunuch. Note:

> But an angel of the Lord said to Philip, "Rise and go toward the south to the road that goes down from Jerusalem to Gaza"; And the Spirit said to Philip, "Go up and join this chariot"; And when they came up out of the water, the Spirit of the Lord caught up Philip (Acts 8:26,29,39).

See how the Holy Spirit led Philip, the evangelist, to introduce this high official of Ethiopia to Christ.

One of the most remarkable passages in the Bible about how the Holy Spirit leads Christian workers to those persons and places where they are to evangelize is Acts 16:6-10. There it is said of Paul, Silas, Timothy, and perhaps also of Doctor Luke:

And they went through the region of Phrygia and Galatia, having been forbidden by the Holy Spirit to speak the word in Asia. And when they had come opposite Mysia, they attempted to go into Bithynia, but the Spirit of Jesus did not allow them; so passing by Mysia, they went down to Troas. And a vision appeared to Paul in the night: a man of Macedonia was standing beseeching him and saying, "Come over to Macedonia and help us." And when he had seen the vision, immediately we sought to go on into Macedonia, concluding that God had called us to preach the gospel to them.

I take it that the vision which led them into Macedonia was a vision which the Holy Spirit gave them because in Acts 2 Peter quoted the prophet Joel as saying that one sign of the outpouring of the Holy Spirit would be: "Your young men shall see visions,/and your old men shall dream dreams" (Acts 2:17).

I believe the Holy Spirit still leads us to those to whom we are to witness. Pastor Herschel H. Hobbs tells how the Holy Spirit guided him one afternoon to a woman in need of salvation. He was out visiting when he received an impression that he should go to the church building. Ignoring it, he continued to visit. Soon the impression almost became an audible voice. Finally he went. Five minutes after arriving, a woman came to see him. She poured out her story of a life of sin. The night before she had heard the pastor's sermon on the radio. From that moment she had been impressed to see him. That afternoon she was saved, and that night she joined the church. Later she was baptized and subsequently lived an exemplary Christian life.[3] You can call that coincidence if you choose, but I call it the leadership of the Holy Spirit.

But let me go one step further and suggest that the Spirit not only guides us to those who need our witness but he also guides us to those who are to be evangelists and missionaries. Have you caught the full significance of those words in Acts 13:2? "While they were worshiping the Lord and fasting, the Holy Spirit said, 'Set apart for me Barnabas and Saul for the work to which I have called them.'" Later that same chapter says of Barnabas and Saul: "So, being sent out by the Holy Spirit" (v. 4).

Perhaps this is the reason our Lord taught us to pray for laborers. Let us pray that the Holy Spirit will call out from our midst those laborers whom we are to send out to gather the Lord's harvest in our own Jerusalem and to the ends of the earth.

Summary and Conclusion

We have been thinking about the role of the Holy Spirit in evangelism as he interacts with and through us and as he

works with the unbelieving world. I have made six statements about the role of the Holy Spirit in evangelism. First,
the Holy Spirit empowers Christians to bear witness to Jesus
Christ. Second, he convinces the lost world of sin, righteousness, and judgment. Third, he regenerates those who are
dead in trespasses and sin and effects the new creation.
Fourth, he equips the church with the necessary spiritual
gifts for building up the body of Christ. Fifth, he inspires us
with what we are to say. And, sixth, the Holy Spirit guides us
in our evangelism.

There are, of course, many other points which might
have been made about the function of the Holy Spirit in
evangelism. No one can even confess Jesus as Lord apart
from the Holy Spirit (1 Cor. 12:3). He helps us to know that
we are saved (Rom. 8:15-16). He guarantees our inheritance
(Eph. 1:13-14). He helps us to maintain self-control and to
overcome our timidity (2 Tim. 1:7). He guides us into all
truth (John 16:13; 1 John 2:20). He enables us to live a
Christian life (Gal. 5:22-24). He brings joy into our lives
which is greater than all of our sorrows. Someone has said,
"The only infallible sign of God's presence is JOY!"

Suggestions for Further Reading

"The Spirit in Evangelism" in David Watson, *I Believe in
Evangelism* (Grand Rapids: Wm. B. Eerdmans Publishing Co.,
1976), pp. 168-188.

"Impartation" in Robert E. Coleman, *The Master Plan of Evangelism* (Westwood, New Jersey: Fleming H. Revell Co., 1963), pp.
61-72.

"Have You Got the Baptism, Brother?" in Lewis A. Drummond,
The Awakening That Must Come (Nashville: Broadman Press,
1978), pp. 33-44.

"Dependency" in Delos Miles, *Master Principles of Evangelism* (Nashville: Broadman Press, 1982), pp. 59-69.

Notes

1. This chapter is a revision of two lectures originally presented to an associational Conference on the Holy Spirit at First Baptist Church, Anderson, South Carolina, on September 17, 1974. The reader's attention is called to some overlapping of this chapter with a portion of chapter 7, "Dependency" in Delos Miles' *Master Principles of Evangelism* (Broadman, 1982), pp. 59-69.
2. W. Stanley Mooneyham, "Getting More Hooks in the Water Is Not Enough: World Evangelization Requires the Right Tackle," *Christianity Today,* Vol. XXV, No. 16, Sept. 18, 1981, p. 19.
3. Herschel H. Hobbs, *New Testament Evangelism* (Nashville: Convention Press, 1960), pp. 34-35.

17
The Messenger's Prayer Life

2 Chronicles 7:11-18; John 15:12-17

Introduction

Someone has said that prayer is the most unpopular activity in the church. Is that really true? If we judge by attendance at most prayer meetings, it is.

Little praying may be worse than no praying because a little prayer can salve the conscience. It can become a farce and a delusion.

One reason our evangelism is so weak is that our prayers are so sporadic, and our praying is so weak and nonexistent. We may have not because we ask not. Jesus said: "Ask, and it will be given you; seek, and you will find; knock and it will be opened to you" (Luke 11:9).

The Need for Prayer

More Christians on their knees praying may mean more evangelists on their feet evangelizing. Robert Speer, a great Presbyterian missions pioneer and leader wrote:

> The evangelization of the world . . . depends first of all upon a revival of prayer. Deeper than the need for men; deeper, far, than the need for money; deep down at the bottom of our spiritless lives, is the need for the forgotten secret of prevailing, worldwide prayer. Missions have progressed slowly abroad because piety and prayer have been shallow at home.[1]

Pad 39 at Cape Canaveral has become famous as the place for launching Saturn 5 rockets. It is 390 by 325 feet of reinforced concrete, which is 48 feet deep. The launch pad is almost the size of a football field covered with 48 feet of concrete. That's what it takes to launch a giant Saturn 5 rocket.

What about your launching pad? What are its dimensions? Is your prayer launch pad more like a sugar cube than a Pad 39?

"The single most important factor in growing to Christian maturity," said a Nigerian pastor, "is prayer." Do you believe that? My friend from Nigeria does.

No amount of Bible study or devotional reading can make up for a lack of prayer in a Christian's life. We need definite times and places for prayer. The growth of the Christian church in South Korea illustrates that.

Korea is one of the great success stories in church growth during this century. In 1966 approximately 11 percent of the Korean population was Christian. By 1978 it was 19 percent; in 1981 it was 22 percent. Some are projecting that it will be 30 percent by 1984, which will be the one hundredth anniversary of Protestant missions in Korea.

That country is rapidly emerging as the first evangelical nation in Asia. It is now predicted that by 1991 Christianity in Korea will have reached the point where there is an average of one evangelical church for every 1,000 citizens. Also by that year 35.9 percent of the citizens will be church members.[2]

Korea now has the largest Presbyterian, Methodist, and Assemblies of God churches in the world. Presbyterianism began in Scotland, but its largest congregation is one in Korea with over 50,000 members. Methodism began in England, but its largest congregation is one in Korea which has a sanctuary that seats 4,000 persons. The Assemblies of God began in the USA, but their largest congregation is Full Gospel Central Church on Yoido Island in Korea. Its membership is now in excess of 165,000, with 5,000 new members being added each month.

I do not cite these statistics to exalt bigness, but to show
that the church is growing by great leaps and bounds in
Korea. If there is any one secret to such rapid growth, it is
the prevailing prayer of the Korean Christians. Peter
Wagner, one of the leading church growth authorities in the
world, visited Korea in 1981. "I think my deepest impression
of Korea," said Wagner, "was the extraordinary, pervasive
sense of prayer I found in the churches." Wagner continued,
"Every church has a dawn prayer meeting at 4:30 or 5:00
every single day. It is considered very important that the
senior pastor of most multiple-staff churches visits or leads
that meeting every morning."[3]

Most of the Korean churches also have an all-night
prayer meeting every Friday. Some of the churches even
have prayer mountains in the countryside to which persons
can retreat for prayer and fasting up to a forty-day max-
imum. Some Korean pastors are literally building prayer
closets in their studies. One pastor has a prayer closet with a
picture of Jesus on the wall, a small, low stand for an open
Bible, and a kneeling cushion on the floor. He spends an
hour and a half a day in that closet. Every Saturday night in
preparation for Sunday services he sleeps in his study and
fasts all day.

Why do these Korean Christians devote so much time
and effort to their daily, weekly, and special prayers? You ask
them and they will answer, "That's where the power comes
from."

Korea's greatest gift to the whole church today is the
example of prayer. I believe the explosive growth of the
Korean churches is due to the power of God released
through fervent, enthusiastic, extensive, intensive, and believing prayer.

In 1916 there was a Korean church which had a weekly
prayer meeting of over a thousand in attendance for more
than three years. Most of us would have been rather thrilled
with that kind of midweek prayer meeting. However, the

pastor felt that his church was growing cold and a bit indifferent. So each morning at four he went to church to pray until six. A few of his members observed his practice and joined him in it. On Sunday morning the pastor told his people what he was doing and invited others who wished to join him. That Monday over a hundred were present from 4:00 AM to 6:00 AM. By Saturday morning nearly six hundred gathered for prayer. Many of those were busy businessmen. The next month more than three thousand persons were added to the Pyeng Yang churches.

We need to start praying with that kind of intensity and seriousness if we want God to revive our cold hearts and heal our sin-sick land. I agree with John G. Hallimond that, "Prayer—earnest, steadfast, and believing prayer—on the right lines, and in the right spirit, is invariably and inevitably followed by revival."[4]

If we would have power with God and with men, we must pray. If we would have revival in our time or anytime, we must pray.

Jesus promised the early Christians that they would receive power when the Holy Spirit had come upon them— power to be witnesses to him everywhere (see Acts 1:8). That power came after a ten-day prayer meeting in the upper room (see Acts 1:13-14; 2:1 *ff.*).

Evangelism is spiritual work which requires spiritual power in order for it to be effective. That spiritual power is often in direct proportion to our prayers.

The Bible connects spiritual power with both prayer and the Holy Spirit. Acts 4:31 reads, "And when they had prayed, the place in which they were gathered together was shaken; and they were all filled with the Holy Spirit and spoke the word of God with boldness."

That colorful and controversial evangelist, Billy Sunday, once said in a sermon on prayer: "If you are a stranger to prayer you are a stranger to the greatest source of power known to human beings."[5] Sunday and his co-workers insisted that preparatory prayer circles be formed, one circle for every block, long weeks before he arrived to begin a crusade.[6] They knew that their power came through prevailing prayer to God.

I have often been intrigued with how the Lord answered Solomon's prayer when the Temple was dedicated to him. "When I shut up the heavens so that there is no rain, or command the locust to devour the land, or send pestilence among my people, if my people who are called by my name shall humble themselves, and pray and seek my face, and turn from their wicked ways, then I will hear from heaven, and will forgive their sin and heal their land" (2 Chron. 7:13-14).

But only recently have I seen the parallel between that passage and what is said in John 15 about the vine and the branches. Jesus said, "You did not choose me, but I chose you and appointed you that you should go and bear fruit and that your fruit should abide; so that whatever you ask the Father in my name, he may give it to you" (v. 16).

Both of those passages connect prayer with fruit bearing. The Johannine passage teaches that as we branches abide in the vine of Christ, the Father who is the Vinedresser will cause us to bear fruit that abides forever. One reason for that fruit bearing is "so that whatever you ask the Father in my name," said Jesus, "he may give it to you."

Therefore, as we bear the fruit of obedience to the commands of Christ, we can expect answers to our prayers. One of his commandments is that we love one another. As we obey that commandment to love our brothers and sisters in the church, we shall find our prayers answered in proportion to our fruit of love for one another.

Another of his commandments is that we love God supremely and neighbor as self (see Matt. 22:37-40). As we obey those commandments and produce that fruit of obedience, we can expect our prayers to be answered in proportion to the fruit of *agape* love which we bear. Still another of Christ's commandments is that we disciple all nations, baptizing them in the name of the holy Trinity, and teaching them to keep his commandments. As we bear that abiding fruit, so will our prayers be answered in proportion to our obedience.

The 2 Chronicles passage is even more corporately oriented than is the Johannine one. But note how God prescribes that we humble ourselves, pray, seek his face, and turn from our wicked ways when the land ceases to bear fruit and bring forth its harvest. The forgiveness of our sins by God and the healing of our land are tied together.

Evidently sin is both an individual and a corporate phenomenon, and so is prayer. One of the means which Charles G. Finney used to promote revivals was "much prayer, secret and social." Finney knew that both private and public prayer was needed.

We need to pray just now because our beloved land of America is in need of healing. This land of plenty is not bearing its fruits for all of its citizens. An average of over 10 percent of our people are unemployed. Our land is sprinkled with poverty. Our cities are festering with great slums. Our streets have become the dwelling place of many homeless persons. The great James River from Hopewell, Virginia, to the Chesapeake Bay has been polluted with 20,000 to 40,000 pounds of the deadly chemical kepone which will remain with us for centuries. PCBs have been dumped indiscriminately in many areas. We have found no certain, safe way to store our nuclear waste. In spite of all that, we continue to proliferate nuclear weapons and to produce dread gases for possible chemical warfare. Our land is sick, and its healing depends on our healing and on our prayers.

We need to pray because we are not bearing the fruit of obedience which Christ commands. We know that we do not love God above all else and all others. We know that we do not love our neighbors as we love ourselves.

Please note that neither passage says we can't pray

unless we are abiding in a perfect relationship with God. They do not rule out anyone praying. However, they do connect answered prayer with fruit bearing.

Prayer and Revival

Let me say a bit more about prayer and revival. One of the important truths about revivals and spiritual awakenings is that they are answers to the prayers of God's people.

A most remarkable spiritual awakening began in America in 1857. Some called it "the greatest revival since Pentecost." Others called it "the great prayer revival" and the Fulton Street revival of 1857-1858. It began in the old Dutch Reformed Church on Fulton Street in New York. Jeremiah Calvin Lanphier issued a call to noonday prayer to a few businessmen. Lanphier was there alone for half an hour. Then, five other persons came in. That prayer meeting grew and expanded until it shook the whole earth.[7]

Samuel Irenaeus Prime wrote an eyewitness account of the great prayer revival in 1858. He says it was directly connected with the economic crash of about that same time. It was largely a lay movement with little preaching but much prayer and testimony. D. L. Moody was caught up in those prayer meetings which had spread to Chicago and even across the ocean.[8]

The Welsh revival of 1905 was like one prolonged prayer meeting. Again, there was little preaching. G. Campbell Morgan, who attended several of those meetings in Wales, said: "If you ask me the meaning of the Welsh revival I say it is Pentecost continued." Its most noticeable characteristic was prayer and more prayer. There was singing, but it was singing in the spirit of prayer. Testimonies were given, but they were testimonies to the power of prayer. Within five weeks, twenty thousand were added to the churches in that atmosphere of prayer.[9]

So far as I can tell, there never has been or will there ever be a great and lasting renewal of God's people apart from earnest and heartfelt prayer. R. A. Torrey said: "I have a theory, and I believe it to be true, that there is not a church, or chapel, or mission on earth where you cannot have a revival, provided there is a little nucleus of faithful people who are holding *onto* God till it comes."[10] If Torrey spoke the truth, and I believe he did, then what prayer warriors ought you and I to be.

Prayer and Evangelism

So very much depends upon our prayers. Spiritual power eludes us because we do not pray as we ought. Personal and corporate spiritual healing passes us by because we do not more earnestly seek God's face. Revival and spiritual awakening tarry, awaiting greater devotion in our prayer life. The same is true of the evangelistic harvest. Little or no prayer means little or no evangelistic fruit.

Jesus said, "The harvest is plentiful, but the laborers are few; pray therefore the Lord of the harvest to send out laborers into his harvest" (Matt. 9:37-38). Have you asked the Lord to send you out after the lost? Are you praying daily for God to raise up laborers and send them out to reap the evangelistic harvest?

Are we not all an answer to our Lord's high priestly prayer in John 17? "I do not pray for these only, but also for those who believe in me through their word . . . so that the world may believe that thou hast sent me" (vv. 20-21).

New Testament scholar, A. B. Bruce, tells us that the events of Pentecost were an answer to the ten days of prayers on the part of the disciples. About three thousand souls were added to the church on that first Pentecost Sunday in answer to prayer.

Since 1976 the Lausanne Committee for World Evangelization (LCWE) has sponsored annually on Pentecost Sunday a Day of Prayer for World Evangelization. This is not some magic talisman guaranteed to bring world revival. Nor is it designed to be a mere form of godliness without the power of God flowing through it. It is a deliberate attempt to give some structure to the deep heart cry for revival and spiritual awakening in the world.

The eighteenth-century missionary exploits of the Moravians grew out of an around-the-clock, around-the-calendar chain of prayer that continued for more than a century. That chain of prayer touched and sparked the Wesleyan revival in eighteenth-century England. Who knows but that John Wesley and George Whitefield were answers to those Moravian prayers? Those praying Moravians influenced William Carey, the Baptist trailblazer and pioneer missionary to India. Those prayers may well have stoked the fires of revival under Theodore J. Frelinghysen, Gilbert Tennent, and Jonathan Edwards in eighteenth-century New England.[11]

I know, not only from history but also from firsthand accounts, that prayer and evangelism must go together. The grandmother of one of my former students prayed for his salvation twenty-seven years. When he was saved, his grandmother quietly told his wife, "Now I am ready to die." Such prayer warriors are unsung blessings to God's kingdom.

Emmett Johnson, director of evangelism for American Baptists, prayed eighteen years every day for the salvation of his father. He thought it would take maybe a couple of weeks. It took eighteen years.

One of my students told me about God's answer to prayer in an unusual witnessing experience which he had in 1981. Joe was enrolled in a four-night lay witness training school in South Carolina. The school introduced him to one intentional technique for sharing his faith with lost persons. A part of that technique included prayer and the use of a small green booklet entitled, "How to Have a Full and Meaningful Life." Joe said:

> On Monday and Tuesday of that week we were encouraged to think of individuals that we knew who were lost. By the end of Tuesday night's class, I had a burning desire to tell

five men at work about Jesus Christ. Before leaving that
night, I asked my pastor and the instructor if they would
pray for these five men. I asked them for five booklets to
use while witnessing to these men the next day at lunch.
They handed me some and assured me that they would
pray for these men.

On a normal day at Hayes Food Products, Inc., all
workers except five men would go out to lunch. These five
men would bring their lunches and talk while they ate. On
Wednesday I hurriedly ate a sandwich. Then I knelt down
in my office and asked God to give me the strength to use
my words in speaking with them, and to deal with each
man's heart individually.

After praying, I went into the plant and found not just
the usual five, but six men. I asked the men if I could have
ten or fifteen minutes to share with them the most
meaningful experience in my life. They agreed, so I
proceeded by taking the booklets out of my shirt pocket.
To my amazement, I had six booklets instead of five. After
handing them out, I shared the gospel with them. The five
I had prayed for accepted Jesus Christ, but the sixth man
did not.

I was thrilled that these men had accepted Jesus
Christ, and I thanked God that he had used me as his
instrument to reach them. I could hardly wait to share this
with my pastor and the instructor. When I arrived at
church that evening and told them what had happened,
my pastor told me that he and about sixteen other pastors
met for lunch that day and had a group prayer meeting for
the five men at about the same time I was witnessing to
them. He said they had only prayed for five because that
was the number I had given them.[12]

You may choose to call that account coincidental. I
prefer to call it providential and to view it as an answer to
prayer. "The prayer of a righteous man has great power in its
effects" (Jas. 5:16). Another jeweled promise on prayer and
evangelism is Psalm 2:8, "Ask of me, and I will make the

nations your heritage, and the ends of the earth your possession." Stephen Olford was correct, "No soul is ever born into God's kingdom unless there has been prayer."

Everybody Can Pray

One of the encouraging aspects of prayer is that everybody can do it. You may not be gifted as a public speaker. You may never be able to teach a class or preach a public sermon. You may be no singer or musician. You may have little or no money to offer God. Yet, whoever you are you can pray. The work of prayer is every Christian's job.

Those who can't read or write can pray. Those who are physically handicapped and confined to bed can pray. Physical invalids can be mighty prayer warriors.

Hallimond said the most wonderful man of prayer he ever knew was a little, bowlegged coal miner in the north of England. That man was Hallimond's Sunday School teacher when he was a boy. He was uneducated and suffered from a speech impediment. When he prayed, however, he had eloquence and power equaled by none other whom Hallimond knew.[13]

Perhaps you have heard that it was the prayers of a bedridden, shut-in, pain-racked, invalid woman in the north of London which started D. L. Moody on his career as a worldwide itinerant evangelist. Twisted and distorted by much suffering, that lady had lain for many years unable to do anything else but pray. She had read in the paper about Moody's work in Chicago. Unknown to Moody or to others, she had placed that paper under her pillow and prayed, "O Lord, send this man to our church."

It seemed unlikely that Moody would ever come to London. She had no means of contacting him. She just kept praying to the God for whom all things are possible.

Moody did go to London in 1872, when his church building lay in ashes. While speaking to the YMCA in the

Strand, a pastor invited him to preach to his congregation. Nothing much happened that Sunday morning. Moody was a bit sorry he had agreed to preach in the same church on Sunday night.

Following the morning service, the sister of the invalid woman informed her that a Mr. Moody of Chicago had preached and that he was to speak again that evening. The invalid turned pale and said, "If I had known, I would have taken no breakfast. I would have spent all the time in prayer. Send me no dinner. Leave me alone. Lock the door. Don't have me disturbed. I am going to spend the whole afternoon and evening in prayer."

The building was packed that evening to hear Moody. There was a different atmosphere. The powers of the unseen world seemed to have fallen on the people. Five hundred gave themselves to Christ in the after meeting. A great revival broke out. That was one of the events which launched Moody's career as an itinerant evangelist.[14]

If that sick lady could pray like that and do so much good, how much more can you and I pray? We should encourage every Christian to be a prayer warrior. Intercessory prayer is our secret weapon against Satan. He can't touch it, and persons for whom we pray can't stop us.

Conclusion

Prayer is the key which unlocks heaven's door. But it isn't the key to simply gain the things which we want and need. Rather, it is a key to finding out what God is doing and how to get in on it.

Prayer is an essential link in the chain of causes which lead to revival. The Holy Spirit is given in answer to prayer.

Four out of five American congregations are not growing. We need to pray for that church growth which pleases God. Some church prayer meetings sound like infirmary roll calls. One reason we don't have more new, countable disciples is that we have not asked God for them.

Suggested Study Questions

1. George Muller began praying for the salvation of five men in 1814. He prayed every day without fail for each man by name, no matter where he went or how busy he was. One of the five was converted after eighteen months; a second after five years; a third after five years and six months; a fourth just before Muller's death in 1898; and the fifth a few years after his death. How do you connect Muller's prayers with the salvation of these five persons?
2. Briefly relate the growth of the church in South Korea to prayer.
3. How does the author seek to tie prayer and fruit bearing together in this chapter?

Notes

1. W. Stanley Monneyham, "Getting More Hooks in the Water Is Not Enough: World Evangelization Requires the Right Tackle," *Christianity Today,* Vol. XXV, No. 16, Sept. 18, 1981, p. 20.
2. James H. Montgomery's editorial in the *Global Church Growth Bulletin,* Vol. XIX, No. 1, Jan.-Feb., 1982, p. 159.
3. C. Peter Wagner, "Where Growth Flows from Prayer Mountain," *Global Church Growth Bulletin,* Vol. XVIII, No. 5, September-October, 1981, p. 137. See also p. 136.
4. J. G. Hallimond, *The Miracle of Answered Prayer* (New York: The Christian Herald, 1916), p. 65.
5. Cited by Daniel Wade Armstrong, *An Examination of Evangelism in America Beginning with the Eighteenth Century in the Light of New Testament Principles of Evangelism* (an unpublished doctoral thesis at Southern Baptist Theological Seminary, Louisville, Ky., 1955), p. 154.
6. Hallimond, p. 67.
7. Ibid., p. 66.
8. Samuel Irenaeus Prime, *The Power of Prayer* (New York: Charles Scribner, 1858, fifth ed.).
9. Hallimond, pp. 66-67.
10. Ibid., p. 65.
11. "Day of Prayer for World Evangelization," *World Evangelization,* Information Bulletin No. 25, Dec., 1981, pp. 14,7. This is a publication of the Lausanne Committee for World Evangelization. For further information write Day of Prayer, LCWE, Box 1100, Wheaton, Ill. 60187.
12. This is a slightly edited version of the written account of Joe F. Hayes, Jr., dated Jan. 21, 1982, and done for my M 4540 course in the spring semester of 1982.
13. Hallimond, pp. 67-68.
14. Ibid., pp. 69-71.

Section VI
The Methods of Evangelism:
How Shall We Evangelize?

18
Methods in Historical Perspective

Habakkuk 3:2; Acts 20:17-35

Introduction

No comprehensive history of evangelism has been written.[1] Such a task may, indeed, be impossible.

Perhaps the nearest attempt at a comprehensive history of evangelism is that of Paulus Scharpff in his 1964 *History of Evangelism.*[2] Wilhelm Brauer in his "Foreword" to Scharpff's work boldly asserts: "The book deals with a subject on which there was previously no work of similar scope. Hence it definitely fills a serious gap in the literature of church history."[3] Scharpff, himself, states the limits to his work:

> In this volume we have discussed evangelism particularly and awakenings only incidentally. The story of spiritual awakenings throughout the world requires another special project. . . . the evangelistic movements in countries geographically adjacent to Germany must be presented in another volume.[4]

Evangelism is defined by Scharpff as "the function of man, distinct from the function of the Holy Spirit evidenced in spiritual awakenings."[5] Scharpff finds the roots of "present-day" evangelism in seventeenth-century Pietism.[6] The first eleven hundred years, including the Protestant Reformation, he dismisses in sixteen pages.[7] It soon becomes clear to the reader that Scharpff is writing a history of Pietism which is highly subjective and sometimes inaccurate.[8] Those who look to Scharpff for a history of evangelism will be disappointed, though not unrewarded. For Scharpff does

229

succeed in showing that modern evangelism has deep roots in Spenerian Pietism. Furthermore, his work is the only single volume which treats the history of evangelism during the last three centuries in Germany, Great Britain, and America. One of its strengths is that it focuses upon the involvement of the laity in evangelism.

Most of the histories of evangelism in America are histories of revivalism and spiritual awakenings which have swept across the country. W. L. Muncy, Jr., in 1945 wrote what he called A *History of Evangelism in the United States*.[9] Basically Muncy's book is a history of revivalism. His "Introduction" launches right into the Great Awakening and singles out "the Pietistic movement in Germany, a vital evangelical awakening in Ireland, and the Wesleyan revival in England" as the sources of it. Muncy treats his subject under the three divisions of "colonial development" (1607-1775), "national beginnings" (1775-1860), and "national maturity" (1860-1944). Its main weaknesses are dependence upon secondary sources, a failure to take seriously secondary causes, and the lack of any definition of evangelism.

Muncy does make an effort at providing a history of evangelism that is broader than revivalism. Evidences of this are his attention to Indian missions, home missions, the underprivileged, youth movements, training for evangelism, and the use of radio.

One unique feature of Muncy's work is his attempt to correlate the decline of evangelism with the American wars. Another helpful contribution of Muncy is his succinct summaries of evangelistic methodology.[10]

Both Scharpff's and Muncy's efforts illustrate some of the difficulties in treating the history of evangelism. There is no recognized or common definition of evangelism. There is considerable overlapping with the history of missions. The tendency is to conflate evangelism with revivalism. It is easier to treat one country than many. Writers on the history of evangelism seem to be especially tempted to subjectivism.

I shall attempt only to identify and sketch eight strands of evangelism in American church history. Roughly each of these strands corresponds to a separate methodology. They are more or less in chronological order: pastoral evangelism, revival evangelism, missionary board evangelism, educational evangelism, youth-group evangelism, visitation evangelism, mass-media evangelism, and lay-group evangelism.

Pastoral Evangelism

Who knows exactly where pastoral evangelism begins? Our most trustworthy model for this kind of evangelism is Jesus himself as he is revealed in the Bible. John T. McNeill in *A History of the Cure of Souls* points out that in primitive societies the functions of curing for both body and soul were commonly assumed by the same person. The shaman of American Indians or primitive Siberian tribes and the African medicine man may have been ancient forerunners of the pastoral evangelist.[11]

Pastoral evangelism has played a large role in American church history. It is not so easy to document this aspect of evangelism because so few have written about it. Samuel Southard's *Pastoral Evangelism* comes close to it.[12] But Southard's book is not confined to the pastoral office.[13] Edgar Whitaker Work barely touches the pastoral role in his *Every Minister His Own Evangelist*.[14] I am thinking here of the pastoral office. Probably the reason so little is said concerning this strand of evangelism is that it is almost always assumed.

Southard is wrong in his statement that "itinerant evangelism began with Charles Finney." But he is surely correct in the statement: "In the first awakening, pastors who preached with zeal in their own churches were then invited to preach in neighboring towns."[15] The itinerants up to Finney were primarily pastors except for George Whitefield, who was in a class by himself. Therefore, even the revivalists prior to Finney were settled pastors. Theodore J. Frelinghuysen, Gilbert Tennent, John Rowland, Jonathan Dickinson, and Jonathan Edwards were pastors.

Moreover, it must be assumed that faithful pastors before the Great Awakening and up to the present, whether sympathetic with revivals or antagonistic to them, have done "the work of an evangelist." If pastors had not preached the Word of God, administered the ordinances, and shepherded their flocks, there might have been no churches to pay the vocational evangelists or to help them with revivals and crusades.

I find myself very much in agreement with McNeill's conclusion:

> The physician of souls has not taken his duties lightly. His has been the most demanding of all professions. Nobody would engage in it for wages alone. The hirelings in the pastorate have neglected this ministry, whatever else they have been willing to do. Only an inward compulsion drives men to it and holds them in it. Deeply conscious of their own limitations, but sustained by high faith and heroic devotion, countless numbers of our race have spent themselves in this spiritual service to damaged or endangered souls.[16]

Revival Evangelism

Revival evangelism in America has its taproot deep in Pietism. By Pietism is meant:

> . . . a type of religion which places the principal emphasis upon what is often termed the religion of the heart. It is a religion which appeals primarily to the emotions. Its principal theme is redemption for individuals. Its object is to awaken men and women to a personal repentance.[17]

Scharpff traces such Pietism back to: William Perkins, the English Puritan, who is known as the "Father of Pietism";

William Amesius and Willem Tellinck in the Netherlands; Jean de Labadie in France; Theodor Untereyck (1635-1693), the "Spener of the Reformed" who influenced Theodore J. Frelinghuysen; Philipp Jakob Spener (1635-1705) of Frankfort and his *Pia Desideria* of 1675; and August Hermann Francke of Halle fame whose most notable pupil was Count Nikoulas Ludwig von Zinzendorf.[18]

Pietism came to America largely through the German immigration and through the Dutch and the English. The Mennonites, Moravians, Dunkers, Lutherans, Reformed, Quakers, English Baptists, and English Methodists who came to America had drunk deeply of Pietism.

Revival evangelism may be dated from around 1720 when Theodore J. Frelinghuysen landed in New York and began to preach his Pietism among the Dutch Reformed there and later in the Raritan Valley of New Jersey.[19] When the pietistic revival among the Dutch was at high tide in 1726, Frelinghuysen influenced Gilbert Tennent who became the foremost Presbyterian promoter of the Great Awakening. The revivalistic Presbyterians formed the New Brunswick Presbytery in 1738, the same year in which John Wesley had his heartwarming experience.

Fuel was added to the fires of revivalism when God began his work in Northampton in 1734 under Jonathan Edwards. However this revival was limited to the River Valley in Massachusetts and extended less than thirty miles to the east of that valley in Connecticut. The Great Awakening didn't really begin until George Whitefield made his first tour of New England in 1740.[20]

Revival evangelism has attained four great peaks in American history. Each of these peaks has been national in scope, and each has lasted about one generation. William G. McLoughlin dates them roughly as follows: 1730 to 1760; 1800 to 1830; 1890 to 1920; and 1960 to, perhaps, 1990.[21]

These four revival peaks roughly correspond to what

McLoughlin and others call four great spiritual awakenings. A 1982 article by Walker Knight differentiates between revivals and awakenings this way:

> Revivals and awakenings are not identical occurrences. Revivals alter lives of individuals; awakenings alter the world view of a whole people or culture. Hundreds or even thousands of revivals, along with many other happenings, are part of a spiritual awakening. Revivals are usually limited to a short period, while awakenings stretch over years, even decades.[22]

The outstanding revivalists in the first Great Awakening were Theodore J. Frelinghuysen, Gilbert Tennent, Jonathan Edwards, and, above all, George Whitefield. The outstanding revivalists in the second Great Awakening were James McGready, Barton W. Stone, Lyman Beecher, Asahel Nettleton, and, above all, Charles Grandison Finney. The outstanding revivalists in the third Great Awakening were Dwight L. Moody, J. Wilbur Chapman, R. A. Torrey, and Billy Sunday. The outstanding revivalists of the fourth Great Awakening have so far been Oral Roberts, Kathryn Kuhlman, perhaps Fulton Sheen and Norman Vincent Peale, and, above all, Billy Graham. Naturally there are a great host of other revivalists who labored during each awakening and in between them.

Frelinghuysen introduced two new methods to American revivalism. The first was private meetings for prayer patterned much after the *collegia pietatis* of the German revival. The second was the introduction of lay exhortation and lay preaching.[23] George Whitefield introduced to American revivalism itinerant evangelists and open-air preaching.[24]

Jonathan Edwards introduced to American revivalism the method of personal counsel with individuals about their spiritual condition.[25] This method became widely used by most of the pastors during the high tide of the Great

Awakening. Jonathan Dickinson said during the high tide of the Great Awakening: "I have had more young people address me for direction in their spiritual concern within these three months than in thirty years before."[26] It was under Edwards that emotionalism first became so intense in American revivalism,[27] though he is not to be blamed with the excesses of James Davenport.[28]

The "camp meeting" method of revivalism was the creation of James McGready, though it had a forerunner in Virginia under Samuel Harris.[29] Charles Grandison Finney was the evangelist who inaugurated modern revivalism. Up to Finney revivals had been a "surprising work of God."[30] Finney wrote in his *Lectures on Revivals of Religion*: "It (revival) is not a miracle, or dependent on a miracle, in any sense. It is a purely philosophical result of the right use of the constituted means."[31]

Finney institutionalized revival. Under him a sense of urgency became a sine qua non of revival preaching.[32] He insisted on a new style of preaching, the utility of protracted meetings, and the anxious seat or bench. Finney did not invent the anxious seat. It had come from the mourner's bench at the Methodist camp meetings. Nevertheless he institutionalized it.

What Finney did invent was protracted meetings. Not even Asahel Nettleton's revivals included an extended series of meetings night after night. The protracted meetings of Finney were the frontier camp meetings come to town and city. Only here the visiting specialist came to be exalted. And eventually the protracted meetings of Finney were extended into two or three weeks of nightly meetings led by an outside expert. "After 1835 the generic term 'revival meeting' was applied indiscriminately to all such efforts."

Finney had two other noteworthy contributions to the revival. He trained his members in New York to "go out in the highways and hedges to bring people to hear preaching." He also gave a large place to the use of music and singing in his work. Thomas Hastings was the first of a long line of musical "co-evangelists." Moody, of course, had Sankey. Sunday had Rodeheaver and Graham has Shea and Barrows. From Hastings through Finney has come a whole new corps of full-time Christian workers called "gospel singers."[33]

Moody was the first evangelist after Finney to change revival evangelism. Finney reigned supreme as the dean of American evangelists until his death in 1775. Moody perfected the use of a soloist and music in his campaigns. In the early years of his career, he preferred not to preach in church buildings. He boasted that no collection was taken at his services. Moody held prayer meetings at noon and in the mornings during his campaigns. As he conducted them, they were a new departure in revival technique. Moody abandoned Finney's anxious bench and made large use of the inquiry room. Moody also began the use of decision cards which marked a major innovation in revivalism. The founding of Moody Bible Institute in 1886 for the training of Christian lay workers also marked a new departure in evangelism.[34] Moody was the first, great city evangelist. He said, "Cities are the centers of influence. Water runs downhill, and the highest hills in America are the great cities."[35]

B. Fay Mills, an evangelist who made a concerted effort to combine the social aspect of the gospel with its personal aspects, contributed to revival evangelism the "Mills District Combination Plan of Evangelism." This was based somewhat upon Moody's methods in London, Baltimore, and Saint Louis. Yet it was the forerunner of J. Wilbur Chapman's simultaneous evangelism plan. Chapman dispensed with inquiry rooms and held only "after-meetings."

Billy Sunday brought tabernacle revivals into their heyday. His only other contribution to the revival was to make it more mechanical and secular. The *New York Times* in his obituary called him "the greatest high pressure and mass conversion Christian evangel that America or the world has known."[36]

Billy Graham's contributions to revival methodology are primarily in the use of mass media, such as newspapers, radio, television, motion pictures, magazines, and books. He has incorporated his work and placed himself on a fixed salary. He does seek to follow up his converts more effectively than Sunday or Moody.

Missionary Board or Society Evangelism

Missionary board or society evangelism was begun in America by various societies from Europe. Cromwell's Parliament created "The President and Society for the Propagation of the Gospel in New England" to Christianize the Indians of the American colonies. When Charles II came to the throne, that society was abolished. Nevertheless the society was rechartered with the name, "The Company for Propagacion of the Gospell in New England, and the parts adjacent to America." John Eliot worked among the Massachusetts Indians under this society. They published the Bible which he translated for the Indians in 1661 and 1663. The work among the Indians of Martha's Vineyard received some assistance from this society. Jonathan Edwards labored among the Indians at Stockbridge, Massachusetts, under the New England Society after he lost his pulpit at Northampton. American Presbyterians after the Great Awakening secured the help of the Society in Scotland for Propagating Christian Knowledge to Evangelize the Six Nations. Samuel Kirkland was quite successful in this work. The Moravians worked among the New York Indians in 1740. Christian Henry Rauch, the first Moravian missionary in America, began this work. Roman Catholic Jesuits and Franciscans worked to convert the Indians in Florida, Texas, New Mexico, Arizona, California, New York, around the Great

Lakes, and along the rivers flowing into the Gulf of Mexico.

"The Society for the Propagation of the Gospel in Foreign Parts" worked among the Indians, Negroes, and white colonists in America. The SPG was an Anglican society. The "Society for Promoting Christian Knowledge," the "Associates of Dr. Bray," and the "Society for Promoting Christian Learning" were allied with the SPG.[37]

The years 1795 to 1830 were "The Era of Organization" for American churches. Home and foreign missionary societies were formed. The New York Missionary Society began in 1796, composed of Presbyterians, Dutch Reformed, and Baptists. Its immediate object was to evangelize the southern Indians. The Missionary Society of Connecticut was formed in 1798. This was a Congregational society "to Christianize the heathen in North America, and to support and promote Christian knowledge in the new settlements within the United States." Within a few years, eight such societies were formed in New England supported by numerous local societies. Some of the Presbyterian synods and Presbyteries and some of the Baptist conventions and associations were organized to promote missions. The Massachusetts Baptist Missionary Society was launched in 1802. The Methodist Missionary Society was formed in 1819. The American Board of Commissioners for Foreign Missions was formed in 1810. The "General Missionary Convention of the Baptist Denomination of the United States of America for Foreign Missions" met in 1814. In 1817 plans were laid by the General Missionary Convention to evangelize the West. John Mason Peck had a distinguished career as a Baptist home missionary. Muncy says Peck was the man who adopted and developed the Methodist circuit system for Baptists.[38] The American Home Missionary Society was organized in 1826. It was the first home missionary organization on a national scale. Like the American Board of Commissioners it was interdenominational. By 1835 the AHMS was employing

719 agents and missionaries. By 1855 the number had increased to 1,032 missionaries serving in 27 states or territories.[39]

Most of today's missionary boards, societies, commissions, divisions, and so forth have their genesis in these societies and boards. Each major denomination now has boards or a board for missions. They also have some person heading up a division or board of evangelism. Southern Baptists even have one or more full-time workers in each state convention who is responsible for evangelism. The National Council of Churches also has a division responsible for evangelism.[40]

Board evangelism has played and is playing a significant part in evangelizing America and the world. Probably we are safe in saying that board evangelism has not been and is not now primarily revival oriented. Note that most of these missionary boards and societies began ecumenically and only later were adopted or followed by denominational boards.

Educational Evangelism

Educational evangelism centers around the Sunday School movement and Horace Bushnell's concept of Christian nurture. The Methodists apparently introduced the Sunday Schools to the United States in 1786.[41] Sunday Schools began in 1774 with the Methodists, but Robert Raikes in 1780 gave them new impetus.[42] By 1816 schools were formed across America and societies for promoting them and providing literature were organized in New York and Philadelphia. In 1824 the American Sunday School Union was formed to promote Sunday Schools and provide literature.[43] The National Teaching Mission of the National Council of Churches reminds Sunday School teachers of their evangelistic responsibility. So does the National Sunday School Association and the National Association of Christian

Schools of the National Association of Evangelicals.[44] Christian day schools and Vacation Bible Schools also present evangelistic opportunities. Edwin Dozier said, "Undoubtedly the Sunday school has made the greatest single contribution to evangelism outside the regular ministry of the church itself."[45] Moody began his great work as a Sunday School worker. While he was yet a traveling collector, he built one of the largest Sunday Schools in the country in Chicago.[46]

Bushnell provided an alternative to revivalism almost in the midst of Finney's glory.[47] His *Christian Nurture* appeared in 1847. A Congregational minister in Hartford, he did not entirely discount revivals. His point was that too much emphasis had been placed on the experience of conversion. Ideally, a child should grow up in a Christian home and become a Christian without ever having known he was lost. More emphasis should be placed upon Christian character.[48] A. E. Kernahan sums up the impact of Bushnell's theory:

> Some of us have been under the influence of a heresy, one of the worst heresies that has ever attacked the Christian Church. We have thought that a child had to be converted. Notice what Jesus says: "For of such is the Kingdom of Heaven." What does He mean? Just precisely what he says. Children are Christians, children do not need to be converted unless we allow them to go astray. This is a big challenge to the home and to the church. It is the business of parents and of churches to keep children so near Jesus through Christian nurture and example that they will never become lost.[49]

Bushnell's point of view was not that of the Sunday School movement in his day however. "Sunday School instruction must be regarded as only a means to an end *and that end the conversion of the soul*," so said an *Annual Report* of the Sunday School Union in 1857.[50] It was not until 1946 that Willard L. Sperry, dean of Harvard Divinity School, claimed a triumph for Bushnell's principles and the substitution of religious education for religious revival: "At the present moment the more sober and less ecstatic types of church expect their children to grow up into the Christian life and thus into church membership as a result of their training in church schools."[51]

Youth-Group Evangelism

Youth-group evangelism had its American beginnings in the YMCA movement which was begun in London in 1844 by George Williams. Captain Thomas V. Sullivan, a Christian worker among American seamen, organized the first YMCA in America in the Old South Meeting House in Boston, December 29, 1851. Within three years twenty-six associations had been organized. The international organization was formed in Paris in 1855. The United States Christian Commission, under which D. L. Moody worked during the Civil War, was formed at the urging of the YMCA.

The Student Volunteer Movement for Foreign Missions was formed at Mount Herman, Massachusetts, in 1886, under Moody's urging. John R. Mott became the leader of this group.[52] Pollock says that from the Student Volunteer Movement came the Student Christian Movement, Inter-Varsity Christian Fellowship, and, as "the far outcome," the ecumenical movement.[53]

W. F. Howard says: "Historically, there have been four organized Christian approaches to the campus scene: non-denominational, interdenominational, denominational, and ecumenical. These have come to life in the order named."[54] The name of John R. Mott is inseparably connected with the nondenominational, interdenominational, and the ecumenical approaches.[55] Out of the eighteenth-century secularism and unbelief and out of the nineteenth-century evangelical revival numerous campus groups sprang up. The campus YMCA and YWCA were formed.[56] Under Mott's leadership the World Student Christian Federation was formed in 1895.[57] The WSCF was both nondenominational and inter-denominational. The United Student Christian Council, organized in 1944 but with its roots in the WSCF, has been the chief exponent of the interdenominational approach. The ecumenical approach is represented by United Campus Christian Fellowship. This is a structure which proposes to make possible an organic union of all student Christian movements.[58] Today's chief exponents of the nondenomina-tional approach are Inter-Varsity Christian Fellowship, the Navigators, Campus Crusade for Christ, and the Fellowship of Christian Athletes.[59] The denominational approach to campus evangelism is a phenomenon which originated in the early twentieth century.[60]

Youth for Christ has exerted a large influence upon youth in evangelism. This organization began in 1943 in Indianapolis under the leadership of Roger Malsbary. Tor-rey Johnson was elected president in 1944. He made it an international movement. Billy Graham was their first "field secretary." The main strength of YFC is still in the North but it is growing in the South.[61] Some insight can be gained into the approach of this group through reading *Reaching Youth for Christ,* a book which grew out of "Chicagoland Youth for Christ."[62]

The Epworth League may also be mentioned. It is one of many youth groups originating since 1890.[63] A textbook on evangelism, prepared for the Epworth League Institutes, was Elmer Archibald Leslie's *Acquainting Youth with Christ.*[64] Every major denomination now has its own youth group. Three other books prepared for these youth groups are: *Evangelism of Youth,*[65] *Winning Youth for Christ,*[66] and *Evange-lism for Teen-Agers.*[67]

The Oxford Group Movement, which began in 1908 with Frank Buchman, catered primarily to youth. House parties, open confession of sin, teamwork, and quiet times have characterized this group. They have produced many books and exercised a powerful influence in the past. Today the emphasis is upon moral rearmament rather than conversion.[68]

Visitation Evangelism

Visitation evangelism began with D. L. Moody in the 1870s.[69] Asahel Nettleton had used it effectively, but he was a pastor and only one man.[70] Finney had trained his people in New York to visit but apparently only to "bring people to hear preaching." Between 1913 and 1916 "the ministers of Indianapolis, having decided not to invite Billy Sunday to their city, conducted a protracted city-wide visitation campaign based on house-to-house evangelism by groups of church members." They added 20,000 members to their churches during the three years. In 1914 Elmer T. Clark wrote *The New Evangelism,* a book describing a "one-to-one" campaign conducted by the Church Federation of Saint Louis. Clark claimed 10,000 new members were added to the churches. A religious census was made of the city to discover prospects. A course of instruction was given to the lay visitors. Systematic visitation was made by the laymen and laywomen who sought to persuade the prospects to sign a pledge to join one of the churches. The pastors followed through on the pledges by writing or visiting those who signed. According to Clark, twenty-five cities were planning to use the plan in 1915.

A. Earl Kernahan and Guy H. Black became professional organizers of visitation evangelism with an office in Washington in 1923.[71] Kernahan, who had been active in revivals and had worked to support Sunday, resigned his Methodist church in Boston to devote full time to organizing and conducting visitation campaigns.[72] His office was called "Directed Survey and Visitation Campaigns."[73] Kernahan instructed his visitors to make only four appeals: the appeals to conscience, a Christian home, service, and to be prepared for the hereafter.[74] Other details of his plan are found in his *Christian Citizenship and Visitation Evangelism.*

The churches soon grew tired of Kernahan's high-pressured approach to visitation evangelism. The city-wide, interdenominational campaigns were abandoned, though many of the churches continued to use some kind of visitation approach.[75] The major denominations, following the demise of the ecumenical campaigns, developed their own approaches to visitation evangelism. A. C. Archibald, an American Baptist, wrote *New Testament Evangelism* in 1946. That book goes into much detail on visitation evangelism.[76]

Dawson Bryan led the Methodists in evangelism and built a large church in Houston, using the methods described in *Building Church Membership Through Evangelism.* Some churches still depend upon an annual visitation campaign to make converts and church members. Others have built into their Sunday Schools the idea of visitation evangelism. Like any other method, its motives and theology must constantly be reexamined.[77]

One of today's prime successors to visitation evangelism is Evangelism Explosion (EE), a highly structured lay witness training program, founded by Pastor D. James Kennedy of Coral Ridge Presbyterian Church in Fort Lauderdale, Florida. Evangelism Explosion is a new ecumenical approach to evangelistic visitation which began in the early 1960s. A somewhat comparable program to EE within a major denomination is CWT (Continuing Witness Training) among Southern Baptists.

Mass-Media Evangelism

Mass-media evangelism began with the invention of the printing press. The cinema, radio, television, and satellites have added new dimensions to evangelism through mass media.

The American Bible Society was organized in 1819 and

the American Tract Society in 1825. Today the American Bible Society is one of the most useful allies the church has in evangelism.

The First Baptist Church of Shreveport, Louisiana, was the first local church in America to own and operate a broadcasting station. Pastor M. E. Dodd began this work and from 1921 preached evangelistic sermons every week.

The Department of Religious Radio of the Federal Council of Churches of Christ in America (now the National Council) began broadcasting religious programs through the National Broadcasting Company on May 23, 1923. Ralph Sockman was a leader in this work. During the first fifteen years, they broadcast more than six thousand programs via radio. Some of these were evangelistic programs.

Moody Bible Institute entered the field of radio evangelism in 1925. WMBI was licensed in 1926. WDLM was licensed in 1943. Many evangelistic programs are broadcast through these stations, and programs are produced for other stations.

Charles E. Fuller's *Old Fashioned Revival Hour* began in 1933. Fuller broadcast regularly from 1928 until his death. Percy B. Crawford's *Young People's Church of the Air* began in Philadelphia in 1931. *The International Lutheran Hour* was inaugurated in 1935 by Walter A. Maier.[78] Southern Baptists have a Radio and Television Commission in Fort Worth which produces *The Baptist Hour, Master Control,* and numerous other programs.

Billy Graham broadcasts weekly *The Hour of Decision.* Special television programs of the Graham crusades are shown annually. He has a daily column entitled "My Answer" in many papers. World Wide Pictures distributes his films around the world.

Evangelicals and charismatics thrust the church into the electronic age. Religious broadcasting was neither pluralistic nor tolerant until the early 1970s. The Communications Act of 1934 had sought to bring order to the burgeoning broadcasting industry. Local and national councils of churches were formed to, in effect, become broadcasting units. "The result," says William C. Winslow of the United Church of Christ, "was that these units, representing liberal Protestantism, became the de facto voice of Christianity over the nation's airwaves."[79] Fundamentalists were frozen out. What time they secured, they purchased. Today, the situation is quite different. Commercial religion now controls 93 percent of all religious programming, and the mainline denominations are out in the cold.

M. G. "Pat" Robertson founded the Christian Broadcasting Network (CBN) in 1960 in Virginia Beach, Virginia. By 1961 he was on the air with *The 700 Club*, named after the 700 supporters who donated ten dollars a month during the first several years of operation. CBN has grown from a tiny UHF station in Portsmouth, Virginia, to a network of 150 television affiliates, 2,900 local cable systems serving nearly 15 million homes, and eighty radio affiliates. It has its own satellite.

The 700 Club is a daily talk and variety show with a religious theme. CBN carries news, weather, kiddie shows, and even a soap opera. Robertson's latest major project was the establishment of CBN University in 1977.

Today The 700 Club has more than 100,000 members. Robertson is the son of the late U.S. Senator A. Willis Robertson of Virginia. He is a graduate of Yale University Law School and an ordained Southern Baptist minister.[80]

Robertson dreams of CBN becoming a "fourth network." His network now has potential access to fourteen million households able to receive cable television programs. He and his co-workers were asking in 1982, "What impact are we really making in response to the Great Commission?" The answer appeared to be "not much." So, CBN continues to make shifts in its format and style to reach the secular audience and to break out of the Christian ghetto. "You have to deal with people as they are and not as you would like them to be," said Robertson, "because the world is not a giant church service."[81]

Jeffrey K. Hadden and Charles E. Swann in their book, *Prime Time Preachers,* call the electronic church "televangelism." Hadden and Swann distinguish the leading actors in televangelism as follows: "The Supersavers" (Billy Graham, Oral Roberts, Rex Humbard, Jerry Falwell); "The Mainliner" (Robert Schuller); "The Talkies" (Pat Robertson, Jim Bakker); "The Entertainers" (Jimmy Swaggert, Ross Bagley); "The Rising Stars" (James Robison, Kenneth Copeland, Jack Van Impe). All of these they separate from "The Teachers" such as Richard De Haan and Paul Van Gorder of *Day of Discovery,* and Frank Pollard of *At Home with the Bible.*[82]

The 1982 ABC television movie *Pray TV* demonstrated some of the problems and possibilities of televangelism. Fifteen thousand viewers dialed a vacant code number within a four-hour period. Such numbers normally could be expected to receive about nine hundred calls in a three-hour period. Actor Ned Beatty flashed on the TV screen the number 800-555-6864. Viewers were urged to call "if you have a problem of any kind." Ten thousand of those calls came in during the actor's appeal. The other five thousand came in the next two hours.[83]

Cable television and low-power television (LP TV) are revolutionizing the television industry and in turn televangelism. Americans are now watching TV more than six hours a day. And with cable TV now linked to 28 percent of the country's homes, it is predicted that the big three networks share of the prime-time audience will shrink from 83 to 59 percent by the end of this decade.[84]

Low-power TV stations may be the biggest thing in the history of broadcasting. The first, of what promises to be many, went on the air in tiny Bemidji, Minnesota, in December 1981. For as little as fifty thousand dollars and a license from the Federal Communications Commission (FCC), you can have your own ministation.[85]

There is now a fast-growing Christian Media Network (CMN) in Minneapolis which never asks the TV audience for contributions of money. Founded by Chuck and Joseph Wilkerson in 1980, CMN is a cable religious TV network. All program time is sold to sponsors, such as churches, religious organizations, and businesses. Salespersons are employed on commission across the country to sell time to sponsors.

The Wilkerson brothers were using over eighty-two miles of videotape per week in March 1981. Joseph Wilkerson pointed out that in 1970 about 14 percent of all Americans with a television had cable TV. That figure had grown to 21 percent in 1979 and was expected to reach 33 to 40 percent in 1981. By 1985 some 70 percent of Americans with a television may have cable TV.[86]

There are those who feel that satellite/cable distribution is not the best way to reach large, secular audiences.[87] On the other hand others are moving forward into this field with the object of helping churches and evangelizing the masses.

Lay-Group Evangelism

Lay-group evangelism is a growing thing in America. This is not the same thing as visitation evangelism. Lay groups—such as the Yokefellows, Christian Men Incorporated, the Fellowship of Christian Athletes, the Navigators, the Full Gospel Businessmen's Fellowship International, Women Aglow, and Christian Businessmen's Committee—are included in this aspect of evangelism.[88]

These are nondenominational groups composed of men and women who are concerned about witnessing to others and bringing new life into the church. They are not "in-house" denominational groups. On the contrary, they are ecumenical, growing, and concerned with theological rather than denominational points of view. Again, notice how much evangelism is taking place across and even outside of denominational lines today.

Suggestions for Further Reading

"Evangelistic Methods" in Michael Green, *Evangelism in the Early Church* (Grand Rapids: Wm. B. Eerdmans Publishing Co., 1970), pp. 194-235.

"Historical Illustrations of Evangelism" in Roland Q. Leavell, *Evangelism: Christ's Imperative Commission* (Nashville: Broadman Press, 1979 rev. ed.), pp. 55-104. Especially chapter 8, "Evangelism Has Been Dominant in American Christianity," pp. 92-104.

"Renewed, Revitalized, Rededicated" in Lewis A. Drummond, *The Awakening That Must Come* (Nashville: Broadman Press, 1978), pp. 20-32.

D. James Kennedy, *Evangelism Explosion* (Wheaton, Illinois: Tyndale House Publishers, 1977 rev. ed.), esp. pp. 1-15.

Charles L. Goodell, *Pastor and Evangelist* (New York: Harper & Brothers, Publishers, 1922). One edition will be found in *Cyclopedia of Evangelism* (New York: Harper & Brothers, Publishers, n.d.). This edition contains three volumes by Goodell, the third of which is *Pastor and Evangelist*.

Notes

1. While this volume was in process, I learned of a major new work proposed for publication in 1983 by Missouri Synod Lutheran historian Professor Milton Rudnick and entitled *A History of Evangelism*. Through the courtesy of Dr. Erwin J. Kolb, executive secretary for Evangelism, the Lutheran Church—Missouri Synod, I have seen this manuscript in its unfinished form and can recommend it most highly to prospective readers. However, a thorough critique of the volume must await its publication.

2. Paulus Scharpff, *History of Evangelism,* translated by Helga Bender Henry (Grand Rapids: Wm. B. Eerdmans Publishing Co., 1966). German edition 1964 by Brunnen-Verlag, Giessen, and Basel.

3. Ibid., p. IX.

4. Ibid., p. XII.

5. Ibid., publisher's jacket. I cannot find this statement anywhere in the text. Nearest thing to it is on p. XII in the "Author's Statement of Purpose."

6. Ibid., p. 23. Also see p. 4.

7. Ibid., pp. 5-21.

8. For proof of subjectivity see p. XII, "Our treatment," says Scharpff, "is intended . . . also to communicate new incentive to believers." So p. 11, Luther wrote
thirty-seven "glorious spiritual songs." Inaccuracies may be seen on p. 33 where the date
for the "great revival" at Northampton is given as 1732; p. 57, was Theodore J.
Frelinghuysen really the inventor of "circuit preaching"?; p. 60, Whitefield is said to
have visited Edwards at Northampton in 1734!; p. 70, speaks of "Whitefield's *six*
evangelistic trips to America (1740-1770) . . . "; p. 72, did Cennick leave or was he
excommunicated by John Wesley?; p. 83, did John Wesley *compose* no hymns?; p. 104,
was Moody a "boy" when converted or a young man?; p. 174, Moody was not won to
Christ "during a call at the Moody home."
9. W. L. Muncy, Jr., *A History of Evangelism in the United States* (Kansas City, Kansas:
Central Seminary Press, 1951 ed.).
10. Ibid., pp. IX, XIV, 14-19, 91-98, 127-132, 133-139, 157-165, 166-175, 37-38, 40,
44, 54, 83, 90, 98, 110, 130, 139, 141, 145-146, 148, 155-156, 158-159, 175.
11. See John T. McNeill, *A History of the Cure of Souls* (New York: Harper & Brothers,
Publishers, 1951), pp. vii-viii.
12. Samuel Southard, *Pastoral Evangelism* (Nashville: Broadman Press, 1962). John
Knox Press published a revised edition of this book in 1981.
13. Ibid., pp. 7-8.
14. Edgar Whitaker Work, *Every Minister His Own Evangelist* (New York: Fleming H.
Revell Co., 1927).
15. Southard, p. 139.
16. McNeil, p. 330.
17. William Warren Sweet, *Revivalism in America* (New York: Abingdon Press, 1944
paperback ed.), pp. 24-25.
18. Scharpff, pp. 23-31.
19. Charles Hartshorn Maxon, *The Great Awakening in the Middle Colonies* (Gloucester,
Mass.: Peter Smith, 1958 reprint), pp. 13-14. This book was originally published by the
University of Chicago.
20. Edwin Scott Gaustad, *The Great Awakening in New England* (Gloucester, Mass.: Peter
Smith, 1965 reprint), pp. 18f., 23, 25 *ff.* Original edition by Harper & Row, 1957.
21. William G. McLoughlin, Jr., *Revivals, Awakenings, and Reform* (Chicago: The
University of Chicago Press, 1978), pp. 10-11. See also McLoughlin's *Modern Revivalism*
(New York: The Ronald Press Co., 1959), p. 8. Note that the 1959 work used the dates
for the four peaks as 1725 to 1750, 1795-1835, 1875-1915, and 1945 to perhaps 1970.
22. Walker Knight, "Prelude to Spiritual Awakening," *Missions USA*, Vol. 53, No. 2,
Mar.-Apr., 1982, p. 20.
23. Maxon, pp. 17-18.
24. Muncy, pp. 37-38.
25. Jonathan Edwards, *Edwards on Revivals* (New York: Dunning & Spalding, 1832),
pp. 87-104.
26. Maxon, p. 63.
27. Edwards, pp. 248-250; also see Sweet, p. 30.
28. Sweet, p. 31.
29. Muncy, pp. 83, 50-51.
30. McLoughlin, *Modern Revivalism*, p. 11.
31. Charles G. Finney, *Lectures on Revivals of Religion*, ed. by William G. McLoughlin
(Cambridge, Mass.: The Belknop Press of Harvard University Press, 1960), p. 13.
32. McLoughlin, *Modern Revivalism*, p. 73. Finney's words were, "Another moment's
delay and it may be too late forever."

33. Ibid., pp. 87, 95, 92-93, 94, 98, 99. Finney was pastor of Chatham Street Chapel at the time. He does not discuss this method in his *Lectures on Revivals of Religion*. Also see Muncy, p. 146.

34. McLoughlin, *Modern Revivalism*, pp. 223, 227, 231, 244-245, 260 *ff.*, 264, 272-273.

35. Bernard A. Weisberger, *They Gathered at the River* (Boston: Little, Brown and Co., 1958), p. 178.

36. McLoughlin, *Modern Revivalism*, pp. 331-334; also see pp. 378-379, 382, 415.

37. William Warren Sweet, *The Story of Religion in America* (New York: Harper & Brothers Publishers, 1939 ed.), pp. 222-231, 232-233, 236-237, 239-244.

38. Muncy, p. 105.

39. Most of the above paragraph is based on Sweet, *The Story of Religion in America*, pp. 351-362.

40. Scharpff, pp. 312-313. This section of Scharpff is by Kenneth L. Chafin of Houston, Texas.

41. Sweet, *The Story of Religion in America*, p. 367.

42. Scharpff, pp. 86, 187.

43. Sweet, *The Story of Religion in America*, pp. 367-368.

44. Scharpff, p. 187.

45. Edwin B. Dozier, *Christian Evangelism*, Vol. I (Tokyo: The Jordan Press, 1963), p. 57.

46. J. C. Pollock, *Moody* (New York: The Macmillan Co., 1963), p. 30.

47. McLoughlin, *Modern Revivalism*, p. 152.

48. Weisberger, pp. 142-143.

49. A. Earl Kernahan, *Visitation Evangelism Its Methods and Results* (New York: Fleming H. Revell Co., 1925), p. 154.

50. McLoughlin, *Modern Revivalism*, p. 157.

51. Ibid., p. 462.

52. Muncy, pp. 133-139.

53. Pollock, chapter 27, "Student Volunteers," pp. 249-260, but esp. p. 260.

54. *The Quarterly Review*, Vol. 18, No. 1, January-March, 1958, p. 22.

55. Ibid., p. 22 and Pollock, p. 260.

56. Kenneth Scott Latourette, *A History of the Expansion of Christianity*, Vol. IV (New York: Harper & Brothers Publishers, 1941), pp. 35-37.

57. Basil Mathews, *John R. Mott World Citizen* (New York: Harper & Brothers Publishers, 1934), p. 104 *ff.*

58. *The Quarterly Review*, pp. 21-22.

59. Ibid., p. 22; Pollock, p. 260; Scharpff, pp. 315, 320.

60. Latourette, p. 37; *The Quarterly Review*, p. 22.

61. Scharpff, pp. 315-316.

62. Torrey Johnson and Robert Cook, *Reaching Youth for Christ* (Chicago: Moody Press, 1944).

63. Muncy, p. 139.

64. Elmer Archibald Leslie, *Acquainting Youth with Christ* (New York: The Methodist Book Concern, 1927 paperback).

65. Albert H. Gage, *Evangelism of Youth* (Philadelphia: The Judson Press, 1922).

66. Paul Judson Morris, *Winning Youth for Christ* (Philadelphia: The Judson Press, 1930).

67. Howard W. Ellis, *Evangelism for Teen-Agers* (New York: Abingdon Press, 1958 paperback).

68. Elmer T. Clark, *The Small Sects in America* (New York: Abingdon Press, 1959 ed.), pp. 83-84. Also see Scharpff, pp. 304-305, 277-280.

69. McLoughlin, *Modern Revivalism*, p. 456. See also Scharpff, p. 321.

70. Sweet, *Revivalism in America*, p. 127.

71. McLoughlin, *Modern Revivalism*, pp. 98, 456-457.

72. Kernahan, pp. 15-25, 45.

73. McLoughlin, *Modern Revivalism*, p. 457.

74. Kernahan, pp. 60-72.

75. McLoughlin, *Modern Revivalism*, pp. 457-462.

76. Arthur C. Archibald, *New Testament Evangelism: How It Works Today* (Philadelphia: The Judson Press, 1946).

77. Scharpff, pp. 321-322.

78. Muncy, pp. 93, 166-175. See also Scharpff, pp. 313-314.

79. William C. Winlow's "Christians on the Air" in the Reader's Response Section of *The Christian Century*, Vol. 98, No. 35, Nov. 4, 1981, p. 1135.

80. Jane A. Welch, "Different Faces of Christianity," *The News and Observer*, Mar. 22, 1982, p. 10A, Raleigh, N.C.

81. "Pat Robertson's Network Breaks Out of the Christian Ghetto," *Christianity Today*, Vol. XXVI, No. 1, Jan. 1, 1982, pp. 36-37.

82. William F. Fore, "A Critical Eye on Televangelism," *The Christian Century*, XCVIII, No. 29, Sept. 23, 1981, p. 939.

83. "15,000 Call TV Preacher," *The Baptist Messenger*, Vol. 71, Feb. 11, 1982, p. 4.

84. "Bad Times for the Big Three," *Newsweek*, Feb. 12, 1982, p. 77.

85. "Lining Up for Power," *Newsweek*, Dec. 21, 1981, p. 76.

86. *CMN Net Work*, Vol. 1, No. 3, March, 1981. Published by CMN in Minneapolis, Minn. See esp. p. 4.

87. Theodore Baehr, "Tangled Christian Telecommunications," *Christianity Today*, Vol. XXV, No. 20, Nov. 20, 1981, p. 35. For more detailed information on mass media evangelism see chapter 20, "Twenty-One Theses on Media Evangelism."

88. Scharpff, pp. 319-321. The reader will note some overlapping between this group and youth-group evangelism because organizations such as the Navigators and the Fellowship of Christian Athletes do not confine their ministry to youth.

19
Deductive Versus Inductive Methods of Personal Evangelism

Ruth 1:15-17; John 1:35-51

Introduction

Have you ever thought much about how the church looks to outsiders? Ralph Neighbour shares a true story which may throw some light on that question. Neighbour was visiting with a Chinese pastor in a Singapore stall, far from areas where tourists are usually seen. The two of them were eating bitter gourds when a man in his late twenties pulled up a flimsy wooden stool and joined them. It became obvious that this man was a government agent checking them out.

Neighbour and the Chinese pastor shared openly with the agent, without yet mentioning the Christian faith. Finally, the man said, "You puzzle me! Are you Christians?"

"Yes," they said, "we are. How did you know?"

The agent replied, "Your attitude is one of love and concern, and that would make you Christian. But you have not acted like all the other Christians I have known."

"Oh!" said the Chinese pastor, "how did all the others act?"

"Well, they remind me of tigers who hide in the bush, waiting to spring on you as you innocently walk by them. Usually when I find a Christian, I plan to get away fast—before they pounce!"[1]

Contrasts Between Deductive and Inductive

That story illustrates some of the differences between deductive and inductive methods of personal evangelism.

253

The literature on personal evangelism offers a large variety of methods. "Yet, underneath the variety," said George G. Hunter, "most of the literature teaches essentially two basic approaches that are analagous to the two ways of logical thinking—deduction: beginning general and moving particular, and induction: beginning particular and moving general."[2] Neighbour and the Chinese pastor used the inductive approach. The government agent had been accustomed to the deductive approach. A Christian witness may pounce on persons unexpectedly like a hiding tiger, or he may treat persons like Aslan, the strong but gentle lion in C. S. Lewis's *The Chronicles of Narnia.*

While it is arbitrary and caricatured, we may for analytical purposes place all personal evangelism in the following model:

Personal Evangelism
(Intentionality)

Deductive	vs.	*Inductive*
Receptivity (high)	vs.	Receptivity (low)
Monological (telling)	vs.	Dialogical (listening)
Short-term Gains	vs.	Long-term Gains
Canned	vs.	Spontaneous
Instant	vs.	Incarnational
Religious Persons	vs.	Secular Persons
Proclamation	vs.	Affirmation (Petersen)[3]
Propositional	vs.	Point-of-Need (Hunter)[4]
Stereotyped	vs.	Service (Armstrong)[5]
Contact	vs.	Conversational (Pippert)[6]
Functional	vs.	Friendship (McPhee)[7]
Rational	vs.	Relational (McDill)[8]
Traditional	vs.	Target-Group (Neighbour)[9]
Individual	vs.	Household (Green, *et al*)[10]
Lips	vs.	Life-style (Aldrich)[11]

The above model shows all personal evangelism methods on a continuum between the deductive and the inductive approaches. Some of the authors who should be connected with the various terms are in parentheses. Key and contrasting words or terms are utilized to catch up the two focuses of the respective continuum.

Examples of the deductive approach may be seen in most books on soul winning,[12] in the program of lay witness training called Evangelism Explosion,[13] in Campus Crusade's Lay Institutes for Evangelism (LIFE), and in the Lay Evangelism Schools and Continuing Witness Training (CWT) of Southern Baptists.

Both Neighbour and Hunter are outspoken representatives of the inductive approach. Neighbour calls for "Target-Group Evangelism." He argues that what we need is "arc evangelism" as over against what we have, which he calls "circle evangelism." He says what we need is evangelism where "believers go *from* the church sanctuary to *structure relationships* with outsiders" until they are exposed to the indwelling Christ in us.[14]

Hunter posits what he calls an "Inductive-Grace Model" and an "Inductive-Mission Model," which he builds around Abraham Maslow's hierarchy of human needs. The grace model meets persons at their points of lower or maintenance needs, such as physiological, safety, love, and belongingness needs. The mission model meets persons at their points of higher needs, such as esteem, self-actualization, knowledge, and aesthetic needs. One model meets them at their points of weakness; the other meets them at their points of strength. Hunter believes these two inductive models will appeal to more persons in our world than the older deductive model.[15]

Other noteworthy representatives of the inductive method are Wayne McDill, Arthur G. McPhee, Rebecca Manley Pippert, Jim Petersen, and Richard S. Armstrong. McDill's book is *Making Friends for Christ*. He says, "The missing ingredient in much of today's evangelism is relationship. *Evangelism will be effective to the extent that it depends on the establishment and cultivation of meaningful relationships.*"[16] That is, indeed, the thesis of McDill's book. His subtitle is "A Practical Approach to Relational Evangelism."

McPhee, a Mennonite pastor, is bold to say, "The best evangelism is . . . friendship evangelism." Indeed, the thesis of McPhee's book, *Friendship Evangelism,* is that your deepest relationships are your best witnessing opportunities.[17]

Pippert, a national evangelism consultant with Inter-Varsity Christian Fellowship, calls this inductive approach "Evangelism As a Way of Life,"[18] "Pizza Parlor Evangelism,"[19] and "conversational" evangelism, as opposed to "contact" evangelism.[20] Pippert wants to see Christians get out of the saltshaker and into the world.

Petersen of the Navigators calls inductive evangelism "affirmation" evangelism as over against "proclamation" evangelism. Proclamation evangelism, according to Petersen, is primarily effective among the prepared people—those who are prepared to hear the gospel and to receive it. Whereas, affirmation evangelism "is a *process* of incarnating and demonstrating the Christian message."[21]

Armstrong of Princeton Theological Seminary calls this kind of evangelism "service evangelism" as over against "propositional" evangelism. The aim of service evangelism is service, not conquest. Armstrong thinks the servant model of Christ himself should be our model.[22]

Characteristics of the Two Methods

If you will look closely at the preceding model, you will see a contrast in style. The deductive style is tighter, quicker, more highly structured, employs "transferable concepts" which can be passed on immediately to other Christians, uses more religious language, requires more memorization, and so forth. The inductive style, on the other hand, is looser, longer, more flexible, less transferable, more secular, more spontaneous, and so forth.

The three *p*s of presence, proclamation, and persuasion, which church growth theoreticians like to connect with evangelism, may aid us in characterizing deductive versus inductive methods of personal evangelism. Deductive methodology accentuates proclamation, persuasion, and presence in that order. Its primary concern is the accurate proclamation of the gospel; its secondary concern is persuading the unreconciled to become Christians; and its tertiary concern is to exhibit a Christian presence.

Inductive methodology lifts up presence, persuasion, and proclamation more or less in that order. Therefore, presence is primary, persuasion secondary, and proclamation tertiary. Establishing credibility is a big thing with those who prefer the inductive approach. Much of their persuading is done before the gospel is ever verbally proclaimed.

Please note that this model insists on intentionality as characterizing both deductive and inductive evangelism. The deductive appears to be more intentional, but need not be. One reason some Christians have shied away from the inductive is that they perceive it has no sharp cutting edge of intentionality. I admit that I once thought of most inductive evangelizing as a cop-out and a subterfuge. Study, personal experience, and observation have changed my mind.

Surely no one would dare to accuse Evangelism Explosion of lacking intentionality. EE is the most intentional approach to witnessing which I know. Yet, the 1977 revised edition of *Evangelism Explosion* has a long chapter on "The Gospel for the Secular Mind." That chapter recognizes that forty million Americans may be classified as "pagans," that is totally secular in their life-style. Also, it admits that many additional millions function as if there were no God. D. James Kennedy and Archie B. Parrish learned from much experience that the standard EE approach was not reaching these secular persons.[23] This is where the inductive approach really comes into its own, namely with today's secular humans who are not at the moment very high on anybody's gospel receptivity scale.

Hunter clearly recognizes that the deductive approach is no longer working with many Americans. He believes it is no longer indigenous to the mental processes of many American peoples and subcultures.[24] Also, I find it significant that Kennedy and Parrish included a new chapter on "Relational Evangelism" in their 1977 updating of EE.[25]

We definitely have two contrasting styles in the two approaches. And although the essential substance of the gospel is the same in both, the actual content of what is shared will necessarily vary depending upon the approach used and the needs of the individuals with whom we share. There can be only one gospel. We dare not share what Paul called "another gospel" (see Gal. 1:6-9). Nevertheless, our content must be tailored to our prospects as much as it must remain true to the divine revelation. We cannot communicate that which persons are unable to hear and understand. We have to begin with persons wherever they happen to be at that time and place.

One other way to characterize the deductive and inductive poles of personal evangelism is to observe that the deductive focuses more on *content,* whereas the inductive throws the light more on *context.* Deductive evangelism is concerned more with the content of the message to be shared. Inductive evangelism believes that the context will determine to a great extent what is to be shared and when.

Timing is important to both methods. However, chronological time tends to be emphasized more in the deductive approach; whereas seasonal time, or what the Greek New Testament calls *kairos,* seems to fit more neatly into the inductive approach.

The Need for a Technique

The index finger pointed up toward heaven was made a familiar sight by the Jesus people in the 1960s. There is now at least one congregation which has chosen the name One Way Church.

Jesus in talking about our Father's house said: "I am the way . . . no one comes to the Father, but by me" (John 14:6). So, the one-way sign is true. Jesus is the door to the Father's sheepfold, and anyone who enters in "by another way, that man is a thief and a robber" (John 10:1).

Although it is true that there is only *one* way to enter our Father's house, it is equally true that there are *many* ways through which one can come to know Jesus Christ. To put the same idea another way, one may use many different techniques to introduce persons to Jesus Christ. There is no *one* correct way to tell the story of God's wonderful deeds for man's salvation.

However, the trouble with most Christians is that they don't have even one conscious technique for introducing strangers, relatives, or friends to Christ. Someone once criticized D. L. Moody for the way he made converts to Christ. Moody asked the man what method he used, to which the man replied, "I don't have any method."

Moody then said, "Well, I like my method better than yours." Perhaps we ought to be hestitant about criticizing the techniques of others, especially if we have no technique of our own.

John Wesley, the founder of Methodism, was a contemporary of George Whitefield who sparked the first Great Awakening in America. Whitefield was a Calvanistic Methodist, whereas Wesley was Arminian in his theology. Whitefield even had Lady Huntington on his side. He was by far a more popular and sparkling preacher than Wesley. Nevertheless, when Whitefield died Calvanistic Methodism died with him. Why? Part of the answer I would suggest is to be found in the systematic and superior methodology of John Wesley.

Persons do not ooze into the kingdom of God. They have to choose. Our part is to confront them with the choice. Persons are not saved by a plan, but by the person of Christ. However, a plan of salvation may help us to point persons to the Savior. We do need to have a way to present Christ to persons who are lost.

I have found that many Christians want a witnessing track on which to run. They welcome a simple technique which enables them to put the witnessing encounter all together.

A Combination Model

I believe that what we need is a combination model for personal evangelism which merges the strengths of both the deductive and inductive methods. The one conscious technique which I have used, taught, and developed for a dozen years is an anagram built around the word *FORM*. The *F* stands for Family, the *O* for Occupation, the *R* for Religion, and the *M* for Message—the message of the gospel. The *F* and the *O* are "small" talk, while the *R* and the *M* are "big" talk. It looks like this:

The FORM Anagram

F—Family
O—Occupation   ("small" talk)
R—Religion
M—Message   ("big" talk)

Note that the arrow moves downward. The goal of the FORM technique is to share the message of the gospel.

I shall briefly structure the use of FORM in a home visit to a stranger with two trainees accompanying the trainer. The first thing to do at the door is to introduce yourself and the two persons with you. Then, immediately, tell the person being visited that you are visiting from your church and give the name of your church. A church has a testimony as well as an individual Christian.

If we are not invited to come in, a simple question like, "Would it be convenient for us to come in and visit with you a while?" might be appropriate. That request is seldom denied. If so, we might be able to set a convenient time later.

What do you say after you have said hello? This is where FORM comes into play. Begin with the *F*. Engage in some friendly talk about family and home—both theirs and yours. Usually that is nonthreatening to most persons. The only problem I've had was in a home where the husband had left his wife and children that day and I didn't know it. One beginning place in the F may be the family pictures on the coffee table, end tables, mantel, or walls. Find out about the various members of the family, the children, parents, grand-children or grandparents, brothers and sisters, and so on. Most persons whom we meet will have a web of kinfolk, friends, or colleagues even if they live alone. If not, we certainly need to take note of that important fact.

Next, focus on the *O* part of FORM. Find out what your prospect's occupation is. Everybody does something, if not for a living then perhaps for a hobby or a pastime. Even those who don't now work for a living may have once worked or may be preparing for some occupation. If persons love their work, they'll light up their countenance and voice when they tell you about it. If they dislike their work, they'll welcome the opportunity to tell you just how much they hate it.

I recall talking one evening to an elderly gentleman who grew soybeans for a living. He told me more about raising soybeans than I really wanted to know. And yet if I had not spent that time in small talk, listening to him tell about his occupation, my guess is that he would not have done any "big" talk at all with me when I got to the *R* and *M* of my visit. He was resistant. I did not lead him to Christ. But I did have the opportunity to share my testimony and the gospel with him.

Some techniques prefer to substitute an *I* here for the *O* and to focus on interests rather than occupation. I see no problem at all with that, especially if you are dealing with older children and youth.

The most difficult transition in the FORM technique is

from the *O* to the *R*. Here are two lead questions on how this can be done. You might ask: "Where did you attend church when you were a child?" Or, you may say: "Of what church are you now a member?" If that is too sharp, inquire: "Have you found a church home since you came to our community?"[26] It is OK at this point to discuss one's church relationship.

Start listening for clues for this transition from the very beginning of your visit. Often the prospect will say something onto which you can later tie in order to make the transition. Also, use Socratic evangelism at this point. Ask leading questions which will generate data that may help you to discover your prospect's religious and spiritual background. I recommend the following five questions, and in this order:

- Have you come to that place in your life where God has become more than a word to you?
- In your opinion, who is Jesus Christ?
- In your opinion, what does one have to do in order to become a Christian?
- Have you reached the point in your life where you know for certain you will go to heaven when you die?
- If you were to die and stand before God in the judgment and he were to say to you, "Why should I let you into my heaven?" what would you say?

You may not need to ask all of those questions. I seldom do. Once you find out where your prospect is in relationship to Jesus Christ, you should use your personal testimony as a bridge into the message of the gospel. The testimony comes then precisely between the *R* and the *M* of the technique. It offers an excellent transition into the message. For example, following your testimony you might ask: "Has anything like that ever happened to you?" You are continuing to find out where your prospect is without being offensive. If the answer is no, you are ready to proceed to the *M* part of your dialogue.

Before we move to the *M,* however, a word of caution should be uttered against improper questions in the *R* part. George W. Truett counseled against rushing up and asking, "Are you a Christian?" I strongly counsel against that also. Remember the writer of Proverbs said, "He that winneth souls is wise" (Prov. 11:30*b,* KJV). Besides there are so many different ideas about what a Christian is that the question is virtually meaningless.

Furthermore, worn-out and hackneyed phrases such as, "Are you saved?" should be avoided. One writer tells of hearing a zealous young fellow saying to a rather intelligent-looking man, "Are you saved, Sir?"

The man replied, "Are you?"

"Thank God, I am," the zealous one answered.

"Not from impertinence," came the cutting reply.[27]

The presentation of the message in the *M* part of the technique may be done through a memorized outline such as in Evangelism Explosion;[28] with a marked New Testament using verses, such as Romans 3:23, 6:23, 10:8-13; with one single verse, such as John 3:16; or through reason, common sense, and an expansion of your testimony. An increasingly popular way to share the message is through the use of a booklet, such as "The Bridge to Life,"[29] "How to Have a Full and Meaningful Life,"[30] "The Four Spiritual Laws,"[31] or "The Steps to Peace with God."[32]

Advantages of the Combination Model

- The FORM technique can be used in almost every personal witnessing encounter: the home, the airplane, the restaurant, the bus, on vacation, on the coffee break, almost anywhere and anytime. It fits most formal and informal witnessing situations.
- It is a transferable concept which can be passed on quickly to another Christian, even to a brand-new disciple. Therefore, it assists with the process of spiritual reproduction.

- It gives the Christian a witnessing track on which to operate or one familiar road on which to travel. Think of the gospel train having a witnessing track on which to travel back and forth across the earth. Most Christians have no track at all.
- It allows us flexibility to depart from it and does not lock us into an inflexible method. If we are using it with kinfolk, friends, or colleagues with whom the F and the O do not so much apply, it still gives us some suggested structure whenever we may need the R or the M. The Christian faith is not an infectious disease. Not even our loved ones and friends can catch it merely by being with us. We still have to tell them the gospel at some point. Another example of its flexibility is that, when we are dealing with the M parts, we may use the witnessing tools which best suit our prospect and fit our personality.
- It does not require a lot of memorization of outlines, illustrations, or Scripture verses. Nor does it intimidate the person who has difficulty with memorization. All you have to memorize is the anagram and what the letters stand for.
- It provides a simple but useful plan for the Christian who is just beginning to acquire some skills in witnessing. If there is some initial feeling of discomfort with it, that also may be a learning experience.
- FORM seeks to combine the best of the "telling" and "listening" models. The $F\,O\,R$ parts are basically listening, while the M part is primarily telling. If appropriately utilized, it helps us to avoid "dump truck" evangelism.
- This technique accentuates the intentionality of evangelism. Its intentional goal is to share the message of the gospel with those who are unreconciled to God. But it allows the gospel train to stop and, if necessary, to tarry for a while at the other three stations of $F\,O\,R$. Plenty of time is allowed for building relationships along the way. FORM may take thirty minutes, thirty days, or it may in

some cases take thirty years. It is designed for both those who are very high and very low in their receptivity to the gospel.

Conclusion

I have discovered that when witnessing to teenagers and adults, especially to men, it is often wise to talk with them privately when we reach the *R* and the *M* sections of the technique. If we are in a family situation, following the *F O* parts of the dialogue, we might quietly ask the prospect if we can see him or her privately.

We may conclude with this word of Paul to Titus: "But avoid stupid controversies, genealogies, dissensions, and quarrels over the law, for they are unprofitable and futile" (Titus 3:9). There are some mysteries which no one has been able to solve. They take the form of questions that no one has yet answered. Examples are: What happened to Amelia Earhart? What's the Mona Lisa smiling about? Does the Loch Ness monster really exist? A perpetual religious question in that category is: Where did Cain get his wife? Do not waste your time on such questions. They will inevitably sidetrack you.

Suggested Study Questions

1. A Christian man named Wayne was following a truck down a mountain. The truck wrecked and pinned the driver in the cab. As Wayne rushed up to the scene, the truck driver said, "I'm going to die; they aren't going to get me out of here alive; can you tell me how to die?" Wayne didn't know what to say. He stammered and hesitated. He wept, but he didn't know what to say. The truck driver died and went out into eternity. Wayne determined that never again would that happen to him. He learned how to share his faith.

Suppose Wayne had come to you and said: "Please teach me how to share my faith with any lost person." Based on the chapter you have just read, what would you say to him?

2. How important is intentionality in both deductive and inductive methods of personal evangelism? Why?

3. List and discuss several characteristics of both deductive and inductive approaches to personal evangelism.

4. What are three advantages of the FORM anagram, according to the author?

5. Give the five questions which the author says may be used to discover a person's religious background, and state them in their suggested order of difficulty.

Notes

1. Ralph W. Neighbour, Jr., "Encounter with the Unchurched," *Trinity World Forum*, Vol. 6, No. 2, Winter, 1981, p. 1. Published by the School of World Mission and Evangelism, Trinity Evangelical Divinity School, 2065 Half Day Road, Deerfield, Ill., 60015.

2. George G. Hunter, III, *The Contagious Congregation* (Nashville: Abingdon, 1979), pp. 37-38.

3. Jim Petersen, *Evangelism as a Lifestyle* (Colorado Springs: Navpress, 1980). Petersen sets proclamation evangelism over against affirmation evangelism.

4. Hunter, esp. pp. 35-39. These are not Hunter's actual terms. He prefers the terms *deductive* and *inductive*, but his new inductive-grace model and inductive-mission model boils down to a point-of-need approach.

5. Richard Stoll Armstrong, *Service Evangelism* (Philadelphia: The Westminster Press, 1979), especially chapter 4. Armstrong bases his service evangelism on the model of Jesus Christ, the Suffering Servant. His is also very much a point-of-need approach.

6. Rebecca Manley Pippert, *Out of the Saltshaker & into the World* (Downers Grove, Ill.: Inter-Varsity Press, 1979), pp. 127-151 and 173f.

7. Arthur G. McPhee, *Friendship Evangelism* (Grand Rapids: Zondervan Publishing House, 1978).

8. Wayne McDill, *Making Friends for Christ* (Nashville: Broadman Press, 1979). McDill prefers the term *relational evangelism*.

9. Ralph W. Neighbour, Jr., and Cal Thomas, *Target-Group Evangelism* (Nashville: Broadman Press, 1975).

10. Michael Green, *Evangelism in the Early Church* (Grand Rapids: Wm. B. Eerdmans Publishing House, 1970), pp. 207-229. Green uses the term *household evangelism*. See also: Thomas A. Wolf, "Oikos Evangelism: Key to the Future," Ralph W. Neighbour, Jr., compiler, *Future Church* (Nashville: Broadman Press, 1980), pp. 153-176; Ron Johnson, Joseph W. Hinkle, and Charles M. Lowry, *Oikos: A Practical Approach to Family Evangelism* (Nashville: Broadman Press, 1982).

11. Joseph C. Aldrich, *Life-Style Evangelism* (Portland, Oregon: Multnomah Press,

1981). See also: W. Oscar Thompson, Jr. *Concentric Circles of Concern* (Nashville, Broadman Press, 1981); C. B. Hogue, *Love Leaves No Choice* (Waco, Texas: Word Books, Publisher, 1976).

12. See, for example, the chapter on "Let's Go Soul Winning" in Jack Hyles, *Let's Build an Evangelistic Church* (Murfreesboro, Tenn.: Sword of the Lord Publishers, 1962), pp. 31-80.

13. D. James Kennedy, *Evangelism Explosion* (Wheaton, Ill.: Tyndale House Publishers, 1977 rev. ed.).

14. Neighbour and Thomas, pp. 17-18.

15. Hunter, pp. 35-63.

16. McDill, p. 14. Italics are McDill's.

17. McPhee, p. 101.

18. Pippert, "Evangelism as a Way of Life" is Pippert's subtitle.

19. Rebecca Manley Pippert, *Pizza Parlor Evangelism* (Downers Grove, Ill.: Inter-Varsity Press, 1976, 1978).

20. Pippert, *Out of the Saltshaker,* 127-151 and 173 *f.*

21. Petersen, pp. 42-43.

22. Armstrong, pp. 83, 63, 38-50, esp. 51-69.

23. Kennedy, pp. 164-185. Parrish is coauthor of the 1977 rev. ed.

24. Hunter, p. 39.

25. Kennedy, pp. 199-203.

26. I am indebted to Darrell Robinson's notebook, *The Total Church Life: People Sharing Jesus* (Pasadena, Texas: Total Life Ministries, 1979), pp. 96-97, for these two questions, though one of them is slightly revised.

27. Related by Arthur C. Archibald, *New Testament Evangelism: How It Works Today* (Philadelphia: The Judson Press, 1946), p. 103.

28. See Kennedy, pp. 16-44.

29. Available from The Navigators, Colorado Springs, Colorado 80901.

30. Available from all Baptist Book Stores, and from the Materials Services Department of the Baptist Sunday School Board, 127 Ninth Ave. N., Nashville, Tennessee 37234.

31. Available from Campus Crusade for Christ International, Arrowhead Springs, San Bernardino, California 92404.

32. Available from The Billy Graham Evangelistic Association, Box 779, Minneapolis, Minnesota 55440.

20
Twenty-One Theses on Media Evangelism

Habakkuk 2:1-5; 1 Peter 2:9-10

Introduction

The *Detroit Free Press* once offered $500.00 to 120 families in its reading area if they would turn off their TV sets for one whole month. Naturally, every family agreed. Right? No! Ninety-three families turned the offer down flat. Actually, the average family in America keeps its TV on forty-four hours a week.[1] By 1985 30,000,000 of us will have 100 TV channels to which we may subscribe.

1. Fashions Soul of Country

The soul of our country is being fashioned by the electronic media. Especially is that true of television, which some wag has called "our squat electronic Buddha." Tom Brokaw says the religious radio-TV audience numbers an estimated 130 million per week. Forty-seven percent of Americans regularly tune in to religious programs, while by contrast only 41 percent of the population attend church services.[2]

We are told that Jesus may have talked to as many as 30,000 persons during his lifetime, while Jerry Falwell may talk to 30,000,000 in one broadcast. Jimmy Allen, president of the SBC Radio and Television Commission (RTVC), thinks the broadcast media "is fashioning the mind-set of society."[3] This shaping influence makes it so important that the denominations seek to offer a viable alternative to much of the X-rated programming which comes at us through the secular, electronic media.

269

An editorial in *Christianity Today* sums up thesis 1 this way:

> Radio and television, with current developments of multiple channels and cable lines, present new challenges and unlimited possibility for the Christian church. The already significant role of religious broadcasting has not begun to peak. Its potential for evangelism can scarcely be exaggerated. There are 50 to 60 million unchurched Americans, but they all watch television.[4]

2. Controlled by Charismatics

The denominations have up until now just about let the charismatics and the parachurch organizations take over the TV medium in America. *Time* magazine has estimated that Jim Bakker's Praise the Lord (PTL) takes in $51 million annually, Pat Robertson's 700 Club $47 million, Rex Humbard $25 million, Jimmy Swaggart $20 million, and Jerry Falwell's Moral Majority $46 million.[5]

It hasn't always been that way. In the infancy of television, the independent evangelicals were frozen out. What little free air time the national networks were willing to devote to religion was primarily divided among Roman Catholics, Jews, and mainline Protestant denominations.

Then, the charismatics moved vigorously into television with Pat Robertson of *The 700 Club* taking the lead. Jim Bakker of *PTL* once worked with Pat Robertson. Kathryn Kuhlman had begun to move into a television ministry prior to her death. Oral Roberts, whose charismatic ministry spans a much longer time than any of these, has pioneered in the religious TV "special" during prime time.

However, the situation is rapidly changing. Denominations and local churches are beginning to set up their own networks and stations.

United Methodists were at one time seeking to purchase their own commercial network-affiliated TV station.

"Our thrust will be getting nonmembers into the churches," says Charles Cappleman, president of the United Methodist Commission on Communication.[6]

There is now a Catholic Television Network of Chicago. Also, a Los Angeles based Jewish Television Network seeks to reach Jews who are unaffiliated with any Jewish organization.

Southern Baptists, under the leadership of Jimmy Allen, are seeking to establish ACTS (American Christian Television System). ACTS is to be a subsidiary of the SBC's Radio and Television Commission. One hundred and nineteen applications have been filed for low-power television stations which would be tied together in ACTS through a satellite and through local cable systems.

The ACTS network will charge an affiliation fee. However, no requests for money will be made from viewers of the ACTS programming.

A long-term contract has been signed for satellite transmission by the Southern Baptist Radio and Television Commission and the Baptist Sunday School Board. In the spring of 1984 two satellite transponders will be under contract for twenty-four-hour-per-day transmission, one for Baptist TelNet (BTN) and one for ACTS. The BTN transponder will be available for communicating with SBC churches and agencies. This moves the Southern Baptist Convention closer to establishing a denominational telecommunications network to churches.

Presently, the receiving dish and other equipment a church would need to receive telecommunications via satellite can be purchased at prices ranging from $3,000 to $9,000.

It is now even possible for a local church to buy and operate its own television station. A church can go on the air with its own low power station for a cost of $40,000, even less if it purchases used equipment. All it needs is a license, a low-power transmitter, a videotape player, and an antenna.

Six thousand applications for such stations were made before the end of 1981. These low-power TV stations are capable of reaching audiences within a radius of three to twenty miles, depending on the quality of the antenna and the terrain.[7]

3. Cannot Replace Incarnation

No media or combination of media can ever replace the incarnation of the Christian faith. The bottom line in all media evangelism is one person telling another person face-to-face about Jesus Christ.

Richard Jackson and his people at North Phoenix Baptist Church in Arizona started knocking on doors four-teen years ago, telling persons about Jesus Christ. During the past ten years that congregation has baptized over six thousand persons. "Today the church uses television, radio, newspapers, and billboards to share Christ," says Jackson, "but there is still no substitute for the personal witness of an individual Christian."[8]

Mark Sills has expressed the opinion that the "elec-tronic church" is a new form of Docetism. Docetism, it may be remembered, was an early Christian heresy which taught that Jesus only *seemed* to be flesh and blood. It taught a phantom Christ which denied the reality of the incarnation. "This new Docetic heresy does not attempt to deny the reality of the historical Jesus," says Sills. "Rather, it denies the reality of the Body of Christ, the church itself."[9]

Where is the local incarnation in the electronic church? Where is the real, physical presence of the church in local communities where persons live, work, play, struggle, and die? Indeed, where is the visible corporate body of Christ? Is not the electronic church all too often a mirage, a phantom, a mere appearance? If the church is to be a continuation of the incarnation of Jesus Christ, it must be manifest in a particular space and time. It must leave its footprints and reveal its nailprints wherever it goes.

One noteworthy feature about the electronic church has been the accelerated pace toward a largely passive, vicarious religious life. Martin Marty suggests that what we have is a Christianity of clienteles instead of congregations.

There is a difference between communication *to* and communication *with* someone. The postal carrier can do the first; whereas, the second is like baking a German chocolate cake and inviting your neighbors to come and share it with you.

4. Wise to Use Variety of Media

It is wise to use a variety of media in evangelism: television, radio, videotapes, cassettes, recordings, computers, billboards, telephones, newspapers, books, and so forth. For example, during the 1980 Good News Missouri Campaign conducted by the Missouri Baptist Convention, newspaper ads were combined with television very effectively in the Saint Louis area. Two telephone banks were also set up and combined with television, radio, newspaper ads, and billboards on both the west and east sides of Missouri.

Direct-mail campaigns combined with an outstanding musical concert or religious drama may be a winning combination of media for some churches. Third Baptist Church in Saint Louis combined a direct-mail campaign with tickets to a musical concert in 1980. Follow-up visits were made into the homes of the newly discovered prospects. It was an expensive campaign, but it did turn up some prospects and increased the visibility of the church.

Most churches who use the mail direct their messages to church members. Very few utilize direct-mail evangelism. Yet, a Roper survey polled two thousand adults and asked which of a series of daily events and activities they enjoyed most. They chose from a list of twenty-one events and activities. Sixty-three percent said "checking to see what you got in the mail" was one of the activities they looked forward to each day.

Some pastors are inundated with so much junk mail that they forget many citizens don't receive that much mail. Most Americans look forward to seeing what is in the day's mail.

There are several approaches to direct-mail evangelism. One approach is to maintain a list of nonmembers and prospective members. Send every general bulk mailing to these people, as well as to your members. A second and relatively inexpensive approach is to mail your monthly program schedule to every household in your zip code area. Another approach is sending invitations to a special program. That was the approach used by Third Baptist Church, Saint Louis.

However, the approach which seems to pay the largest dividends is to mail first-class letters. A church located in a city may use a "crisscross" directory for such mailings. It is better to have them addressed personally, perhaps by volunteers. The response rate to a highly sophisticated direct-mail campaign may run as high as 10 to 20 percent.

Two points should be kept in mind in direct-mail evangelism. Each letter should be directed to the needs of the recipient and not at the needs of the sender. Moreover, direct mail is not a system for getting more church members. We can use it to identify potential members. But all contacts generated through direct-mail must be personally followed up if these prospective members are to be evangelized.[10]

Videotapes are a fast growing medium for equipping witnesses, training leadership for evangelization, and for use with certain evangelistic prospects. A Southern Baptist Video Tape Service (VTS) was formed in 1981 to serve as a cooperative effort by state conventions and Southern Baptist Convention agencies to produce and distribute at least sixty videotapes each year for use by the churches.[11]

Computers are also becoming more available to churches to assist them with their program needs in evangelism. The Institute for American Church Growth added a Department of Church Growth Information Management in 1981. Jack Gunther left an executive position with IBM after fourteen years to head the new department. That department is now suggesting to us that there may be computers in the future of many local churches. Insight 2000 is the name given to the new computer and program which is being pushed.[12]

Gospel music is another medium which the church should not overlook. Gospel music has become big business in our time. Christian record companies now gross $100 million a year on record and tape sales. Sheet music sales reach $75 million a year. The 500 Christian artists on the road take in gate receipts of $50 million a year. Some "Jesus music" artists sell 200,000 to 300,000 albums a year. A Jesus concert can turn a profit in excess of $200,000.[13]

5. Will Help Make Church More Visible

The media will help make your church more visible. I have heard that there is a certain church building in Houston which is difficult to find. That church has wisely turned its liability into an asset by advertising itself as the "hard-to-find" church.

One purpose of all media use is to make your church visible. Through TV and radio and billboards, your church's name and even your pastor's name can become a household word. No matter how well located your church may be, you still need all of the visibility you can get with the public and with individuals.

6. Soft Sell Versus Hard Sell

The soft sell is more effective than the hard sell in reaching secular persons. A one-minute parable may be more valuable than a one-hour service.

James Pleitz of Dallas, Texas, is a master at the soft sell

on both TV and radio. Through the soft-sell approach, Pleitz has been able to get on all of the network TV stations in Dallas. While it is impossible to catch the full impact of his parables without both hearing and seeing them, one of them goes like this:

> Hello, I am James Pleitz. The size of the universe just staggers the imagination. If it costs a penny to ride a thousand miles, a trip around the world would cost twenty-five cents. But a trip to the nearest star at one cent per thousand miles would cost two hundred and sixty million dollars. It makes you feel sort of insignificant, doesn't it? Listen, in the heart of God no planet is as important as a single person, including you.[14]

There are, of course, other examples of the soft-sell approach. A Canadian evangelist by the name of Terry Winter conducts a popular TV show on Sunday afternoons. The format is simple. Music is keyed to the gospel theme for the day. Someone tells how he or she became a Christian. Frequently that witness is a young person. The testimony sets the stage for a clear-cut explanation of the gospel. Often this explanation is set in interview format involving well-known Christian scholars in the discussion. Michael Green, for example, was featured in a six-part series in 1980.

Winter always concludes with the recurring theme: "What will you do with the claims of Christ?" No wonder Winter is referred to as the thinking-person's evangelist.[15]

7. Secular Audience More Valuable

The secular audience is more valuable than the religious audience. Our objective in evangelism is to reach unbelievers. Most of the unbelievers are in the secular audience.

Media evangelists like to boast about their large audiences. There is increasing evidence that these audiences may not be as large as some have claimed. Furthermore, these audiences remain largely composed of active church members. Therefore, their usefulness as tools of evangelism is highly questionable.[16]

"Make-believe mission" is a phrase used to describe those televangelistic stars who aim their programs at reaching the known Christian market. One authority, the president of the Episcopal Radio-TV Foundation, categorically says: "If the program dedicated to evangelism is not in the market place or the forum reaching the secular public, then it is clearly involved in 'make-believe mission.'"[17]

Televangelism may have peaked. The combined audience size for all syndicated religious programs reached a growth peak in 1977-1978. While individuals and different programs may have attracted an increased audience, the combined total audience reflects the saturation point.[18] A 1981 report by the A. C. Nielsen Company found that the ten most popular religious TV programs lost more than 600,000 viewing homes between May, 1980 and May, 1981. Oral Roberts's audience declined 12.3 percent for the year and Jerry Falwell's 16.8 percent.[19]

8. Sponsoring Versus Producing

You may get more mileage out of your media dollars by sponsoring an acceptable program than by producing a program. That is the only way a church can buy prime time in some markets. Perhaps you could sponsor a music program or a sports program. I have heard, for example, the Saint James Anglican Catholic Church in the Kansas City area sponsoring a classical music program on KXTR.

9. Using Rank-and-File Christians

Straight advertisement campaigns through the media may be more effective in using rank-and-file Christians rather than big-name celebrity Christians. For example, "Good News Texas" used celebrities like Eldridge Cleaver, whereas "Good News Missouri" used lesser-known Chris-

tians who lived and served in the state of Missouri. A former
Black Panther may get the attention of more persons more
quickly. However, a plain Christian who is clearly "one of us"
may not have the same credibility problem as a "soul on ice"
who became a "soul on fire" and who subsequently joined
the Mormon Church. He is now a member of the Unification Church.

First Baptist Church, Slater, Missouri, participated fully
in the 1980 Good News Missouri Campaign. That congregation even went a step further. They held their own media
campaign on a radio station. They spent one thousand
dollars above what was given to the statewide effort. Time
was purchased for thirty-second spots which were repeated
over and over during several weeks. Church members were
used to write and record their own words about the Christian faith.

10. Should Be Accompanied by Invitation

Any use of TV or radio should be accompanied by an
opportunity (or an invitation) for viewers and listeners to call
or write a person. Programs sponsored by a church or a
denomination should always seek to establish dialogue with
listeners. If you are going to get on TV and radio regularly,
you must have a follow-up plan which will enable persons to
contact you.

When Jimmy Allen was pastor of First Baptist Church,
San Antonio, he was highly visible in the media. Yet, he
never had an unlisted telephone number. At one time all of
his staff had unlisted numbers. Allen ended up getting all of
their calls, so they went back to listed numbers. If you want
to evangelize through the media, you will have to find a way
to let persons get in touch with you.

11. Trained Volunteers

Almost every technical aspect of the media can be
handled by trained volunteers in your congregation. For

example, First Baptist Church, Ferguson, Missouri, in 1981 involved 150 persons in their widely viewed program *Think About Tomorrow.* That congregation now has over one quarter of a million dollars in sophisticated equipment. Only one full-time staff person is paid to work with the production. All other workers are volunteers who have learned to operate the equipment and to do whatever is required.

You don't need a large paid staff to handle the technical aspects of media. You don't have to pay high wages at double the regular rates for weekend work. Your own people can do the job.

12. Must Never Usurp the Local Church

The media must never usurp the local church in evangelism. There can be no substitute for a local fellowship of Christians. The missing element in network televangelism is the involvement of hundreds and thousands of local churches. ACTS is an effort to fill that missing link.

13. Avoid Hucksterism

The media offers unique opportunities for hucksterism in evangelism. Avoid that like you would the plague. There is no place in media evangelism for the Elmer Gantry or the Marjoe Gortner types.

14. Impossible to Use Without a Star

It is almost impossible to use the media without having a "star." Especially is that true of TV. We must accept the burden of that and do the best we can with it.

15. Room Now for Called Persons to Work

There is now room for God-called men and women to work full time as media directors for local churches and for parachurch organizations. If ACTS becomes a reality, that one network will provide opportunities for many who wish to devote their lives and talents to media evangelism and ministry.

16. Quality Programs Versus Quantity

Quality programs are more valuable than quantity of programs. Style and substance are more important than the number of stations.

David W. Clark, dean of the graduate school of communications at CBN (Christian Broadcasting Network) University in Virginia Beach says, "We tend to worship technology. There's something about the lights and the cameras that consumes people. People who have two-color cameras say, 'Boy, if I had three-color cameras, then I could really win the world for Christ.'" Clark thinks broadcasters should start giving more attention to content and less to technology.[20]

We should guard against what Frederick Ferré calls "technolatry," the belief that "every apparent evil brought on by technique is to be countered by yet greater faith in technique."[21] I agree with Harry Hollis who said television is "neither a one-eyed tyrant to be feared nor a one-eyed god to be served."[22]

17. Capturing a City

The lifeline of any church which wants to capture a major city for Christ may be TV. If you are serious about reaching your city, you'll have to get on TV regularly.

"No one . . . questions the power of television over the minds of Americans today," says Donald Kimmick. "There are an estimated 138 million black and white and color sets. TV sets are in use for an average of 6 hours and 10 minutes a day in 99.9 percent of the homes in our country—up from 5 hours and 30 minutes in 1965."[23]

Robert Schuller has said that those churches which wish to start a television ministry need to answer four questions: "Who do you want to impress? What kind of impression do you want to make? How do you make that impression? And are you willing to pay the price?"[24]

18. Same Logo or Symbol

All media used by a church should use the same logo or symbol. Use it on everything you do. Its purpose is to establish your identity and to create familiarity with you and your church. Business corporations spend millions of dollars on logos.

19. A Catchy Phrase

A catchy phrase may be helpful to use in media evangelism, if it is true. One such phrase which became omnipresent to me when I lived in Columbia, South Carolina, was "The Fellowship of Excitement." That was the way First Baptist Church, Columbia, wanted to be known. Another such phrase is "The Church Where People Care."

20. Personal Testimonies

Personal testimonies communicate better than anything else in using the media for evangelism. Those who may tune out all sermons will often listen to a personal testimony. I believe personal testimonies, coupled with inspiring music and appropriate short readings, appeal to more secular and religious persons than do most of our media sermons and lectures.

If you will log a typical television hour, you may be surprised to discover that as many as fifteen pieces of information will be shoved at you. Seldom will any solid block of input last more than twelve or fifteen minutes. Some messages are only fifteen seconds and many only thirty seconds.

21. Telephone Most Neglected Tool

The telephone is perhaps the most neglected technological tool which churches could readily use in evangelism. Alan Walker, a Methodist pastor, was the founder of "Lifeline" in Sydney, Australia. Walker designed a way to use the telephone as an instrument for communication around the clock, seven days a week. That movement has spread to other countries. Some Christians in America minister to persons through a program called "Fish."

Yet, scores of towns and cities and churches have no one on duty at all times to hear the lonely, to comfort those who mourn, to prevent suicide, to help a stranger find his way, to feed the hungry, to help persons bear their burdens and thus fulfill the royal law of love for one's neighbor.

Only a handful of churches in America offer an opportunity for anyone in need to call and talk with a live human being any time day or night. Robert Schuller's church does. The School of Christian Unity does.

"If most pastors would only spend an hour a day in the creative use of the phone," wrote Dennis Benson, "their ministries would be expanded vastly."[25]

Jimmy Allen has said that he believes the time will come when "anywhere in America a person with a need will be able to call a number and someone in his area will immediately get in touch with him."[26] Only the local churches can turn that dream into a reality. The electronic church cannot respond to such needs in person.

The Billy Graham Evangelistic Association began a telephone counseling ministry in 1980 in conjunction with crusade telecasts. This is a natural extension of Billy Graham's crusade ministry.[27]

We are now told that within a few years, entry-level salesmen will start their careers selling by telephone. When a face-to-face call can cost from $40.00 to $100.00, as over against an average cost of $7.00 for a telephone call, economics alone move businesses toward the telephone.[28] If businesses are discovering the utility of the telephone, how much more should those of us who are on the King's business?

Conclusion

Newspapers, advertisements, commercials, comic strips, comic books, movies, radio, and TV are all art forms. News *is* managed, if only by juxtaposition on page 1 of the newspaper and by size and shape of headlines and letters. All of the world is compressed into one page of a newspaper. The ads carry a powerful psychological wallop. The church should help people to be aware of potential slavery to all of these art forms. Propaganda is going on all of the time. Fallout from such propaganda makes it more difficult to get a hearing for the gospel. Insofar as lies within our means, we should seek to enlist all media in the service of evangelism.

Suggested Study Questions

1. We live in a media saturated environment. Most of us have been changed radically by the media, especially by television. Television has changed us by orienting us toward stories. It has given us more pictures and chopped things up for us more. Most pictures on television will last only seven seconds at most. Sensationalism has invaded our lives through TV. It has also given us a new appreciation for the well-prepared script. All of this impacts the way we share the gospel. List at least three ways in which evangelizing may be impacted by television.

2. Japanese in Japan watch television an average of three hours and 25 minutes per day. Housewives average five hours. Actually 98.2 percent of Japanese households in Japan have color TV sets. Based on the chapter you have just read, or other resources, give whatever corresponding statistics you can for the United States.

3. List the five theses from this chapter which you consider of greatest importance, and rank them in your order of priority, on a descending scale from 1 to 5. Be prepared to discuss your choices and to give a rationale for your ordering.

4. Write down the ways you now use (or have used) the telephone in evangelization. Then, add all of the ways you would like to see the telephone used to evangelize your Jerusalem.

Notes

1. See the editorial, "Why Johnny Can't Listen to the Sermon," *Ministry*, Vol. 54, No. 5, May, 1981, p. 22.

2. See the editorial, "Making the Most of the Electronic Church," *Christianity Today*, XXV, No. 3, Feb. 6, 1981, p. 14.

3. Quoted in *The Baptist Courier*, Vol. 113, No. 6, Feb. 5, 1981, p. 6.

4. Vol. XXV, No. 3, Feb. 6, 1981, p. 15.

5. Quoted in an editorial, "Making the Most of the Electronic Church," *Christianity Today*, XXV, No. 3, Feb. 6, 1981, p. 14.

6. Reported in *Newsweek*, Feb. 9, 1981, p. 101. However, that effort appears now to be in grave difficulty and may not be consummated. See Jean Caffey Lyles, "Will United Methodists Buy a Television Ministry?" *The Christian Century*, Vol. 99, No. 15, April 28, 1982, pp. 505-509.

7. "Broadcast Deregulation Touches Off Mad Scramble for Local TV Stations," *Christianity Today*, XXV, No. 4, Feb. 20, 1981, p. 40.

8. "'Tell the Jesus Story,' Charges Jackson," *Word and Way*, Vol. 118, No. 44, Nov. 5, 1981, p. 12.

9. Mark R. Sills, "The Docetic Church," *The Christian Century*, XCVIII, No. 2, Jan. 21, 1981, pp. 35-36.

10. Lyle E. Schaller, "Direct Mail Evangelism," *The Lutheran*, June 3, 1981, pp. 11-12. I am indebted to Schaller for much of the content in the preceding five paragraphs.

11. "60 Topics Selected for Use on Baptist Video Network," *The Baptist Courier*, Vol. 113, No. 5, Jan. 29, 1981, p. 11. Originally VTS was called Video Network.

12. *Church Growth: America*, Vol. 7, No. 1, January, 1981, pp. 2-6, and 14.

13. Richard D. Dinwiddie, "Moneychangers in the Church: Making the Sounds of Music," *Christianity Today*, Vol. XXV, No. 12, June 26, 1981, p. 17.

14. Used by courtesy of the Radio and Television Commission of the SBC. An announcer says after the parable by Pleitz, "This was brought to you by Park Cities Baptist Church in Dallas."

15. Lloyd Mackey, "The Thinking Person's Evangelist: Terry Winter," *Christianity Today*, Vol. XXV, No. 15, Sept. 4, 1981, p. 53.

16. "The Electronic Pulpit: Does It Preach to a Smaller Audience Than Claimed?" *Christianity Today*, Vol. XXV, No. 11, June 12, 1981, p. 34. See also Rodney Clapp, "Who's Kidding Who about the Size of the Electronic Church?" *Christianity Today*, Vol. XXVI, No. 13, Aug. 6, 1982, pp. 44 and 46.

17. Theodore Baehr, "Tangled Christian Telecommunications," *Christianity Today*, Vol. XXV, No. 20, 1981, p. 35.

18. Peter G. Horsfield, "Religious Broadcasting at the Crossroads," *The Christian Century*, Vol. 99, No. 3, Jan. 27, 1982, p. 87.

19. "Electronic Audiences," *The Christian Century*, Vol. 98, No. 42, Dec. 23, 1981, p. 1335.

20. Quoted in "Broadcast Deregulation Touches Off Mad Scramble for Local TV Stations," p. 40.

21. Quoted by Horsfield, p. 89.

22. See the Baptist Press release, "Broadcast Meeting Features Use of Media," *The Word and Way*, Vol. 118, No. 20, May 14, 1981, p. 8.

23. *Evangelism News*, No. 26, Winter, 1981, p. 1. A bimonthly newsletter of evangelism and renewal, Episcopal Church Center, 815 Second Ave., New York, N.Y. 10017.

24. Quoted by a Baptist Press release, "Broadcast Meeting Features Use of Media," p. 8.

25. Dennis C. Benson, *Electronic Evangelism* (Nashville: Abingdon Press, 1973), p. 101.

26. "God's Word Is Alive and Real," *Baptist Courier,* Vol. 112, No. 39, Oct. 2, 1980, p. 2.

27. "Just a Phone Call Away," *Decision,* Vol. 22, Nos. 8 & 9, August-September, 1981, p. 6.

28. Tom Wolf, "Marketing Exec Sees More Sales 'Calls' by Phone," *The Kansas City Star,* Mar. 10, 1981, p. 7A.

21
Suggestions for Successful Revivals

Psalm 85:6; Ephesians 4:25 to 5:2

Introduction

Methodist evangelist Sam P. Jones was once told, "Revivals just don't last."

Jones replied, "Neither do baths." T. DeWitt Talmadge, a former pastor of the famous Brooklyn Tabernacle, may have been right when he said "people who criticize revivals need them most."

More than thirty-five years ago A. C. Archibald wrote: "Revivals and the vogue of itinerant evangelists were essentially a nineteenth century product. They grew out of the camp-meeting custom and the ways of pioneer preachers. On the whole, they served their day and generation well. But that day has passed."[1]

Revivals Today

What Archibald said about the day of revivals having passed may be true of some denominations, but it is certainly not true of Southern Baptists and denominations such as the Nazarenes and the Free Will Baptists. Nor is it true of most of the independent churches in America and Canada. Southern Baptist churches reported over 40,000 local church revival meetings in one recent year. The majority of Southern Baptist churches still hold one or more revival meetings each year.

It is true, however, that in some cases the revival has degenerated into a form of godliness without the power of God flowing through it. When any means of grace is institutionalized, you always run the risk of routinizing it and losing its dynamic. That may be one reason some churches have discontinued holding revival meetings. Furthermore, revivals are now more occasions than causes for professions of faith in Christ.

But let us not make the mistake of concluding that every revival meeting which begins on the third Sunday in August or on the second Sunday in October is as dead as the dodo. Two of the most memorable revivals of my ministry were held in Virginia during the late 1950s. One was in a town church in October, and the other was in a rural church in August. They were held at traditional times of the year. I baptized forty-nine converts, most of them adults, following the town revival. The power of God was so evident that week that it shook the town to its foundations. The church house overflowed every service. The invitation on the last Sunday morning of that revival continued for nearly ninety minutes following the sermon. It was not contrived. We were not begging persons to respond. God broke our hearts and opened the fountains of heaven upon us. As the song says, "Heaven came down and glory filled [our] soul[s]." No one went home; no one wanted to go home. We had meat to eat that the world knew nothing about.

About the same things could be said of that rural church revival in August. It was not on as large a scale. But God opened the floodgates of heaven every service. Nearly thirty persons made public professions of faith or other significant public decisions. There was standing room only in the church house. It was a blessed and never-to-be-forgotten week.

I was in another revival meeting in South Carolina in the 1960s which had to be extended an extra three days. A lay leader in that congregation responded to God's call to preach during the extended part of the revival. He has planted one church from scratch, which is now a strong congregation. Presently, he is pastor of another church in

North Carolina. Everyone who participated in that ten-day revival meeting would tell you that there was no drudgery or deadness to it. It was as though God gave wings to the gospel through music and sermon during those days. We were caught up in the Spirit and surprised with overflowing joy and love. I must tell you that a bond was cemented between and among some Christians during that revival which not even death itself is strong enough to break.

Today's revivals have grown shorter in duration. Many of them are now four-day meetings, Sunday through Wednesday. Back in the early to mid 1950s, some denominational leaders of evangelism were promoting two-week-long revival meetings. The first week was to focus on revival and renewal among the people of God, whereas the second week was to turn outward toward the undiscipled in evangelism and witnessing. Some churches did hold two-week meetings back then. However, such churches were definitely in the minority in the southeastern United States.

I find it interesting that the first protracted revival meetings conducted by Charles G. Finney were four-day meetings. Another name, in fact, for the revival at one time was "the Four-Day Meeting." Now after 150 years, the length of the revival meeting has gone full circle.

The pace of life today is too fast for lengthy revival meetings. Technological changes have revolutionized our culture and made it more difficult for long revivals. Occasionally we hear of a forty-day-long revival, or even of one lasting 120 days, but those are noteworthy exceptions rather than the norm.

Not only has the length of revivals changed drastically but also the purpose has slowly shifted. Technically, revival has to do with renewal among the people of God. Nevertheless, almost from the beginning of protracted revivals, the church leaders have used them to revive the Christians and to save the lost.

One of the questions I always ask about the revival

meetings in which I participate is: Do you want this to be geared toward the church members or toward the outsiders? Occasionally a pastor will say: "The church members." More often they want a two-pronged approach, both toward the church and the unbelievers.

I can tell you that the revival has been a potent evangelistic tool among the churches of America. And especially has that been true of Southern Baptists. While we have in the last decade or two supplemented, or even substituted, the revival with lay renewal weekends, retreats, bus ministry and lay witness training, revivals continue to be a major means of evangelization for the churches.

Purpose

It seems to me that the first step in preparing for a local church revival should be to determine its purpose. If you don't know where you are going, almost any road will take you there.

The pastor may decide the purpose. If it is a very large congregation, the Church Council or the evangelism committee, should be involved in determining the purpose. If the deacons are spiritual leaders in the congregation, they will want to have a voice in deciding the purpose for a particular revival.

I believe each revival meeting needs a specific purpose. Ask questions, such as the following, to clarify your purpose: Will we direct this meeting toward our church members or toward outsiders or both? Do we want to make this primarily a time of harvesting or a time of sowing and planting? Shall we focus on the inward journey or the outward journey?

Date

A second step in revival preparation is to set aside a tentative date on the church calendar. Try to find a date which will be suitable to the largest number of persons in the congregation and in the community. Watch out for possible conflicts with events such as elections, sports events, school activities, major holidays, and local festivals.

I believe the date should be tentative until it can be firmed up with any outside personnel which you hope to secure. Unless you have to lock the date into a traditional time, such as one coinciding with an annual homecoming service, it would be better to set two or three tentative dates until you can enlist your evangelist and musicians. Those dates could be prioritized into first, second, and third choices.

Two other points need to be made about the date. First, plan as far in advance as you can. You will come closer to securing the evangelist and music leader of your choice if you will plan two or three years in advance. Many churches wait until a few months before a revival and then try to put it together at the eleventh hour. Most churches do not plan far enough in advance.

Second, don't think you simply can't have a revival meeting except in the early fall or early spring. One of the good revivals in which I was privileged to participate was held during a Thanksgiving week. Sam P. Jones conducted a powerful revival in Brooklyn during the month of January. It lasted for four weeks. Passion Week, or the week before Easter, is a good time for a revival in many places. Yet, we often overlook this natural time for a revival in the Christian calendar. Summertime is a good time for a local tent revival or for a stadium revival.

Personnel

Step 3 in revival preparation is to enlist the personnel who will lead the revival. Most churches give their pastor the privilege of selecting the preacher. The pastor may confer with other church leaders before he invites someone. He will, of course, welcome suggestions from any member of the congregation.

I believe the pastor should schedule himself from time

to time to be the preacher for revival services in his own congregation. This can be especially fruitful at the beginning of his ministry with a congregation. Moreover, no one knows the congregation and the community like the pastor who has been ministering there for some years. Therefore, he is in an enviable position after a few years to be especially effective in preaching his own revival. If the pastor can refuse to accept an honorarium for such meetings, the financial arrangement will not encumber his decision to preach in his own church.

We should not overlook vocational evangelists when we set out to secure a preacher. A reputable evangelist who has a gift for preaching and itinerant evangelism can be a choice blessing to a church. If in doubt about an evangelist, check with the pastor of the local church in which he holds membership. Inquire of pastors who have used that evangelist. Ask your associational chairman of evangelism and your state director of evangelism if they can recommend particular vocational evangelists. Probably there are more full-time professional evangelists serving the churches today than ever before.

Others to consider as possible revival preachers are: staff members of associational, state, and denominational agencies and boards, college or seminary professors, retired pastors, and, above all, pastors who have hearts for evangelism.

Some pastors and denominational leaders are not comfortable leading revivals. A friend of mine once said to me, "I have stopped doing stand-up revivals." That was his way of telling me that he felt uncomfortable preaching in a revival meeting. Well, I wouldn't invite such persons to preach in revivals. God will use them to do some other things which need to be done in the church.

What we want in a revival preacher is ideally one who has both a heart and a head for evangelism. He may not have the spiritual gift of an evangelist; but, if he has a heart for evangelism, that will do. I think the pastor has an obligation to bring a variety of preachers to his pulpit. He ought to bring the best preachers he can enlist to help his people celebrate their faith and to cast the gospel net for the lost.

If an outside music leader is needed, some of the same things said about the preacher may be said of the musician. He ought to be able to select appropriate hymns and songs. He should respect the time allotted to him.

Soloists and special musical groups should be carefully chosen. The revival is not a time for showmanship. Nor is it a musical talent hunt. Whoever the organist and pianists and guest singers or musicians may be, they should, except in emergencies, stay throughout the entire service. It is rude for them to come and perform and then depart before the sermon.

When you enlist outside revival personnel, you should have a clear understanding about finances on the front end. The invitation should be confirmed in writing. These two front-end items: finances and exact dates, if confirmed in writing, will avoid possible misunderstandings and confusion later.

One other reminder should be interjected at this point. Don't make the mistake of thinking you can import a revival or evangelism to your church. Both revival and evangelism are more exportable than they are importable. You can't package them in persons and buy them as though they were labeled, retail items.

Organization

Step 4 relates to the organization. Set up whatever organization you need to get the job done. Small churches will obviously not need as extensive organizations as will large churches.

An evangelism committee may be all that some churches need. An increasing number of churches are setting up continuing committees on evangelism. Most Southern Baptist churches do not have organized, functioning Church Councils. If you do have such a council, it might act as a coordinating group for the revival.

Consider whether you need the following committees: prayer, publicity, attendance, music, hospitality, ushers, finance, and special events.

Even if you don't need a separate committee to handle such items, you will have to have one or more persons who will be responsible for those items.

The prayer committee would mobilize the people to pray. The publicity committee would make definite plans to let the church and the public know about the revival. An attendance committee would lead in specific plans to get the church members and the undiscipled to attend each service. A music committee would coordinate the music and singing for the revival. The hospitality committee would arrange for the hospitality and transportation needs of all outside revival personnel. An usher's committee would welcome and minister to those who attend the revival services. A special events committee would seek out opportunities to present the gospel during revival week to the larger community.

Finances

A fifth suggestion which I offer has to do with finances. Whether handled by a finance committee or by an individual, this is such a significant aspect of revival preparation that I feel it needs to be singled out separately. A revival can be torpedoed more quickly by misunderstandings over finances than almost any other way.

I believe it is wise to place in the church budget an item which will cover revival expenses. These expenses would include revival publicity, any materials, rooms, meals, and travel expenses of the evangelist and musicians. All expenses of the revival team should be allowed for in this budgeted item.

If the honoraria for the revival team is not budgeted, it can be handled through free-will offerings. My preference is to make expenses a line item in the church budget, but to handle the honoraria entirely through free-will offerings. This may be done by providing special envelopes and receiving an offering each service of the revival. A better way may be for the pastor and the finance committee chairperson to send a letter before the revival to each member with an enclosed envelope explaining the honoraria. The cover letter would indicate *when* the offering will be received during the revival. Under no circumstances would I permit an evangelist or musician to use his own special offering envelopes in a local church revival. The envelopes should be opened and properly counted and credited by the church.

The guest evangelist and musicians should be given *all* of the honoraria. If you don't take separate offerings for the evangelist and musicians, agree ahead of time how the money will be divided. Make a full report to the congregation on the revival finances following the revival.

I prefer two separate checks to the outside revival leaders: one for all expenses not otherwise cared for and the other the honorarium. We ought to reimburse guest workers at a mileage rate in keeping with prevailing costs. It is a discourtesy to say nothing of being unchristian, to count travel expenses as part of the honorarium.

Wherever revival finances have been handled as I have suggested, I have yet to see an unworthy honorarium. However, if the honorarium should prove to be unworthy and embarrassing, the finance committee may be authorized to supplement it from the church budget.

Finally, on finances, let me suggest that you consider sending your revival team an advance on their travel expenses before the revival, especially if they are to travel a long distance. Also, by all means, give them their checks immediately when the revival is concluded. Do not wait and mail them a few days or a few weeks following the meeting.

The laborer is worthy of his hire, and he shouldn't have to wait on or beg for that which is rightfully his. I also like to see the checks presented to the team by the pastor privately, but not sealed in some envelope with one's name written on it.

Goals

We need to set some goals for the revival. These are bite-sized chunks of work which will help us to achieve our overall purpose. Our goals should be so *clear* that even if one should see them on the run, he could read and understand them. They should be *concise,* rather than lengthy and wordy. They should be *calendared* so that each one is on a time line. They should be *changeable,* in case we need to revise them at the last minute. They should be *challenging* so that they may motivate us to go on to greater heights. If our goals are clear, concise, calendared, changeable, and challenging, they will be measurable and manageable so that we can check up on them and use them to evaluate our effectiveness.

Revival goals which we might set may have to do with Sunday School attendance, the number in the revival choir, the number of ushers, the number of prayer meetings, additions to the church, professions of faith, and total members involved in the revival. It is just as right to set goals for a revival meeting as it is for a church budget or for a church building campaign. Nor should tangible goals rule out intangible ones.

If it's worth doing, it's worth doing right. And one right way to go about planning for a successful revival is to set goals for it. One of my friends who has been very successful in conducting revivals suggests the following four goals:

- Involve total resident membership in revival preparation.
- Enlist every prospect for services.

- Average at least as many each service as attend Sunday School per Sunday.
- Disciple every person who makes a decision.[2]

More Suggestions

One idea which I have seen work is to choose or assign prayer partners for a revival meeting. Any two persons in the church can covenant to pray together each day for a week before the revival and during the revival. It seems to work better if these prayer partners meet together in one place. However, it can be done on the telephone if necessary.

Another idea which one church used was to assign every church member to a Sunday School class and department. This particular church was located in Primitive Baptist territory. Many of its church members were not members of the Sunday School. They called these assigned members "*agape* members." Their purpose was to have someone responsible for ministering to these non-Sunday School members. Even if a church only did this in conjunction with a revival meeting, it could mobilize specific Christians to pray for and befriend and minister to a large number of its own members who may not be very active.

Conclusion

Charles G. Finney said, "It is useless to expect a revival simply by asking for it, without bothering to fulfill the laws which govern spiritual blessings." Revival is both a surprising work of God and the hard work of fervent Christians. All of our local church revivals should seek to preserve this delicate balance between the sovereignty of God and the responsibility of the people of God.

The revivals which have caught fire in my experience have had a kind of *kairos* about them. Everything seemed to come together at a divinely appointed time. The time was right; the people of God were ready; the preacher was ready; the singers and musicians were ready; the prospects were ripe for harvesting.

Furthermore, the significant revivals of my acquaintance have arisen out of heartfelt prayer on the part of some of God's servants. They have been answers to the heartfelt cries and petitions of the saints of God. The effectual, fervent prayers of righteous men, women, youth, and children still avail much.

Suggested Study Questions

1. What are the significant features of the following true case history?

A seven-week revival meeting in Orangeburg Avenue Baptist Church of Modesto, California, recorded 313 professions of faith in 1982. So far, 143 of those have been baptized into church membership. The evangelist was Barry Westbrook, a pastor in Ontario, California, seven hours away. Orangeburg members went to Ontario and drove Westbrook back and forth in a van with a mattress in it so he could sleep and maintain his pastoral duties there. Orangeburg Avenue Church has grown from an attendance of 60 in 1977 to an average of 380. Ninety percent of those professing Christ during the revival were between the ages of nineteen and forty-five. Also, 95 percent of those who were saved had never been to that church prior to the crusade.

Pastor Jim Silvers attributed much of the growth to the personal growth and commitment of two ladies in the church who committed themselves in 1977 "to faithful prayer for awakening, faithful visitation, and faithful witness." Silvers also credits a "strong unity in the leadership, pastoral-deacon ministry, and a great burden for souls and for community."[3]

2. Here is one actual scheme for special nights and days in a local church revival. The scheme is designed to create interest, increase attendance, and enhance the publicity.

SUNDAY . . . . High Attendance
MONDAY . . . . Men's Night

TUESDAY .... Ladies' Night
WEDNESDAY .... Youth Night
THURSDAY .... Children's Night
FRIDAY .... Couples' Night
SATURDAY .... Special Music Night
SUNDAY .... Everybody's Day

You are planning a four-day revival meeting (Sunday morning through Wednesday night) for your church. How will you designate the five services?

3. Why should we have a clear understanding about finances preceding a revival meeting?

Notes

1. Arthur C. Archibald, *New Testament Evangelism* (Philadelphia: The Judson Press, 1946), p. 21.
2. These goals were suggested by Tal Bonham at an evangelism meeting on 12/11/74.
3. "California Revival Goes On . . . and On and On," *The Baptist Courier*, Vol. 114, No. 16, April 22, 1982, p. 10.

22
The Public Invitation[1]

Genesis 3:9; Revelation 22:17

Introduction

D. L. Moody preached one Sunday night on the text: "Then what shall I do with Jesus who is called Christ?" (Matt. 27:22). He exhorted his congregation to take that text home with them, turn it over in their minds during the week, and on the next Sunday to come prepared to decide what they would do with Jesus.

The closing hymn which Ira Sankey sang following Moody's sermon said:

> Today the Savior calls,
> For refuge now draw nigh
> The storm of justice falls
> And death is nigh.

That fateful Sunday evening was October 8, 1871, the night Mrs. O'Leary's cow kicked a lantern over and the great Chicago fire began. The next morning much of Chicago was in ashes.

Moody regretted for the remainder of his life that he had given his audience a week to think about their salvation. He learned in the experience that whenever he preached to try to bring persons to a decision on the spot. Never again did he fail to give a public invitation for persons to respond immediately to Jesus Christ.[2]

"The evangelistic invitation," wrote Farris D. Whitesell, "is an appeal to the will for decisive, wholehearted and

301

immediate action."[3] It is drawing the gospel net to take persons alive for Jesus Christ. In some respects the invitation is comparable to what salespersons call "closing the deal." It is "an appeal to someone to accept the benefits of the Christian gospel," said Roy Fish.[4]

Origin of the Invitation

Two points seem clear regarding the history of the invitation. First and overarching is the point which Whitesell makes when he says: "Modern evangelistic invitations are of comparatively recent origin."[5]

The invitation as we know and use it goes back to the late eighteenth century. It is by and large a product of nineteenth-century revivalism. It cannot be traced all the way back through church history to the apostolic church. The "sawdust trail" and "the trail of blood" are by no means synonymous! The eighteenth-, nineteenth-, and twentieth-century church created and institutionalized the invitation.

A second historical point which seems clear is that the modern invitation traces back through Billy Sunday's sawdust trail, Dwight L. Moody's inquiry room, A. B. Earle's card signing, Charles G. Finney's anxious benches or anxious seats, to Asahel Nettleton's anxious rooms and anxious meetings around 1817.[6]

Apparently, the genesis of the modern invitation was an invitation to those who were anxious about their spiritual condition to attend anxious meetings where anxious rooms were set aside for the anxious to pray and to discuss with the preacher their anxiety over their salvation. This was the method used by Asahel Nettleton, a Congregational preacher.

Charles G. Finney, instead of having folk come to an anxious meeting and to anxious rooms, invited them to come to benches or seats at the front of the assembly. These were called anxious seats or anxious benches. We still use the front pews for those who respond during the invitation.

A. B. Earle, about the mid nineteenth century, asked those who came forward during the invitation to sign cards. Prior to that, the cards which were used in invitations were given to the new convert to take home with him. On the cards were Scripture verses which would help in one's new life.

Moody and Major Whittle added the innovation of inquiry rooms. This was an adaptation of Nettleton's anxious meetings and anxious rooms. They invited inquirers to walk forward to the inquiry room where they were counseled.

Billy Sunday used personal workers to move through the crowd and urge persons to go forward when response to the invitation slacked. "Walking the sawdust trail" originated with Sunday. He had great tabernacles built in which he conducted his meetings. The dirt floor of these tabernacles was covered with sawdust. One who walked the sawdust trail walked forward to confess Christ. Our expression "walk down the aisle" may have some connection with "walking the sawdust trail."

Billy Graham has further perfected the techniques of his predecessors by having trained counselors to come forward during the invitation to personally counsel with every person who makes a public decision. Sometimes, because of the large number of public decisions and the location of Graham's meetings, the inquiry room becomes the very spot on which the inquirer stands when he comes forward and stands before the evangelist. Those making public decisions are given some literature. A vigorous follow-up effort is made with each inquirer.

I share these broken, incomplete sketches of history in order to indicate what the invitation is. The evangelistic invitation is a comparatively recent creation of the church. It is what some of our forefathers called "a new measure." It is a product of revivalism. It encompasses a rich variety of innovative techniques in evangelism. We have institutionalized it because it has served us so well.

Why Give an Invitation?

Now, let us raise the why question. Why should we give a public invitation? Are we preaching for display or for response? United Methodist pastor, O. Dean Martin puts the answer like this: *"Whenever* we approach the pulpit for the period of proclamation we are basically and simply doing one of two things: we are asking people to think we are wonderful, or we are asking them to (right now) say, 'yes,' 'no,' or 'maybe' concerning that which we have proclaimed."[7] There are at least four good reasons for giving an invitation.

The invitation fits our theology. We believe in a seeking God of love who pays persons the supreme compliment of letting them choose between life and death, between heaven and hell. Our God is not some cosmic policeman who walks the beat of the world with a blackjack in his hand knocking persons over the head and dragging them into his kingdom. Rather, he is the Good Shepherd who seeks after the lost sheep until he finds them. That's what the incarnation, the crucifixion, the resurrection, the ascension, and the second coming are all about. From Genesis to Revelation God is seeking persons. In Genesis 3:9 God calls to Adam: "Where are you?" That's the omnipresent, omnipotent, omniscient question which God addresses to every person: "Where are you?"

Then, when we come to the very last chapter in our Bible we read in Revelation 22:17, "The Spirit and the Bride say, 'Come.' And let him who hears say, 'Come.' And let him who is thirsty come, let him who desires take the water of life without price."

R. G. Lee in his introduction to *Sixty-Five Ways to Give Evangelistic Invitations* refers to "the Scriptural sanction of invitations." There is a scriptural sanction for the invitation in Genesis 3:9 and Revelation 22:17 and all the way in between.

We ought to have an invitation because it so beautifully fits our theology. It fits what we believe about the nature of

God and the freedom, dignity, and responsibility of persons.

The invitation fits our psychology. William James in his great psychological study on the *Varieties of Religious Experience* found two basic types of religious experience: the twice-born type and the once-born type. An example which James gives of the once-born type is the Christian Scientist. An example which he gives of the twice-born type is Saul of Tarsus who became Paul the apostle. James seems to conclude that most persons are so psychologically constructed that they require a second birth, a radical new reorientation to life.[8]

We ought to give the invitation because it so perfectly fits the psychological needs of human beings for a new birth and a new start in life. "Once the judgment is decided," wrote James, "let a man commit himself, let him lay on himself the necessity of doing more, let him lay on himself the necessity of doing all. Let him take the public pledge if the case allows. Let him envelop his revolution with all the aids possible."[9]

The invitation fits our pedagogy. We know that one way persons learn is through gestalt, or phenomenal patterns. A gestalt experience is an a-ha experience. Isaac Newton had an a-ha experience when an apple fell on his head and he discovered the law of gravity. All of a sudden, like a bolt of lightning from heaven, the pieces fall into place. It all fits together. The puzzle is completed, and we cry, "Eureka!" The invitation encourages learning through gestalt. God alone knows how many people get themselves together and "get it all together," as we say, in the invitation time.

We know also that persons learn by doing. The invitation encourages persons to have faith, to repent, to love, to confess, to put feet under their prayers, to learn by experiment.

Further, we know that persons learn through models and modeling. The public invitation provides opportunities for persons to see, to be, and to hear living, incarnated models of faith in action.

We ought to extend the invitation because it fits our pedagogy. It helps us to fulfill the teaching function of the church. It is a potent teaching instrument.

The invitation fits our ideology. Two of the biggest planks in our American ideology are individualism and pragmatism. Our ancestors were pioneers. This was true in both the settlement of the colonies and of the Western frontier. What we have come to call "rugged individualism" developed naturally in such a setting. We do not have the sense of corporateness which developed in Asia, Africa, and even Europe because our history is different. So when we call on persons to make individual decisions on the spot, we still have this ideology of rugged individualism going for us.

The other big plank in our ideology is pragmatism. We are unrepentant pragmatists. Almost the first question we ever ask about anything is: Will it work? Well, the invitation certainly will work. It does produce results. One of the first persons I met at the Billy Graham Crusade in Knoxville, Tennessee, a few years ago was Joe Hale. He had been converted in one of Billy Graham's crusades and was at that time working as a staff member of the General Board of Evangelism of the United Methodist Church. So, in extending an invitation we are being pragmatic, and we have the American ideology of pragmatism going for us.

Why give an invitation? It fits our theology, our psychology, our pedagogy, and our ideology. Whitesell sums up our rationale for giving an invitation in these words: "Evangelistic preaching naturally culminates in an invitation. The whole drive of such preaching reaches a logical climax in the appeal. Without the invitation the evangelistic message is incomplete and the effect of the message unknown."[10]

When to Give an Invitation

At what point in the service should the invitation be given? On rare occasions the invitation should come before the sermon or in lieu of the sermon. Almost a decade and one-half ago I was informed about a revival which broke out in Gaffney, South Carolina. I went to Gaffney and talked with the pastor of the church where the revival was in progress. One unusual fact about that revival was that no public sermons had been preached up to that point—several days into the meeting.

Usually, however, the invitation should be given following the sermon. Common sense and spiritual sensitivity should guide us on when to give and when not to give an invitation. Since invitations are primarily for lost persons, the invitation should usually be extended when the preacher knows unsaved persons are present.

Whenever you are reasonably sure of even one response, give an invitation. By all means give an invitation when you feel the convicting presence and power of the Holy Spirit in a service. When you know you have preached with freedom and power, give an invitation.

There are churches where it is customary to give an invitation at every service, but there may be other churches where it would be unwise to give the invitation that frequently. It is usually better in evangelistic meetings and revivals to extend an invitation at every service.[11]

How to Give an Invitation

How should the invitation be given? As to the manner, style, and content of the invitation, John Bisagno, a Southern Baptist pastor who has excelled in giving invitations, has eleven suggestions: (1) give the invitation authoritatively; (2) be specific; (3) give it urgently; (4) get into the invitation; (5) give the invitation positively; (6) give the invitation prayerfully; (7) give it proudly; (8) don't be afraid to give a long invitation; (9) give a good rededication invitation; (10) deal properly with those who come; (11) make much of their decision.[12]

The one point which I would underscore as to how to give the invitation is to never violate one's personality. I have seen forms of the progressive invitation which I believe lock people in so that they may feel they have been manipulated.

Work out for yourself what O. Dean Martin calls "a basic M-O (mode of operation)" for the invitation. Select a specific model of invitation which you can use most of the time. If you have one standard model, it will be easier for you to utilize a variety of models.

Strive for sensitivity to logical complementation in your invitations. In other words, let your invitation flow "logically and sequentially from the context of the proclamation."[13] You may notice, for example, that Billy Graham usually begins to give his invitation when he stands up to preach, near the beginning of his message. The invitation should not be a foreign object tacked onto the sermon.

Do not be afraid of redundancy in extending an invitation. People are bombarded with so much stimuli nowadays that they can't possibly take it all in. Run the same thing by again and again, both in the same way and in different ways.

Learn to use Scripture verses, hymns, and pithy quotations in some of your invitations. One of the really fine features of *Sixty-Five Ways to Give Evangelistic Invitations* is the appendix where Whitesell devotes eighteen pages to suggestions for this kind of thing.

Appeal to a variety of motives in casting the gospel net. Study how others, especially full-time evangelists, give their invitations.

Preach shorter sermons and give longer invitations. John Bisagno says: "I have found that 90 percent of the converts come forward after the third verse of the invitation."[14]

Conclusion

There is a paucity of resource material on the invitation. When Whitesell published his book in 1945, he wrote in the preface: "I have not been able to find a single book devoted exclusively to the topic." Roy Fish, writing his monograph on *Giving a Good Invitation,* said in his preface nearly thirty years later (1974): "To my knowledge, only one book has been written which was devoted entirely to the subject." Presumably Fish did not know about O. Dean Martin's 1973 book on the invitation.

These three volumes are all we have in the way of published books on the topic. They total scarcely 250 pages. Whitesell's covers the most territory but has long since been out of print. Martin writes primarily for Methodist consumption. Fish is the freshest and best written. Each is well worth the effort. One weakness which all three have in common is the lack of a comprehensive chapter on the history of the invitation.

Suggestions for Further Reading

"The Invitation," in John Bisagno, *How to Build an Evangelistic Church* (Nashville: Broadman Press, 1971), pp. 75-88. This chapter is a reprint from Bisagno's *The Power of Positive Evangelism* (Broadman, 1968).

Roy J. Fish, *Giving a Good Invitation* (Nashville: Broadman Press, 1974).

O. Dean Martin, *Invite: What Do You Do After the Sermon* (Nashville: Tidings, 1973).

Faris D. Whitesell, *Sixty-Five Ways to Give Evangelistic Invitations* (Grand Rapids: Zondervan, 1945).

Notes

1. I published this chapter originally as "C.A.R.E. Revival Invitation and Follow-Up," in *Proclaim,* April, May, June, 1977, Vol. 7, No. 3, pp. 40-42. It has been rewritten and revised.

2. Roy J. Fish, *Giving a Good Invitation* (Nashville: Broadman Press, 1974), pp. 29-30.
3. Faris D. Whitesell, *Sixty-Five Ways to Give Evangelistic Invitations* (Grand Rapids: Zondervan, 1945), p. 31.
4. Fish, p. 7.
5. Whitesell, p. 15.
6. Ibid., p. 16; see also Fish, pp. 14-16; and William G. McLoughlin, Jr., *Modern Revivalism* (New York: Ronald Press, 1959), pp. 56-57, 95 *ff*. 238-239, 304, 382, 385, 410, 434.
7. O. Dean Martin, *Invite: What Do You Do After the Sermon* (Nashville: Tidings, 1973), p. 8.
8. William James, *The Varieties of Religious Experience* (New Hyde Park, New York: University Books, 1963), pp. 78-126, 217 *f.*
9. Cited by Leighton Ford, *The Christian Persuader* (New York: Harper & Row, 1966), p. 124.
10. Whitesell, p. 11.
11. For more on this question, see ibid., pp. 38-39.
12. John R. Bisagno, *How to Build an Evangelistic Church* (Nashville: Broadman Press, 1971), pp. 75-88.
13. Martin, p. 70.
14. Bisagno, p. 85.

23
Pros and Cons of Bus Evangelism[1]

Ecclesiastes 1:9-11; 2 Corinthians 10:1-6

Introduction

The Bible Baptist Church in Uniontown, Pennsylvania, in 1982 had a pastor who started coming to that congregation's Sunday School on one of their buses as a "bus kid." Five of the church's seven deacons were also "bus kids." Gary Herring, the church's pastor, was saved and baptized at the church. Seven years ago he became pastor of his home church. This is one example of how bus evangelism has borne fruit in some churches.[2]

Beginnings of Bus Evangelism

"If ever there was a technique that was originated and polished by Fundamentalists," wrote Elmer Towns, "it is the Sunday School bus outreach." At one time Landmark Baptist Temple in Cincinnati, Ohio, published a picture with 100 buses in front of the church building. First Baptist Church of Hammond, Indiana, had 250 buses bringing in 12,000 riders. Thomas Road Baptist Church of Lynchburg, Virginia, conducted a bus clinic in 1972 which drew 5,000 delegates from all across America. The late John R. Rice published a list of churches which baptized over 200 converts a year, and congregations with bus ministries filled the list. Also, churches with buses dominated the list of 100 largest Sunday Schools published by *Christian Life* magazine.[3]

Towns admits that this growing trend of the early seventies has been reversed. He even suggests that the Christian school movement may be the new technique which the Fundamentalists are using in the 1980s. Nevertheless, he insists that busing is "still successful in those churches which work at it."[4]

Burnout is a real problem in bus ministry. If you go out every Saturday and Sunday, you can experience rapid burnout. That is what has happened to some bus ministries. One way some avoid burnout is to visit the routes once a month rather than weekly. Others are rotating teams of bus workers on a weekly or monthly basis.

Some have also quit bus evangelism because of the escalating cost of gasoline. Curtis Hutson, editor of *The Sword of The Lord,* commenting on this wrote: "The value of souls and not the price of gasoline should determine whether or not one stays in the bus ministry."[5]

Bus evangelism among Southern Baptists began in a significant way in the early 1970s. It was copied from the Independent and Bible Baptist churches. William Powell "was probably the first Southern Baptist busing enthusiast with any impact on the Convention," according to Norman Jameson.

Powell, who was then employed by the Home Mission Board, led his home church into busing. That congregation, Woodlawn Baptist Church in Decatur, Georgia, became a model church for bus evangelism. Powell became a busing expert for Southern Baptists. He was shifted to the Evangelism Division to consult with churches on their bus programs.

The first national conference on bus evangelism was led by Powell in February 1971. Between 400 and 500 participants were attracted. Requests for bus evangelism conferences began to pour into the Home Mission Board. Powell led 300 bus conferences in three years.

D. Lewis White was the first person named by the Baptist Sunday School Board in Nashville to coordinate bus outreach. In 1973 the Southern Baptist Convention added bus outreach to the BSSB's program assignment. Up until that time, there was confusion over whether to contact Atlanta or Nashville for assistance in bus outreach. Printed resource material was also scarce.

One Southern Baptist pastor in Florida by the name of J. W. Wynn created a thing called BUS (Blessings Unlimited Service). Lined with books, his bus became a library. Equipped with several hundred feet of electrical cord and electrical outlets, his bus became a mobile sewing classroom. Pull-down shades turned it into a movie theater. A lift on the back made it a boon to transport the handicapped. Wynn's BUS "became to church busing what Boeing was to the Wright brothers," wrote Norman Jameson. "Wynn's multi purpose bus became a symbol of the best that busing could offer."

Bus evangelism peaked among Southern Baptists in 1975. About 7,200 SBC churches were involved at that time. The best estimates are that one quarter of a million persons came to Sunday School on buses then.

The scarcity and high cost of gas and oil drove some churches out of bus ministry. Some quit because they became convinced they were caught up in a numbers racket in the name of God. A few abandoned busing because they discovered that God builds the church rather than General Motors.

Nevertheless, probably a core of 5,000 Southern Baptist churches continue to do bus evangelism. Broadway Baptist Church in Memphis, Tennessee, for example, was bringing 1,100 to Sunday School on buses in 1981. Also, Eastwood Baptist Church in Tulsa, Oklahoma, had 26 buses in 1981. Dauphin Way Baptist Church in Mobile, Alabama, was busing in about 800 on 19 routes in 1981.[6]

Southern Baptists are the only major Protestant denomination to use bus evangelism. Several of the Pentecostal- and Holiness-type denominations are using the technique. So are some of the Free Will Baptists and other smaller denominations. The forte of bus evangelism is still among the Independent, Fundamentalist-type churches.

A Dangerous Method?

George E. Sweazey says, in his book *Effective Evangelism*:

> Every evangelistic method the Church has ever used can do great harm; it may therefore easily be discredited by calling attention to its misuse. Evangelism is always dangerous—though not so dangerous as the lack of evangelism. Any evangelistic method must be taught to a church as a boy is taught to use a gun—the first lessons must be on its safe handling.[7]

Sweazey was obviously not talking about Church Bus Evangelism (CBE) because those words were written in 1953. Yet, what Sweazey said does apply to CBE and to every other evangelistic method.

I have been in evangelism long enough to see that it is like atomic energy. It can be either a creative or a destructive force.

If those who use CBE are ethical, probably the method will be ethical. On the other hand, if those who use CBE are unethical, chances are that the method of CBE will be unethical. CBE may be likened to the analogy of drugs. Certainly, drugs can destroy persons if they are misused. But, on the other hand, the proper use of drugs when prescribed by doctors saves many lives.

It may help us to remember that CBE is not the only evangelistic method which has been questioned. In the eighteenth century, Jonathan Edwards, under whom the first Great Awakening broke out in this country in 1735 at Northampton, Massachusetts, wrote at least three volumes to defend and promote revivals. Those volumes are usually referred to by their shortened titles as *A Faithful Narrative, Thoughts,*[8] and *Religious Affections.*[9]

The full title of the first two volumes is significant. The

first work is labeled: *A Faithful Narrative of the Surprising Work of God in the Conversion of Many Hundred Souls in Northampton, Mass., A. D. 1735.* The second work is labeled: *Thoughts on the Revival of Religion in New England, 1742, and the Way in Which It Ought to Be Acknowledged and Promoted.*

Edwards' *Faithful Narrative* simply documents what happened in 1735 at Northampton, Massachusetts. In the second work, Edwards made no effort to gloss over the weaknesses and faults of revivals. He readily acknowledged the emotional excesses of men like James Davenport. But, he argued that, in spite of its faults, we should support and promote revivals of religion. In his *Religious Affections,* Edwards addressed himself to the subject of how we can distinguish the true converts of revivals from the bogus converts.

My point is that the same books might well be written today about CBE! One could write a book documenting this surprising work of God through CBE in a hundred or more cities. One could write another volume showing how CBE ought to be acknowledged and promoted. Also, one might well write a third volume showing how to distinguish between the good and the bad, the true and the false converts produced by CBE.

It may shock some of us, but many early Baptists in America opposed the revival methodology in the eighteenth century. Nevertheless, revivalism became a major evangelistic method for Baptists. While the parallel to CBE is different in many respects, the similarities are striking.

What's Wrong with CBE?

Let me now share with you some things which I think are wrong about CBE. Then, I will indicate some things which are surely right with CBE. First the negative and the unethical, then the positive and the ethical.

Proselytism is wrong in CBE. It is wrong to use CBE to proselyte riders who are already attending another church or Sunday School. Sheep stealing is never right. And the same thing holds true for the stealing of lambs.

One of my favorite pastimes is watching Westerns. I like stories about cowboys. Have you ever noticed how harshly the good cowboys deal with rustlers? We get upset today if someone steals what is ours. Shouldn't people rustling in CBE upset us also?

Pharisaism is wrong in CBE. Pharisaism is the attitude of the Pharisee toward the publican in Luke 18:9-14. He bragged on himself that he was "not like other men." Pharisaism is the elder-brother attitude in the story of the prodigal son (Luke 15:25-32). It is possible for the CBE churches and workers to become pharisaical toward non-CBE Christians. If you look down your noses at churches and Christians not involved in CBE and exclude them from your circle of fellowship, you are a twentieth-century Pharisee. Be careful that you do not deserve the woes which our Lord himself pronounced upon the Pharisees in the first century (Matt. 23:13-36).

Prejudice is wrong in CBE. Those who use CBE to maintain social and racial segregation in the body of Christ are wrong. The gospel is for all persons, poor and rich, white and black. I am convinced that evangelical Christians who believe the Bible will solve the racial and social problems quicker than those Christians who talk so much about the Bible and do so little. God does not want us to neglect the rich, the poor, or the in between in CBE. He does not want us to neglect any race or color. Prejudice is a sin and is, therefore, wrong.

Penalizing mission giving is wrong in CBE. This is what I call "robbing Peter to pay Paul." I believe it is wrong for a church to penalize state, national, and world evangelization in order to buy buses or to employ a staff member for CBE. If you do not have sufficient funds to evangelize your Jerusalem, the solution is not to cut back on the evangelization of Judea, Samaria, and the uttermost parts of the earth. The solution is to give more sacrificially and to enlist more stewards.

Propagating a kingdom for one's self is wrong in CBE. The kingdom of God will not permit rival kingdoms. The pursuit of a personal kingdom can cause us to magnify numbers out of proper proportion. Building one's own kingdom can destroy democratic procedures. Pursuing one's own kingdom can cause us to neglect new converts, depersonalize persons, and put people on the level of things. The CBE practitioner who wants to make a name for himself may ignore other churches and ride roughshod over the feelings of fellow Christians.

It may be that instead of busing everybody to one church, we should at some point consider establishing new churches. Certainly one should ever be mindful that the kingdom of God is far bigger than any one local church. It bothers me that some CBE churches seem to play down denominational loyalty and minimize giving to worldwide mission causes.

Placing an overemphasis on one evangelistic method is wrong in CBE. CBE practitioners are so enthusiastic that they sometime give the impression that CBE is the only way to make converts. A few of them even leave the impression that CBE should always take precedence over all other activities of the church. This is what we call in the vernacular "putting all of your eggs in one basket." No one method of evangelism will reach all of the lost who can be reached. Church history teaches us that a variety of evangelistic methods are needed. Of every method it may be said: "This, too, shall pass away." Therefore, we should not enshrine any method.

What's Right with CBE?

Now let me mention some things which are right about CBE.

Going out after the lost is right in CBE. We are to seek the lost wherever they may be found. CBE turns the church outward, toward the world.

Loving little children and nurturing them in the Christian faith is right in CBE. Our Lord himself said: "Let the children come to me, and do not hinder them; for to such belongs the kingdom of heaven" (Matt. 19:14). CBE workers incarnate the love of God for children.

Being aggressive and systematic in our evangelistic methodology is right in CBE. Evangelism has but one strategy— conquest. The sweet boldness of CBE is commendable. Going from house to house, street to street, road to road every Saturday is commendable.

The *enthusiasm* of CBE is right. There are no more enthusiastic workers in the church than the CBE workers. Their enthusiasm is like a fresh wind from heaven and is contagious.

The *willingness of CBE churches and workers to help other churches launch and maintain a CBE ministry* is right. Many CBE workers give generously of their time and resources to help colleagues and beginners. They have a missionary spirit. Freely they have received and freely they give.

The *hard work* which CBE workers engage in from week to week is right. Paul said to Timothy, "Do the work of an evangelist" (2 Tim. 4:5). Evangelism is work. And especially is CBE hard work. Probably it is the hardest work many Christians have ever done. We ought to thank God for calling and equipping a great corps of CBE workers who do not mind hard work.

Conclusion

Church Bus Evangelism has made two major contributions to the church. Both of these are often overlooked. First, CBE has created a new class of church-related vocational workers. We call these persons ministers of evangelism, ministers of outreach, church bus ministers, and so on.

As churches expanded their busing, they felt the need to employ workers to direct that ministry. Some pastors who have become successful at bus ministry in smaller churches were called by larger churches as ministers of evangelism. Some lay persons who excelled as volunteer CBE workers were employed by churches to be directors of bus ministry. Churches which never intended to do CBE were motivated to call ministers of evangelism and outreach.

Today's vocation of full-time and part-time ministers of evangelism received its strongest impetus from CBE. We should not overlook this positive contribution of CBE toward world evangelization and the revitalization of an equipping ministry for evangelistic purposes.

A second major contribution of CBE to the church has to do with children's worship. Some churches discovered through CBE that children need and appreciate worship experiences on their level. Graded children's worship services in our churches are by and large a direct result of CBE. CBE resulted in the production of a new literature for children's worship. A few churches even employed part-time staff persons to assist with children's worship. At least one denomination was called upon to provide resource persons on children's worship.

Along with all of that should be mentioned the army of volunteer workers which CBE enlisted in the service of Christ. There are instances where the lost parents of bused children were won to Christ and then became active bus workers themselves.

Suggestions for Further Reading

"Buses Go Out" in Elvis Marcum, *Outreach: God's Miracle Business* (Nashville: Broadman Press, 1975), pp. 59-71.

"Buy a Bus" in John R. Bisagno, *How to Build an Evangelistic Church* (Nashville: Broadman Press, 1971), pp. 107-108.

Jim Vineyard and Jerry Falwell, *Winning Souls Through Buses* (Nashville: Impact Books, 1972).

William A. Powell, *Church Bus Evangelism* (Decatur, Georgia: Woodlawn Baptist Church, 1971).

Notes

1. Portions of this chapter were published under the title, "Some Ethical Considerations of the Church Bus Ministry, in *The Baptist Courier,* May 3, 1973, pp. 6-7. Also, the same article was published under the title, "Church Bus Evangelism: What Is Right? What Is Wrong?" in *The Baptist Program,* Sept., 1973, pp. 7-8.

2. Cited by Curtis Hutson, "Editor's Notes," *The Sword of the Lord,* Vol. XLVIII, No. 18, July 16, 1982, p. 2.

3. Elmer L. Towns, "What Happened to Sunday School Busing?" *Fundamentalist Journal,* Vol. 1, No. 1, Sept., 1982, p. 34.

4. Ibid., pp. 34-35.

5. See Curtis Hutson, "Editor's Notes," *The Sword of the Lord,* Vol. XLVIII, No. 18, July 16, 1982, p. 2.

6. Norman Jameson, "Church Busing: Boon and Bane in the 80s," *Missions U.S.A.,* Vol. 52, No. 6, Nov.-Dec., 1981, pp. 77-80.

7. George E. Sweazey, *Effective Evangelism* (New York: Harper & Brothers, 1953), p. 23.

8. Jonathan Edwards, *Edwards on Revivals* (New York: Dunning & Spalding, 1832). Both *A Faithful Narrative* and *Thoughts* are included in this volume.

9. Jonathan Edwards, *Religious Affections.* The Works of Jonathan Edwards, volume 2. Edited by John E. Smith (New Haven: Yale University Press, 1959).

24
Evangelizing Children

Psalm 78:1-8; Mark 10:13-16

Introduction

Many years ago as a young pastor I had a very young girl, about seven years of age, to come forward on a public confession of faith at a Sunday evening service. Her parents were not present. She was unable to articulate the answers to my questions. I had become extremely sensitive to guard against practicing a Baptist form of infant baptism. Therefore, I did not ask the church to vote on her immediately, as was our custom. Instead I indicated that I would talk further with her and her parents.

This case was further complicated by the fact that another girl, more mature and able to answer my questions satisfactorily, came making a confession of faith immediately prior to the seven-year-old. I did present the older girl to the church as a candidate for baptism.

Now in retrospect, I can see that I handled the situation very poorly. My intention was good, but my judgment was poor. Both the girl and her parents were offended. After all, there was an unwritten custom in that congregation that anyone making a public confession of faith was to be voted on right there on the spot. My actions were interpreted as publicly embarrassing both to the child and the parents.

Several years after I moved away from that pastorate, a pastor who followed me baptized that young lady. The story finally had a happy ending. Nevertheless, ever since that unpleasant incident, I have pondered the question of evangelizing children.

321

The Problem Stated

Theologically the problem focuses on the difference between a conversionist type of theology and a sacramental theology.[1] Baptists hold to a conversionist theology. For Baptists, the usual way to become a Christian is by conversion. Baptist theologian William L. Hendricks states the conversionist type of theology like this:

> There is a time when a child is not consciously a Christian. There is a time when the child, enabled by God's grace, becomes a Christian. Conversionist theology puts a large premium on grace, personal faith, believer's baptism, and the individual conscience . . . assumes an awareness of alienation from God, a recognition of God's provision for our salvation in Jesus Christ, and the cooperation of the human will with the divine will in effecting a conversion.[2]

Sacramental theology also has a conversionist principle, but conversion is gradual. "Sacramental theology stresses grace, infant baptism as a means of receiving grace, the corporate religions experience, and the rites of church tradition as further extending grace," according to Hendricks. Furthermore, in sacramental theology says Hendricks, "a child may be alienated from God by virtue of being born. But this alienation is overcome by infant baptism which places the child in grace."[3]

Melvin Douglas Clark reported in 1975 on his study of the evangelism of children among Southern Baptists. Clark's five conclusions were:

- While conversions of children nine to twelve years of age can be found sporadically throughout the nineteenth century, they became normative only at the close of that century.
- Conversions of children six to eight years old, as more than an extremely rare occurrence, have their origin at the beginning of the twentieth century.
- Professions of faith at ages four to five began to be

accepted about twenty-five years later.

- There is currently a tendency for the six to eight years to replace the nine to eleven years as the normative age for conversion experience.

- There has been in the past thirty-five years a decline of approximately three years in the average age at which persons are baptized in Southern Baptist churches.[4]

There is some evidence that Southern Baptists are now giving more attention to winning adults.[5] Nevertheless, Samuel Southard's statement remains unchallenged: "For the past sixty years there has been a steady drop in the chronological age at which churches will accept a child's accountability for sin."[6]

One big problem with child conversion is that psychological studies offer no support for responsible conversions at an early age.[7] Children are very literal minded until they are about ten or twelve. They take the words we say literally. If you talk with them about a lion preying on other animals, they may picture a lion sitting on a rhinoceros with her head bowed and praying. Piaget said children do not think symbolically.

Yet, some groups, such as Child Evangelism Fellowship[8] which reports outstanding success with children, use a great deal of symbolism. They make black stand for sin; white for purity; red for Christ's shed blood; clean hands for a good life; and dirty hands for the unregenerate life. "Young children simply cannot understand such symbolism," wrote Eugene Chamberlain.[9]

Sin, of course, is not abstract; but the concept of sinfulness is. There has to be a certain maturation of thought processes in order to understand the concept of sinfulness. If you ask a grade-school child what sin is, what kind of answer do you get? One nine-year-old suggested there are degrees of sin: "A sin is when you disrespect the law of God. There are big sins and little sins. Like when you beat up your sisters . . . that's a middle-sized one."[10]

Those of us who hold to a conversionist theology have to wrestle with several theological questions: When is a child ready for conversion? What is the status of the child who dies before conversion? Should children be required to conform to a particular adult crisis model in their conversion? Should children who are church members have the same rights, privileges, and responsibilities of all other church members?

Assumptions We May Make

We may assume that both the conversionist and the sacramental types of theology produce a sizable number of spiritual stillbirths. Hendricks said twenty-one of his eighty-one students in 1973 at Southwestern Baptist Theological Seminary in Fort Worth, Texas, were victims of a spiritual stillbirth when they were young. These students were baptized at an early age, reassured everything was OK, then left to flounder on their own.[11]

On the other hand, Southard cites a Lutheran study in which only 27 percent of 580 respondents who were baptized as infants remained in baptismal grace. Sixty-three percent of those respondents wrote they fell away from God and were converted in adolescence or adulthood.[12]

I think it is realistic and honest for us to assume that neither theological system for child evangelism is fail-safe.

We may assume that the idea of a hands-off policy toward child evangelism is not a viable option for us. "The world is unwilling to assume such a position of neutrality concerning our children," wrote Kenneth Chafin.[13] Furthermore, the majority of our members may now become Christians while they are yet children. A. C. Archibald, as far back as 1946, wrote:

> The most recent statistics reveal that about one-fourth of those joining the church do so while under twelve years of age. About one-half of our accessions are of people

between the ages of twelve and twenty. The median age of conversion seems to be around fourteen.[14]

The anonymous editors of a 1921 volume wrote: "It must be remembered that the majority of the human race die in childhood." They saw that as one reason for child evangelism. However, they made a stronger point for our involvement in child evangelism when they said: "Evangelism finds its finest and most fruitful field among the young life of the world, and the readiest and most eager response to the appeal of Jesus will ever be made by those who stand on the threshold of life."[15]

Jesus told his disciples not to hinder those who were bringing children to him. "Let the children come to me . . . for to such belongs the kingdom of God" (Mark 10:14). His was a hands-on policy rather than a hands-off one. We shall be wise to follow our Lord's example in our dealings with children.

We may assume that infants are safe in God's care and that children continue to be safe in God's care until they become capable of responsible decision making. The child is not "a miniature adult."[16] Infants and young children who die before they are capable of conversion go to heaven. They are a part of God's kingdom. Based on what the Bible tells us about the nature of God, he will not hold a young, immature child responsible for making a decision of which he is incapable.[17]

That nagging suspicion which says the Lord may not have the child's name if we haven't written it on our church roll may trace back to the postbiblical terms of "total depravity" and "original sin." Both Jeremiah and Ezekiel rejected the idea that guilt could be inherited.

It is safe to assume the covenant mercy of God toward infants and all very young children. God is more concerned about our children than we are. He can be trusted to deal adequately with those who have not yet reached accountability. Therefore, let us not become anxious and compulsive about their making professions of faith at very tender ages.

Another assumption which we may safely make is that there is no *one* age of accountability. "The time of accountability," wrote Hendricks, "is the moment of grace when one is brought to a decision for or against Christ by the Spirit."[18] Children reach an age of accountability at different chronological ages.

Polycarp became a Christian at age nine; Matthew Henry at age ten; Isaac Watts at age nine; and Jonathan Edwards at age seven.[19] Pastor William E. Hall of South Carolina said, "I knew well how to be saved at age 6."[20] Religious educator, R. Othal Feather told how his two sons were saved at the ages of eight and seven. "Age is no criterion for the conversion experience," said Feather, "although the great majority are brought under the convicting power of the Holy Spirit after nine or ten years of age and before they reach sixteen years if God's Spirit has a fair chance to deal with them."[21]

There can be no arbitrary age for the conversion of children. Some latch onto age twelve because that was the age of Jesus when he confounded the Temple teachers in Jerusalem (Luke 2:41-51). Occasionally there is a five-year-old, like Baker James Cauthen, who will become a Christian and never doubt it. But so far as I am concerned most children under nine are not evangelistic prospects. I don't think we ought to get uptight about unconverted children until they get to be eleven or twelve years old.

We may further assume that children who are accountable before God can experience genuine conversion. When they reach that level of maturity at which they can recognize their sin and come to Christ through his Spirit, they can and should be saved.[22] Charles H. Spurgeon was a strong believer in early conversions. He said, "Capacity for believing lies more in the child than in the man. We grow less rather than more capable of faith."[23]

You may ask, What does the child know about the deep things of God? Archibald answers: "Salvation is not wholly a thing of knowing. The child possesses that which is of more value to him than knowing, namely, intuition and teachableness. Children enjoy religion and their conversion is more likely to be real than that of adults."[24]

It would be wise for us always to respect the decision and confession of a child. We ought not to say, "Well he is so young he can do it again sometime." Every decision, contended Archibald, should be regarded as final and leading to public confession and baptism.[25] I agree, provided there has been proper counseling with those children and their parents.

Children should not be forced into a crisis-adult model of conversion. That is an assumption which will save us many headaches and some heartaches. The conversion experience which is appropriate for a tender-hearted twelve-year-old may not be appropriate for a hardened fifty-year-old. While there is not one gospel for adults and another for children, there are different models of conversion. Saul of Tarsus, who became Paul the apostle, represents one model of conversion. Timothy, Paul's son in the faith, represents a very different model.

Not every conversion is a crisis like Saul's. Some do have a crisis and enter the kingdom violently, as we might say. Others enter into the kingdom quietly through a process of Christian nurture. Their conversion is a radical turning from faith given to faith owned. They are represented by the young man who said: "My conversion to Christ was not a revolution, but an evolution. I don't really know the date when I became a Christian."

I know it is possible for us to idealize children and forget that they too have an innate tendency to sin. We may also lose sight of the power of the sinful environment in which children live.[26] They do have to repent of their sin and believe in Christ for themselves in order to be saved. But I know of no biblical requirement that they must have a

Damascus-road experience patterned after Saul's.

Observations on Child Conversion

We have stated the problem which those holding to a conversionist type of theology face in evangelizing children. We have attempted to spell out some assumptions which may be made about child evangelism. Now, let us register some observations which may help us to be more faithful in the task.

Some children who respond to a public invitation only want information or affirmation. A five-year-old boy came forward during the invitation one Sunday morning. His pastor asked him why he had come. The boy said, "I want you to see my new suit." Another boy came forward because he wanted to know where the bathroom was.

Every child who makes a decision toward Christ or the church, whether in public or in private, should be affirmed in that decision. W. A. Criswell, pastor of First Baptist Church, Dallas, always affirms any child who comes forward. He calls it a step toward God. But he does not baptize children under nine years of age. Criswell tells parents not to keep their children from going forward during the invitation.

Children who make public decisions should be affirmed and taken at face value. If the church has a policy never to present a child for baptism and church membership until a private conference is held with the child, preferably in the presence of one or both parents (or guardians), all parties involved will be spared unnecessary embarrassment.

My considered opinion is that everyone who comes forward should be joyfully welcomed. However, the wise church will have a policy which allows the vote to take place afterwards. That will especially allow a proper time to counsel with children and their parents.

The most fitting persons to introduce children to Christ are their own parents. There is (or ought to be) a difference between children who grow up in Christian homes and children who are reared in non-Christian homes. Household or *oikos* evangelism is the best kind for children. We are surely wrong when we shift responsibility for the spiritual life of children from the home to the church.

Perhaps you heard it said, "Win the child, win the family." That may be true in some cases. However, much sounder advice would be, "Win the parents, win the family." Where the society is still patriarchial we could say, "Win the man, win the family."

If the parents will not or cannot lead their children to Christ, then the children's Sunday School teachers are the key. Admittedly, parental responsibility comes first, but we have little or no control over that.

Pastor A. C. Archibald suggested that Sunday School teachers of older children utilize three approaches to winning their lost pupils to Christ and church membership. First, they can use their regular class lessons, especially capitalizing on the evangelistic values of lesson material. Second, they can use extra classroom endeavors, such as friendship gestures and occasional planned meetings with their children's parents (guardians). Third, they can hold one or two Decision Days each year in lieu of the regular class lessons and departmental meetings.[27]

Fear is often a real element in conversion, and I think especially in child conversions. One of my former students, who was converted at the age of seven, later looked back at his initial conversion experience and expressed that fear:

> Around the age of seven there were times at night that I could not go to sleep. I was scared! I did not know why I was scared. I was afraid that I would not wake up. This went on for a couple of months. After a while I became so afraid that I asked my parents about it. They knew what was bothering me. Mother and Daddy sat me down and talked to me and prayed with me about God. I knew I was not a bad boy, but I was lost without Jesus Christ as my personal Lord and Savior.[28]

Such fear should not be manipulated. However, it

should be acknowledged, owned, and dealt with lovingly in the power of the Holy Spirit.

When presenting the gospel to children, I prefer to use a little booklet such as "The Real Life."[29] It has diagrams, is multicolored, and uses Scriptures from *Today's English Version* of the Bible. The next best material to use is the child's own Bible.

Simplicity should be self-consciously sought in all child evangelism. Sam P. Jones felt that the greatest compliment he ever heard about his preaching came from a small boy on his first circuit. It was annual conference time. Jones was finishing up the year's work and getting ready to go to conference where the pastoral appointments would be made. The little boy said to his father: "I want Brother Jones to come back to our church. I can understand everything that he preaches."[30] Such simplicity is a goal after which every preacher should strive.

Keep in mind where children are in their mental development when you talk with them about becoming Christians. Ask probing questions which cannot be answered with yes or no. Avoid leading questions, such as You want to be saved, don't you? More appropriate statements might be:

Tell me how you feel.

Please tell me why you want to become a Christian.

What made you start thinking about this?

What do you think one has to do to become a Christian?

Conclusion

Those of us who aspire to evangelize children need to remember that tomorrow will come, and today will pass. Yet, more than that, the hearts of the young are as brittle as glass.

Suggestions for Further Reading

Gaines S. Dobbins, *Winning the Children* (Nashville: Broadman Press, 1953).

John H. Westerhoff, III, *Will Our Children Have Faith* (New York: The Seabury Press, 1976).

"Tell All the Little Children," Kenneth L. Chafin, *The Reluctant Witness* (Nashville: Broadman Press, 1974), pp. 88-103.

Clifford Ingle, ed., *Children and Conversion* (Nashville: Broadman Press, 1970).

Horace Bushnell, *Christian Nurture* (New Haven: Yale University Press, 1966 ed.).

Eugene Chamberlain, *When Can a Child Believe?* (Nashville: Broadman Press, 1973). Cos H. Davis, Jr. *Children and the Christian Faith* (Nashville: Broadman Press, 1979).

Notes

1. For a contrasting statement of the problem, see Samuel Southard, *Pastoral Evangelism* (Atlanta: John Knox Press, 1981 rev. ed.), pp. 72-75. Southard states the problem in terms of patience and responsibility.
2. William L. Hendricks, *A Theology for Children* (Nashville: Broadman Press, 1980), p. 15.
3. Ibid., p. 15.
4. Melvin Douglas Clark, "The Evangelism of Children: A Study in Southern Baptist Practice," *Search*, Vol. 5, No. 3, Spring, 1975, pp. 50-57, esp. p. 54. This article is an abstract of the author's unpublished STD thesis at The Southern Baptist Theological Seminary, Louisville, Ky.
5. Reginald M. McDonough, "Baptisms: Children and Adults," *The Baptist Program*, June-July, 1982, p. 27.
6. Southard, p. 75.
7. Ibid., p. 76.
8. Now located on a 660 acre headquarters in Warrenton, Missouri.
9. Eugene Chamberlain, *When Can a Child Believe?* (Nashville: Broadman Press, 1973), p. 27.
10. G. Temp Sparkman, "Baptists and Baptism," *The Christian Century*, Vol. XCIV, No. 13, April 13, 1977, pp. 349-350.
11. Baptist Press report, "Seminarian Says Young Children Risk Danger," *The Baptist Courier*, Vol. 106, No. 7, Feb. 14, 1974, pp. 5,10.
12. Southard, p. 73.
13. Kenneth L. Chafin, *The Reluctant Witness* (Nashville: Broadman Press, 1974), p. 92.
14. Arthur C. Archibald, *New Testament Evangelism: How It Works Today* (Philadelphia: The Judson Press, 1946), p. 121.
15. *Winning the Children for Christ* (Glasgow: Thomson & Cowan, 1924), pp. 11,13,9.
16. "The Child and the Home" in Clifford Ingle, ed., *Children and Conversion* (Nashville: Broadman Press, 1970), p. 125.

17. See the booklet by Robert G. Fulbright, *Winning Children to Christ* (Nashville: Baptist Sunday School Board, n. d.), p. 3.

18. William Hendricks, "The Age of Accountability," in Clifford Ingle, ed., p. 97.

19. Fulbright, p. 205.

20. "Letters to the Editor," *The Baptist Courier,* Vol. 106, No. 9, Feb. 28, 1974, p. 4.

21. R. Othal Feather, *Outreach Evangelism Through the Sunday School* (Nashville: Convention Press, 1972), p. 127.

22. Tal D. Bonham, "Pitfalls of Child Evangelism," *The Baptist Program,* January 1980, p. 6.

23. Quoted by Archibald, p. 124.

24. Ibid., p. 124.

25. Ibid., p. 125.

26. Gaines S. Dobbins, *Winning the Children* (Nashville: Broadman Press, 1953), p. 51.

27. Archibald, pp. 124-131,122.

28. Lowell Gregg Whitson, "My Autobiography and How It Relates to the Gospel Story," an unpublished research paper done for my course, M 4500, Basic Evangelism, at Southeastern Baptist Theological Seminary, fall, 1981. See esp. p. 3.

29. "The Real Life" booklet is a cost item available from the Home Mission Board, 1350 Spring Street, NW, Atlanta, Ga. 30309.

30. Mrs. Sam P. Jones and Walt Holcomb, *The Life and Sayings of Sam P. Jones* (Atlanta, Ga.: The Franklin-Turner Co., 1907, 2nd rev. ed.,), p. 65.

25
Evangelizing the Cults

Jeremiah 14:13-16; 1 John 4:1-6

Introduction

The time was a Sunday afternoon in 1981. While the place happened to be a beautiful suburb in Wilmington, North Carolina, it might well have been Anytown, USA. Two young men rang the doorbell. Both were well dressed, well mannered, and carried genuine leather cases in their hands. They did not travel on bicycles. Nor were they members of the Church of Jesus Christ of Latter Day Saints. They were, in fact, two Jehovah's Witnesses. One was seventeen, and the other was just two months shy of his thirteenth birthday.

Would you believe that the chief spokesperson was the twelve-year-old? He was extremely articulate, very well trained, and perfectly poised.

The man who answered the doorbell invited them inside. What did they want? They wanted to sell some magazines put out by the Watchtower Society. The man excused himself to get some change. He purchased each of the two magazines for a total of thirty cents. Then, he gave them an adult Sunday School quarterly which dealt with the Gospel of Matthew. That was all he could find at that moment. Next, he engaged the two in conversation.

He promised to read their literature if they would read his. They talked about how bad the world is getting and what persons need to do to escape the coming judgment. The kind of being Jehovah God is and who Jesus Christ is were also discussed. Never had this man encountered two young men so well versed in their faith and so able to dialogue with him.

If some cultists like that haven't yet rung your doorbell, they probably will. Just give them time.

I have been struck with a statement by Lloyd Whyte, who works with the Interfaith Witness Department of the Southern Baptist Home Mission Board. Whyte said, "If you could get the average born-again Baptist to give his time to door-to-door visitation, we would have the greatest revival in the history of mankind."

Whyte made that statement against the background of tireless visitation by the Jehovah Witnesses and the Mormons. According to Whyte, the cults are growing by sheer hard work and volume. He attributes their growth to continued visitation efforts. Over against that persistent visitation, Whyte says of Southern Baptists, "We've got the people, but we're not witnessing 10 hours a month."[1]

Make whatever allowances you must for overstatement by Whyte. The fact remains that too few Christians are ringing too few doorbells and pounding the pavement too infrequently.

Evangelizing the cults is now an important agenda item for the churches. Thirty years ago Walter Martin, who has engaged in three decades of battle with the cults, said that most churches would not take him seriously. Today, Martin and others have more calls for help and information than they can begin to answer.[2]

Signs of a Cult

By cults I mean Christian deviations—or alternatives to the style of Christian discipleship set forth in the New Testament. I do not use the word *sect* because it is primarily a sociological term and is too often confused in speech with *sex*.

A keen observer has pointed out nine signs of a cult as follows:

- Cult leaders claim authority by a direct revelation from God (that is, "God spoke to me," "God appeared to me," "God anointed me!")

- Salvation is by works rather than faith. The follower works out his salvation by such things as attending meetings and begging or selling on the street.
- There is usually a messianic component. Some persons, usually the leader, have been especially appointed by God for this time. His or her authority is God-given and may not be questioned or violated.
- The system of doctrine is ambiguous. It means whatever the leader says it means. It often changes and sometimes contradicts itself with each new situation or revelation.
- All who do not believe are denounced. Those who actively oppose are agents of Satan or the Antichrist.
- Members are given special secret information which is not available to outsiders. They exhibit a type of Neognosticism.
- Bible verses and other sacred writings are isolated from context and reinterpreted.
- Often there is financial exploitation. There are continuous calls for money, money, and more money.
- Members are often made dependent on the leader or the cult not only for spiritual needs but also for the physical and emotional necessities of life.[3]

Some questions which we may ask in order to determine whether a group is a cult are: Is there a totalitarian leader? Do they have an extrabiblical source of authority? Do the members make value judgments for themselves? Do they believe the end justifies the means? Do they fear those who do not share their beliefs? Do they see themselves as the exclusive community of the saved? Do they believe their group has a central role in eschatology? Do they devalue Jesus Christ?[4]

One additional point may be helpful in recognizing cults. Most members of cults are "comeouters" from other religious groups. "It is significant that they first approach known Christians," said theologian Carl F. H. Henry. "Seldom do they attempt to reach the unevangelized, which

should be the first step in any genuine missionary program."[5]

Unpaid Bills of the Churches

The first and most important thing I should like to say
about evangelizing the cults is that we should recognize them
as the unpaid bills of the churches. J. K. Van Baalen in his
now famous book on *The Chaos of the Cults* said the cults
result from "the unpaid bills of the churches."[6]

Heinz Horst Shrey, a German scholar, is even stronger
in saying we ought not to so much seek to convert the cults as
to convert ourselves! Shrey thinks that is the only attitude we
can assume.[7]

Shrey overstates his point. We do need to convert the
members of cults; but we also need to learn some things
about ourselves from them.

What are some of the unpaid bills of the churches which
the cults seek to pay? Whether we like it or not, the cults are
ministering to some real needs of many persons.

One of these unpaid bills is the identity, meaning, and
purpose which the cults give to society's shutouts and
dropouts. Jehovah's Witnesses have always directed their
outreach to the poor, the disenfranchised, the uneducated,
and the marginal citizens of society. In the case of Jehovah's
Witnesses, the whole cult is composed of society's shutouts
and dropouts.

Yet, how many of our churches ignore or disdain those
in the lower economic classes? When I became pastor of a
church many years ago, I was told that there were very few
prospects for membership in that church. I soon personally
discovered more than seventy-six prospects living in that
immediate community. They were unemployed, under-
employed, bootleggers, alcoholics, prostitutes, and invalids,
the kind of folk called "poor white trash" in the movie *Gone
with the Wind*.

Such persons are the unpaid bills of the churches. May

God forgive us for overlooking such folk in our selective evangelism!

A second unpaid bill of the churches is our racial prejudice toward blacks and minority races. The Black Muslims, who now call themselves the American Muslim Mission, was founded by Elijah Muhammed who was born Elijah Poole in Sandersville, Georgia, the son of a black Baptist preacher who was hanged by a white mob.[8] One of the most moving books I've ever read was *The Autobiography of Malcolm X*.[9] Malcolm X probably made more converts to the Black Muslim cult while he was behind bars than some of us have made in all of our years as free people. Malcolm X had more to do with the conversion of Cassius Clay (now Muhammed Ali) to the Black Muslims than any other man. If the Christian churches had been faithful to their Lord in their attitudes and dealings with America's blacks, I don't believe the Black Muslims would have ever started.

It grieves my heart to see blacks and whites worshiping together in practically every Kingdom Hall of the Jehovah's Witnesses because I know there are white churches where blacks are not welcome. If we were as concerned about being Christian and evangelizing the blacks of America as we are about evangelizing the blacks in Africa, we might not have this unpaid racial bill.

A third unpaid bill which is rapidly coming due in our churches is our attitude toward women. The cults, by and large, recognize the role of the woman in their life and work. Christian Science was founded by Mrs. Mary Baker Eddy. More than two-thirds of the official Christian Science practitioners are women. Emma Hale Smith was prominent in founding the Reorganized Church of Jesus Christ of the Latter Day Saints with headquarters in Independence, Missouri. Mrs. Ellen G. White played a large role in Seventh Day Adventism. Myrtle Fillmore, along with her husband, started the Unity School of Christianity. Susan B. Anthony was a prominent female leader among the Unitarians. It is no

accident that 12 percent of all settled ministers in the
Unitarian Universalist Association are females. Also, slightly
more than half of that denomination's 190 theological students are women.[10]

Yet, here we are in the mainline churches arguing over
whether a woman can be (or should be) a deacon or a
preacher. I recall some years ago how a large church refused
to let a female missionary speak in their pulpit on a Sunday
morning in a World Missions Conference. It was all right for
this servant of God to represent her denomination in Africa,
but our cultural bondage made us conclude that she would
desecrate the pulpit of that beautiful Gothic sanctuary.

A fourth unpaid bill of the churches has to do with our
antiintellectualism. Persons do have minds as well as hearts.
The Unitarian-Universalist cult recognizes that fact and
siphons off many of our brightest young men and women.
Christian Science has a powerful appeal to the intellect. It is
the only American cult which publishes a high-quality
newspaper and provides free reading rooms in every major
city in this country. Carl F. H. Henry, founding editor of
Christianity Today, has pointed out repeatedly that one of the
greatest dangers faced by evangelicals is their antiintellectualism. Especially in our day when so many citizens are earning
diplomas and degrees, we must not neglect the minds of
persons. The late C. S. Lewis, an outstanding Christian
intellectual and writing apologist for the faith, will in my
judgment go down in church history as one of the greatest
evangelists of the twentieth century.

A fifth unpaid bill of the churches is the limited and
often sloppy use which we make of such modern tech-
nologies as the telephone. At Lee's Summit, Missouri, the
Unity School of Christianity has someone on duty seven days
a week, twenty-four hours a day, to answer a toll-free
telephone for prayer and counseling to help persons with
real or imagined needs—anywhere and anytime. Almost
any church could install a telephone and tend it day and

night around the clock to pray for persons, to counsel them with their problems, and to mobilize immediate assistance for those in need. The widespread use of Dial-a-Prayer telephones suggests to us that persons may respond even more readily to a real live voice.

An intelligent and wholesome evangelism acknowledges that many of the cults, and perhaps some of the world religions like Islam, represent to a frightening extent the unpaid bills of the churches. It is said that the young man Muhammad (AD 570-632), living in the city of Mecca, was a great seeker after God. He wanted to find God. That was his preoccupation. And in those days there were both Jews and Christians in his hometown.

Muhammad first went to the Jews to find out about God. But they made fun of him and laughed at him. Then, he went to the Christians to find a way to an experience of God. Would you believe that he could find no Christian who could plainly tell him how to find God? They only told Muhammad about their theological opinions concerning the two natures of Christ. He turned away in disgust. The rest of that story is a trail of blood and tears, which spans all the centuries since the seventh, up to this present time. A new chapter to the story is even now being written in the Middle East.[11]

Once-, Twice- and Thrice-Born Types

The second suggestion I have about evangelizing the cults is the recognition that there appears to be three major types of religious experience among humans: the once-born type, the twice-born type, and the thrice-born type.

William James's famous and widely quoted book on *The Varieties of Religious Experience* identified two major categories of religious experience: the once born which he illustrated with the Christian Scientist and the twice born which he illustrated with Saul of Tarsus who became Paul the apostle to the Gentiles.[12]

I want to add a third major type to the two upon which James rang the changes. I call it the thrice born. We have to recall that James was writing around the turn of the century—near the end of the nineteenth and the beginning of the twentieth century. What Henry Pitt Van Dusen, John Mackay, and Bishop Lesslie Newbigin called a "third force" in Christendom had not yet developed. I refer to the Pentecostal and Neopentecostal phenomenon. Also, we must remember that Van Dusen lumps many of the cults with what he calls the "third force."[13] Indeed, the cults have become significant numerically only in this twentieth century.

W. E. Boardman in *The Higher Christian Life* helps illustrate what I mean by the "thrice-born" type of religious experience in his discussion of two conversions. Boardman posits two conversions illustrated by a familiar line from the hymn, "Rock of Ages." The line says: "Be of sin the double cure, Save from wrath and make me pure." The "double cure" represents to Boardman the two conversions. The "save from wrath" equals the first conversion and the "make me pure" equals the second.[14]

Boardman's first conversion is equivalent to what evangelicals call the new birth or the second birth or regeneration. Also, it is essentially what James called the twice-born type religious experience. His second conversion is what the Holiness-type groups call sanctification. If James's typology were extended, we might label it the thrice-born type of religious experience. Then, along came Pentecostalism with its doctrine of the baptism in the Holy Spirit. Couple that with the "higher" or "deeper" life emphasis of Boardman, and you truly have what Frederick Dale Bruner calls subsequent experience theology![15] Indeed, there is a significant number of persons, particularly among the Holiness, Pentecostal, Neopentecostal, and "deeper life" Christians, who espouse what I call the thrice-born type of religious experience.

Most cults fall into either the once-born type or the thrice-born type. An example of the once-born type cult is Christian Science. Actually all of the science-styled cults, those who exalt the metaphysical and debase the physical, belong to the once-born type. This includes the School of Unity, Theosophy, Zen Buddhism, and Unitarian Universalists.

Examples of the thrice-born type cults are Jehovah's Witnesses; the Unification Church; The Children of God; The Way, International; the Local Church (of Witness Lee); The Church of Jesus Christ of the Latter Day Saints; the Peoples' Temple; etc.

I see both the once-born type cults and the thrice-born type as Neognostics. So, what we are dealing with in seeking to convert the cults is two different mind-sets—one which sees no need for the new birth and the other which feels strongly the need for a third birth. Actually, you may have an emphasis on rebirth in some cults almost to the extent that life itself becomes a series of rebirths—a series of reincarnations in the course of one life as it were.

In the case of the once-born type cultist, we have to convince the adherent of the absolute necessity and the real possibility of the new birth—of regeneration. But in the case of the cultist who has already gone through both a second birth and even a third or fourth birth, we have to convince the adherent of the efficacy, power, and sufficiency of an authentic second birth. It may well be that in all of the adherent's births, except the first which was physical, he or she was only stillborn. One may have sought to birth the cultist through violence to his or her personhood.

If the above is valid, the implications for our evangelism are: (1) we should preach, teach, and talk the necessity and possibility of the new creation; and, (2) we should preach, teach, and bear witness to the sufficiency and power of the second birth. One of the problems with which the cults confront us is the superficiality of our Christian education processes in teaching and learning our Christian doctrine.

Other Clues

If we are to successfully evangelize the cults, the following clues may serve as guides in our task:

- Direct your evangelism toward all persons who live around you and near you.
- Direct your ministry toward the whole person in all of his or her needs and concerns and toward the whole family with all of its members in season and out of season.
- Endeavor to determine the basic type of religious experience with which you are dealing—whether the once-born or the thrice-born type.
- Enter into dialogue with cultists. Invite them into your home and church. Ask them their names. Listen to their message. Buy their literature and study it. Be kind to them. Study the Bible with them.
- Use cultivation and demonstration evangelism with the cultist. Incarnate God's love and your love for the cultist.
- Present appropriate gifts to cultists, such as a modern translation of the Bible or a book or tract which may speak to their particular needs. For example, C. S. Lewis' *Mere Christianity*[16] and *Surprised by Joy*[17] may be appropriate for a bright mind caught in the clutches of Unitarian-Universalism or Moonism. A copy of your church or denominational creed, articles of faith, or covenant may be helpful.
- Take with radical seriousness the priesthood of each believer and give all persons in the church a task to do which matches their spiritual gifts.

Conclusion

According to the latest Gallup Youth Survey as many as 500 thousand teens may be involved in the "Moonies" movement. That is 2 percent of the total US teen population.[18] We may want to put down the cults for their aggressiveness in going and making contacts for their faith. But what have we done? What are we doing? Are we going? Are we making contacts with others in order to share our faith? Some heretical cults like the Mormons and Jehovah's Witnesses are telling persons who Jesus is not. We need to tell them who Jesus is.

Christians have nothing to fear from the zeal and competition of the cults. But we do have much to fear from our own apathy and lethargy in this vital area of evangelistic concern.

Suggested Study Questions

1. Analyze the opening illustration used in this chapter. Why would a twelve-year-old Jehovah's Witness be so articulate about his faith? Is it appropriate for twelve- and seventeen-year-olds to propagate their faith? How do you feel about the actions of the man whom they visited?

2. Write up in several paragraphs one encounter, confrontation, visit, or conversation which you have had with a cultist. Then, use the resources of this chapter to evaluate that experience.

3. Select from the signs of a cult in this chapter the four which you consider most revealing. Try to illustrate each of your four signs with one or more actual examples from the cults.

4. List three "unpaid bills" which, if your local church does not pay, some cult may pay for you.

5. Explain what you think the author means by the term *thrice born* as it applies to evangelizing cultists.

Notes

1. "Cultists Surpass Baptists in Zeal," *The Word and Way,* Vol. 118, No. 20, May 14, 1981, p. 8.

2. Rodney Clapp, "Cults: 'A Reality That Has Staggered Our Imaginations,'" *Christianity Today,* Vol. XXVI, No. 1, Jan. 1, 1982, pp. 50, 56.

3. This is a slightly revised list, made in an unpublished paper by Donald J. Welch, the Methodist Campus Minister at Wofford College, Spartanburg, South Carolina, in November, 1976.

4. For a different list of such questions, see Gordon R. Lewis, *Confronting the Cults* (Philadelphia: Presbyterian and Reformed Publishing Co., 1966), pp. 6-7.

5. Carl F. H. Henry, "The Challenge of the Cults," in a *Christianity Today* symposium, *The Challenge of the Cults* (Grand Rapids: Zondervan Publishing House, 1961), pp. 74-75.

6. J. K. Van Baalen, *The Chaos of the Cults* (Grand Rapids: William B. Eerdmans Publishing Co., 1938). This original edition has undergone several revisions. M. Thomas Starkes, *Confronting Popular Cults* (Nashville: Broadman Press, 1972), pp. 9-12.

7. Lewis, p. 9.

8. Starkes, p. 73.

9. Malcolm Little, *The Autobiography of Malcolm X* (New York: Grove Press, Inc., 1966).

10. "UU Ministry Has 100 Women in Fellowship," *Unitarian Universalist World,* Vol. 12, No. 1, Jan. 15, 1981, p. 3.

11. Some of the above two paragraphs is based on Akbar Haqq's "The Two-Fold Mission of the Church," an unpublished and undated message delivered to a Billy Graham School of Evangelism. See esp. pp. 6-7.

12. William James, *The Varieties of Religious Experience* (New Hyde Park, New York: University Books, 1963), pp. 80, 166, 363, 488.

13. Frederick Dale Brunner, *A Theology of the Holy Spirit* (Grand Rapids: William B. Eerdmans Publisher, 1970), pp. 29-32.

14. Ibid., pp. 43-44, 62.

15. Ibid., pp. 62-63.

16. C. S. Lewis, *Mere Christianity* (New York: Macmillan Publishing Co., Inc., 1960 ed.).

17. C. S. Lewis, *Surprised by Joy* (London: Collins, Fontana Books ed., 1959).

18. Cited in *R D Digest,* Vol. IV, No. 3, March, 1982, p. 3, a publication of the Research Division of the Home Mission Board of the SBC.

26
Evangelistic Bible Studies

Isaiah 53:7-9; Acts 8:26-40

Introduction

Bible studies can be used to bring the undiscipled to belief in Jesus Christ. Hundreds of persons, especially adults, have been introduced to Christ through small-group Bible studies during the last two decades. Marilyn G. Kunz, a cofounder of Neighborhood Bible Studies, Inc., says: "It has been for many the appropriate means of evangelism to reach first their minds, then their hearts, and finally their wills."[1]

Peer Bible Study Groups

What I am talking about is a group of six to eight persons. The ideal size is eight, but a group of six to ten can function well. If the group is married couples, it could go up to six or seven couples, but not more. One's commitment to the group will often diminish if the size goes beyond eight or ten persons. This is a group of peers from one's neighborhood, office, factory, school, or club.

Preferably, a group of eight would have two Christians who have some experience in Bible study and six who are beginners. If the ratio is reversed, group interaction will be adversely affected. Christians in the group should not smother the non-Christians. Nor should the Christians come on so strongly that they tend to "freeze" or "squeeze" out the searchers.

There might be a "leader," provided he or she does not dominate or stifle the group. Leadership may be rotated.

345

But if that happens in such a way that an observer would say members took turns being the "teacher," a poor pattern has developed. What we desire is a pattern of discussion which resembles an asterisk, rather than a fan in which all responses come back to the designated leader.

It is important to emphasize that there are no experts in this Bible study group. The initiator should emphasize this to prospective participants. If the initiators bowl the group over with their Bible knowledge, group members will clam up. No one will readily volunteer to lead the discussion next week if the first leader sets a pattern which others feel they can't match.

What we are after is group discussion and participation. One television program on educational excellence showed a large poster which read:

I hear .... I forget
I see   .... I remember
I do   .... I understand

Those who take their turn chairing the group Bible study will "see" and "remember." They will "do" and "understand."

Another facet of the peer Bible study group is to use the inductive rather than the deductive approach. An inductive method of study is investigative, whereas the deductive method begins with generalizations. Avoid exchanges over how the group feels about the Bible passage under study. Approach a passage of Scripture like a good detective would. Begin by observing the clues, and close by making applications to the present-day life of the group. Encourage each group member to ask of the passage *who, what, when,* and *where.* Then ask the question in conclusion, What difference should this make in my life?

The Gospel of Mark is a good beginning place. Take one chapter a week. Cover the whole chapter. Do not jump about for supporting texts from elsewhere in the Bible. Once you have covered chapter 1 of Mark, you can always go back to it. But don't go beyond your frame of reference in that group's study. Keep to this pattern of studying in context. That will condition newcomers to the approach.

Avoid tangents and debates. This, for example, is not a proper place to debate predestination. Let the Bible text under discussion be your authority.

Believe that the discussion mode is important for evangelization because it helps create an atmosphere for change. Our goal is not merely to impart information; we want to effect transformation and to bring about a change in understanding, life-style, and life direction. A change of mind and heart and life is what we are after.

Such inductive Bible study encourages a church to grow in knowledge and understanding through the participation of its members and to grow in numbers as new persons are reached through Bible study. Your first peer Bible study group might become the pilot group for a whole network. Methods and other resources are available, and the pattern is reproducible.[2]

Bible Readings

Another approach to evangelistic Bible studies has been perfected by one denomination for more than a century. Seventh-Day Adventists, under the leadership of Stephen N. Haskell, adopted a catechistic method of Bible instruction in 1883. That method of Bible instruction evolved quickly into a prebaptismal and premembership curricula for both evangelistic and educational purposes. Both pastors and lay leaders used these "Bible studies" to give premembership instruction to prospective church members.

Haskell conducted a ten-day training institute in Battle Creek, Michigan, in 1883 to equip men and women in the work of Bible readings. That institute began with an attendance of 300, which swelled to well over 1,000 by its final days. Those 1,000-plus participants, included "many of the citizens" of Battle Creek. So, evidently not a few lay Christians were involved.

This ground swell of success with the question-and-answer method of Bible study led to increased emphasis upon it. A variety of Adventist schools and summer institutes offered courses on how to give Bible readings. Even "city missions" were held on the work of giving Bible readings. Haskell, himself, led many of these institutes and missions.

By 1980 these "Bible studies" had become so popular and widespread that a new one began on the average of about every three seconds of every minute of every hour of every day of every year since 1969. Adventists frequently call this particular method of one layperson studying the Bible with a nonmember, "Bible Readings." During the period of 1969-1979, over ninety-seven million of these studies were conducted worldwide. Over seven million were in North America. That means that worldwide some 26,575 such Bible studies took place each day.[3] Therefore, lay "Bible Readings" are a potent evangelistic tool among Seventh-Day Adventists.

This is not an appropriate place to enter into argument over whether Seventh-Day Adventists are evangelicals or cultists.[4] Whatever they are, they have some things to teach us about intentional, carefully prepared, one-on-one evangelistic Bible study. So much of our Bible study has been in small groups that most of us have little or no experience teaching unbelievers one-on-one in our homes or in other appropriate settings.

Ballroom Bible Class

Pastor Marshall Edwards of First Baptist Church, Columbia, South Carolina, introduced a new ministry to that city in 1981. It is called Wholeness of Life and is, in essence, taking Bible study to the marketplace. One day a week for five months each year Edwards gathers the city's business and civic leaders at the Wade Hampton Hotel's ballroom for a quick lunch and an expository study of selected Bible passages. The first meeting was prepared for five hundred, but one thousand persons came.[5] Perhaps this is something you could try in your city or town.

The ballroom Bible class could supplement Sunday School Bible classes. It has high potential for adding to a church's visibility in the city. Some unbelievers will more readily attend it because it is conducted on their turf or neutral ground rather than on church premises. Doubtlessly, Christians will find it a bit easier to bring their lost friends with them to such a setting. The teacher of the class may also build some relationships with the unchurched through this approach. I see it as soft-sell, relational, marketplace evangelism which magnifies Christian presence, affords opportunities for Christian proclamation, and enhances Christian persuasion.

Bible Studies in House Churches

Home Bible studies were about the only evangelistic strategy available in mainland China from 1949 almost to the present. Believers banished to Inner Mongolia during the Mao reign started home Bible studies which became and continue as house churches. These few Christians have now grown to more than twelve hundred, meeting in more than forty house churches. Twenty smaller house churches are now intentionally seeking to convert the 2.6 million indigenous Mongolians of Inner Mongolia.[6]

Jonathan Chao, director of the Chinese Research Center in Hong Kong, thinks the house church movement in mainland China is beginning to transform the entire nation. Chao estimates that there are from twenty-five to fifty million believers in China's house churches.

Three facts stand out about these house churches. First, some of them began long before the government completely took over the churches in 1954. They are an extension of the independent church movement in China that began in 1911. The Jesus Church was organized in 1917, the Jesus Family in 1926, and Watchman Nee's "Little Flock" in 1928. Second, they are predominantly a lay movement. Even female leaders loom large in some of them. Third, they have thrived under persecution.[7]

Although these home Bible studies are not identical with so-called "house churches," they do have some similarities. Raymond Fung in his book, *Households of God on China's Soil,* tells many stories about "how small Christian communities, through one of the most radical upheavals in human history, kept their faith in Jesus Christ—and how their faith kept them."[8] The church in mainland China would not have survived, let alone thrived, apart from home Bible studies.

It should surprise none of us that many new churches in the United States began as home Bible study groups. Both the birthing of disciples and the birthing of churches are natural results of Bible study.

Some churches are now intentionally starting home Bible studies which will grow into small house churches rather than into large, traditional congregations. Gambrell Street Baptist Church in Fort Worth, Texas, has started several such house churches. These congregations are designed to reach persons who are "turned off" by the more traditional church. About fifty members seems to be the leveling off point for them.

Members come dressed casually in jeans and slacks. Certain persons seem to respond better to such small, informal gatherings. These churches are autonomous congregations. They tend to be more like a family, with the worship services resembling a family reunion. Everyone knows each other and actively participates.[9]

Nor should we think that home Bible studies are limited to any one branch of Christendom. A Roman Catholic home Bible study magazine has topped the 200,000 subscription mark in its first two years of existence. *Share the Word,* a monthly sixty-four-page magazine, is published by Paulist

Catholic Evangelization Center and is supported by free-will offerings.[10]

Christian Day Schools

Christian day schools or academies are a controversial trend which should be tied to evangelistic Bible studies. Lyle E. Schaller in a 1982 article refers to the proliferation of such schools. He thinks their existence is a foregone conclusion.[11]

Some churches have shifted from a bus ministry to Christian academies. Most of the Christian academies are evangelical. By the end of the 1970s, between seven hundred and eight hundred new private Christian elementary or high schools were being founded each year. Two-thirds of the more than five and a half million students now enrolled in private elementary and secondary schools are in schools which label themselves "Christian."[12]

Christian day schools are growing rapidly. The Association of Christian Schools International indicated that such schools were growing at the rate of three per day in 1981, with an estimated one million students in about ten thousand schools.

The Kansas City area of Missouri, for example, had 1 Christian day school in 1968, with 118 pupils. There were 22 schools in 1981, with about 6,000 students.

Kansas had sixty-five Christian day schools in 1981. Missouri had eighty-five. Most of these were begun in the past several years.[13]

These schools began to mushroom in the South during the decades of the 1960s and 1970s. Many of them were apparent refuges for white supremists. Now, however, the situation is much more complicated. Kent R. Hunter, a Missouri Synod Lutheran authority on church growth, believes "the most significant force influencing the growth of outreach in Christian schools has been the increasing discontent of unchurched people with public education."[14]

A new factor has entered the picture with Christian day schools. Unchurched parents are now lining up to enroll their children in Christian schools. These schools are forming "a new and exciting horizon of opportunity to reach children—whole families—with the gospel of Jesus Christ."[15]

Two missiological principles seem to lie at the heart of this new opportunity in Christian day schools. These schools are meeting a felt need, which makes persons more receptive to the gospel. Many parents are grateful for an educational alternative. Furthermore, a web movement is possible in this kind of school. We know that 70 to 90 percent of all Christians trace their entrance into a church to the influence of a friend or relative. One Lutheran church in Detroit quadrupled baptisms when that congregation used the natural bridges of opportunity afforded by the Christian day school.[16]

According to Kent R. Hunter, director of the Church Growth Analysis and Learning Center in Detroit, Michigan, the Christian day school should be a vehicle for evangelism as well as an agency of nurture. The staff can be trained for evangelism. Their job descriptions can be written so as to go beyond the walls of the classroom. The schools are to be viewed as the church in action and not as a separate agency or arm of the church. Hunter, in short, sees the purpose of these academies as fulfilling the Great Commission to make disciples.[17]

If "a new Christian school is now opening on the average of every seven hours,"[18] and if the philosophy of the Christian day school expressed by Hunter takes hold, a new approach to evangelism will have been created. This new technique may indeed replace the bus ministry phenomenon which flourished in the 1970s.

Whatever else the Christian academy teaches, presumably it teaches the Bible. Whenever that teaching is tied intentionally to evangelism, we have evangelistic Bible study.

Conclusion

An elderly statesman of evangelism from Mexico was once asked, "What is an effective evangelistic method that you've used?" His answer was "distribute the Bible." That wise old gentleman pointed out that all Christians can distribute the Bible. Then he went on to tell the following story.

Years ago near Tampico, a colporteur selling Bibles was attacked by fanatics and his Bibles were destroyed. Some Indians, watching, realized the problems started just because of the book. They picked up some of the charred pieces and took them to a village leader, who recognized them as coming from the Bible. "When I was in the hospital, I was visited by a woman who gave me this book," the leader said. Those Indians got hold of a Bible and that was the beginning of practically the conversion of a whole village. The Indians thought if that book was worth fighting for that it must be worth something.[19]

Suggested Study Questions

1. Sketch on one page in outline form with brief notations what you consider to be the main features of peer Bible study groups.
2. If Bible readings are so old, why do you think we know so little about them?
3. What do you consider to be the minimum requirements for conducting a ballroom Bible class in a town or city?
4. What do we know about Bible studies in house churches on mainland China?
5. How do you relate Christian day schools to evangelistic Bible study?

Notes

1. Marilyn Kunz, "Bible Studies that Bring Them to Belief," *Christianity Today*, Vol. XXV, No. 17, Oct. 2, 1981, p. 20.

2. Ibid., pp. 20-23. I am indebted to Kunz's excellent article for much of the above material.

3. Gordon R. Mattison, *Seventh-Day Adventist Premembership Curriculum: An Alternative Model*, pp. 1-17. An unpublished Doctor of Ministry project at San Francisco Theological Seminary, San Anselmo, Calif., 1981.

4. See the dialogue between Kenneth Chafin and Thomas Starkes, "Interfaith Witness/ Evangelism—An Interrelationship," in *Resource Booklet: Concepts of Interfaith Witness* (Atlanta, Georgia: Home Mission Board of S.B.C., 1972), p. 8. "I can show you a stack of thirty books that say . . . Seventh-Day Adventists are Christian or evangelical, whatever term the author chooses to use. And I can show you another stack that say they are pseudo-evangelical or non-evangelical or non-Christian," said Starkes.

5. See the editorial, "Wholeness of Life," *Baptist Courier*, Vol. 113, No. 36, Sept. 17, 1981, p. 3.

6. David Yat-Ping Wang, "House Churches Grew in China's 'Dumping Ground,'" *Global Church Growth Bulletin*, Vol. XIX, No. 3, May-June, 1982, pp. 186-188.

7. Jonathan Chao, "Churches in China: Flourishing from House to House," *Christianity Today*, Vol. XXVI, No. 11, June 18, 1982, pp. 24-26.

8. *A Monthly Letter on Evangelism*, No. 8, August, 1982, p. 10, World Council of Churches, Commission on World Mission and Evangelism.

9. "Turned Off by Traditional Church, They Get Another," *Baptist Courier*, Vol. 113, No. 36, Sept. 17, 1981, p. 13.

10. Reported in *World Evangelization*, Information Bulletin No. 27, June, 1982, p. 15, a publication of the Lausanne Committee for World Evangelization.

11. "A Look at the Local Church of the Future," *Christianity Today*, Vol. XXVI, No. 4, Feb. 19, 1982, p. 30.

12. Richard G. Hutcheson, Jr., "Where Have All the Young Folks Gone?" *Christianity Today*, Vol. XXV, No. 19, Nov. 6, 1981, p. 33.

13. Helen T. Gray, "Christian Teachers Say Sense of Mission Outweighs Financial Loss," *The Kansas City Times*, May 23, 1981, p. C-13.

14. Kent R. Hunter, "Christian Day Schools: An Open Door to the Unchurched," *Christianity Today*, Vol. XXV, No. 10, May 29, 1981, p. 18.

15. Ibid., p. 18.

16. Ibid., pp. 18-19.

17. Ibid., pp. 19 and 21.

18. Ibid., p. 18.

19. See the interview by John Maust, "An Interview with Gonzalo Baez-Camargo: Mexico's Grand Old Man of Evangelism," *Christianity Today*, Vol. XXVI, No. 5, March 5, 1982, p. 30.

27
Follow-Up and Conservation

Psalm 119:105; Philemon 4-22

Introduction

Follow-up and conservation are what George Sweazey called "the second half of evangelism."[1] Evangelism is never complete until the evangelized turn to Jesus Christ, some local church, the Christian ethic, and the Christian world mission.

"Follow-up evangelism," wrote Pastor W. Hal Brooks, "is the work of a local church in protecting, training, and guiding a 'babe in Christ' in order that he may develop into a growing, useful, victorious Christian in every area of life."[2] I have heard D. James Kennedy, the founder of Evangelism Explosion, say: "Follow-up never ends."

The goal of evangelism is to make disciples. "A disciple is a functionally mature, responsible reproducing member of a local church," according to Kennedy.[3]

One evangelist who has committed his whole ministry to follow-up has said, "It needs to be understood that evangelism's most persistent enemy is poorly planned and poorly executed follow-up." Billie Hanks, Jr., calls this "the unsolved problem of evangelism worldwide." Hanks continues, "Too few are doing the work of many in evangelism."[4] Our members settle into a life of churchmanship rather than a life of disciple making.

I have observed that we are losing about one half of all our converts. Typically, one out of every two persons who joins a Southern Baptist church is lost to meaningful service.[5] The same apparently is true of many denominations and independent-type congregations. Doubtlessly the most serious weakness in today's evangelism is the lack of adequate follow-up and conservation.

Four Follow-Up Gaps

Waylon B. Moore, a pastor who has excelled in follow-up, has identified four major follow-up gaps.[6] The first of these is the gap between winning a person to Christ and getting him into the fellowship of the church. I call this *the church membership gap.* Our first major hurdle is to get the new convert to be baptized and join some local body of believers.

Frequently, if the decision to follow Christ has been made in one's home, the bridging of this gap will begin when we persuade the new disciple to make a public confession of faith. Publicly owning one's faith, being baptized, and formally joining a church are the actions which bridge the church membership gap in many churches. Some churches at this point also require discipleship or new member classes.

A second follow-up gap is between joining the church and being enlisted in its program. I call this *the enlistment gap.* Another term for it might be the assimilation gap. Right here is where so much follow-up breaks down. Lyle Schaller insists that it is unchristian to invite persons to unite with a congregation and then not to accept them into that fellowship.[7]

Whether unchristian or not, the congregations in the dozen largest mainline Protestant denominations in the United States were by action of their governing bodies dropping from their rolls over 700,000 names each year in the 1970s. A "disproportionately large number of these" were names of individuals who had joined those congregations by profession of faith or confirmation or believer's baptism. They either lapsed into inactivity or disappeared from view.[8]

The enlistment gap is often bridged when the new church members become active in one or more of the smaller groups within the church. It may be a Sunday School class, a choir, or any face-to-face fellowship group of the congregation. Sponsors may also be assigned to each member to personally assimilate them into the congregational life. Those Barnabases who have the gift of encouragement are sorely needed in this bridge-building ministry. Those who labor to bridge this gap might even be called encouragers. Care should be taken to match encouragers to new members by sex, age, and interests, insofar as possible.

A third follow-up gap is what I call *the intentional witnessing gap*. Moore points out that "enlisted members are not necessarily soul-winners." Another name for this might be the discipling gap. Church members can be active only in "come"-type church structures. They may mistakenly assume that these "come" structures are sufficient for evangelizing the lost.

A truly evangelistic church will be turned outward toward the unreconciled. It will show intentionality about seeking the lost in order to save them. Its members will witness on the job and on the run wherever they go. It will show and tell new members how to share their faith.

The fourth follow-up gap, I label *the reproducing gap*. "Winning souls is no substitute for producing reproducers," says Moore. You may prefer to call this the multiplication gap. Trained witnesses who are willing to train others through on-the-job experience are necessary to bridging this gap.

Pastors who see themselves as equippers are vital to overcoming the reproducing gap. One pastor said, "I am a proclaimer, not an equipper." He had difficulty with the term "the equipping ministry." Why can't we do both?

If we can get a vision of the fantastic possibilities of multiplying disciples geometrically, that dream may spur us forward and nurture our hope for victory within our lifetime. It has been calculated, for example, that if 35,000 Southern Baptists (not churches) commit themselves to the winning and discipling of two people per year and commit

the new Christians to do the same, by geometric progres-
sion, the Southern Baptist Convention would have over
25,000,000 Christians in six years, and 6,243,885,000 Christians in eleven years, or approximately the world population
by 1992.[9]

Our goal in conservation should be to bridge all four of
these follow-up gaps. We shall be tempted to stop short
before each gap is closed. Particularly will some of us be
blinded and deceived by Satan against even seeing the
intentional witnessing gap and the reproducing gap. Dawson Trotman, who saw gaps four and three perhaps more
clearly than most Christians in this century, said: "No man
ever followed Jesus who didn't become a fisher of men. He
never fails to do what He promised. If you're not fishing,
you're not following."[10]

Counseling New Converts

Let us now shift our attention to the actual, practical
steps which may be followed in counseling new converts who
respond to the public invitation. The follow-up ought to
begin at the point of response to the gospel invitation.

The first thing to do is find out why people have come
forward. Most of those who have responded to my invitations came to confess their faith in Christ, to renew their
baptismal vows, to move their church membership, or to
declare they felt God's leadership into some church-related
vocation. God may have put something in their minds that
you know nothing about. On the other hand, you may
already know why the person came. If so, all you need to do
is touch base and affirm the person in the decision.

Once you have found out the responses which they wish
to make, either talk with them personally or assign trained
counselors to immediately clarify their decisions. If they are
making professions of faith: review the plan of salvation,
lead them to make a prayer of confession, welcome them
into the family of God, share some Scriptures on assurance

(such as John 5:24), introduce them to the disciplines of the Christian life, and present them with a spiritual birthday certificate.[11]

I am a strong believer in helping persons to seal their commitments. When the decision has been clarified, it may be appropriately sealed at this point with verbal agreement, prayer, the shaking of hands, and the spiritual birth certificate. Some churches also require, then or later, that the decision be sealed with the new convert's signature. Later, the decision may be sealed with the convert's verbal testimony to the congregation. Ultimately, the confession of faith is sealed with baptism.

Following the clarification and the sealing of the decision, the new convert should be presented to the congregation in keeping with the church's policy. If time will permit, I like to present the new disciple at the same service in which he responds; and if not then, at the earliest possible time.

It is better to have significant others to stand beside the new converts after they have been properly presented. These may be parents, grandparents, spouses, Sunday School teachers, friends, or the lay evangelists who introduced them to Christ. This gesture will put the new disciple more at ease, build up the fellowship, and affirm faithful witnesses. It makes the most of a teaching moment in the life of the church.

Next, ask the church members to come up after the benediction and share their happiness over the decisions. This is a time for warm handshaking and perhaps a loving embrace or a "holy kiss" (Rom. 16:16). Let us rejoice, make merry, and be glad because a lost brother or sister is found and a dead brother or sister is alive (see Luke 15:6-7, 9-10, 20, 32).

Be sure to have the church clerk, or other designated workers, secure accurate information on each person who has made a decision. Most Christian book stores stock standard forms which may be secured for this purpose. You need as a minimum the full name, address, telephone numbers, sex, birthdate, and marital status.

I recommend that something be placed into the hands of those who respond. It may be a booklet, an appropriate tract, a picture, a Scripture portion, a leaflet, a brochure, or a book. Don't give them more than two items, preferably one, in addition to the spiritual birth certificate.

Contact the persons making decisions within forty-eight hours. This initial contact may be by personal visit, but a telephone call will do. The next best contacts are telegraph, letter, or card. You want to affirm the new converts in their decisions, hear how things are with them spiritually at that point, and make appointments for personal follow-up visits that week.

Have someone from the church visit in the new convert's home within the week, before the next Sunday. This may be a Sunday School teacher and a Sunday School outreach leader. It might be a deacon and his or her spouse. Preferably it will be the witnessing team which introduced that person to Christ.

The visit has several important purposes. You want to affirm the decision which was made, clarify it, further seal it, focus on the disciplines of the Christian life, answer questions about your church, and encourage the convert to follow through on his commitment with baptism and responsible church membership.

Make much of the baptismal service. Christian disciples are baptized only once in their lives. There should be something special about it. We ought not to be casual and unexcited about such a momentous once-in-a-lifetime experience.

I was visiting in a pastor's home one day. A six-year-old by the name of Marion asked his mother in my presence, "When were you ordained?"

Marion's mother, somewhat puzzled said, "Honey, I've never been ordained."

The boy said, "I mean when were you baptized?"

Marion may have been closer to the truth than either he or his mother realized. There is a sense in which baptism is a Christian's ordination into the Christian ministry. If there is any such thing as an ordination into the Christian priest-hood to which all believers belong, it is our baptism in the name of the Holy Trinity.

Loved ones and friends of the baptismal candidates should be invited to witness the event. I recommend that engraved invitations be sent out and a reception held in someone's home following the baptismal service. It is an occasion for celebration and thanksgiving. Moreover, the religious drama of a baptismal service packs a powerful evangelistic wallop. I am hard pressed to think of a better opportunity for the new Christian to bear witness to his lost kin, friends, and associates.

Following baptism, the new Christian should have a brief, basic course in the Christian faith and church mem-bership. This may be done one-on-one or in a small group. An abundance of material is now available for such a course.[12] We now have, in fact, a growing literature which provides curricula for advanced training in discipling.[13]

All new disciples should be assigned sponsors. Some churches use deacons as sponsors. Other churches use Sunday School workers. Some use members of the church's evangelism committee. I believe wherever possible the spiri-tual pediatrician ought to be the same as the spiritual obstetrician. However, some Christians who have the spiri-tual gift of an evangelist are too busy introducing persons to Christ to be the spiritual guardians and guides for all of their converts.

A. C. Archibald especially emphasized the sole duty of the lay evangelist to be a persuader, a reaper, and a harvester. Later, he surprises us when he counsels that the one who does the reaping should also be urged to do the conserving and the keeping.[14] While I wholeheartedly agree,

I caution against not including that in the contract on the front end. When one volunteers for a visitation campaign to be a reaper, we ought at an appropriate time to tell that individual up front that we are also going to ask him or her to help nurture and build those who are won.

Additional Considerations on Conservation

The proper counseling of new converts will go a long way toward bridging the four follow-up gaps mentioned above. However, there are some additional considerations which may also aid us in the abolition of those gaps.

A new babe in Christ needs immediate and continuing attention as much so as a new physical baby. A little girl said to her mother, "Mother, I wish I had never joined the church."

Alarmed, the mother asked, "Why?"

"Because, before I joined the church, everyone was interested in me. Now," said the girl, "no one ever pays any attention to me."

That attitude is not peculiar to little girls. An older man said to his pastor, "Preacher, sometimes I wish I was lost again!" He went on to explain that when he was lost a lot of people from the church expressed an interest in him. They sought him out, visited him, and encouraged him. But once he was saved, those contacts ceased.

We dare not bring new members into the family of God and then abandon them. We are spiritual fathers and mothers to our converts. Is the nursery ready? Do we have licensed and competent obstetricians and pediatricians ready for the delivery and the caring process? Are we prepared to feed these new babes the "pure spiritual milk" (see 1 Pet. 2:2) of the Word of God?

Atmosphere and attitude are vital components of church member conservation. Samuel Chadwick said putting new converts into a cold church "was like putting a baby in the arms of a corpse."[15] What do you suppose would have happened if the prodigal son had met up with the elder brother before he got to the father? "If we treated newborn babies as carelessly as we treat newborn Christians," wrote George Sweazey, "the infant mortality rates would equal the appalling mortality of church members."[16]

Revival and renewal do play a vital role in church member conservation. New persons are needed more than new programs. We can't live off of the spiritual capital of a previous generation—even if that generation was made up of spiritual giants.

Nor is church member conservation a question of quality over against quantity. North Phoenix Baptist Church in Phoenix, Arizona, said when they committed themselves to follow-up, God gave them more new Christians than ever before.

Intercessory prayer should have a larger role in follow-up and conservation. The New Testament church used personal contact, sent substitutes or representatives, wrote letters, and offered intercessory prayer as methods of follow-up. The twentieth-century church uses all of these methods and more. However, intercessory prayer for new disciples is weak, sporadic, or nonexistent in some of today's congregations. Those who would follow Jesus should be able to say with him, "I am praying for them" (John 17:9). A major responsibility of those workers who serve as sponsors of new members should be regular intercessory prayer for them.

One hindrance to the public invitation is the lack of trained counselors other than the pastor. Over the long pull, if the pastor alone does all of the counseling at the altar, the people may grow weary. Besides, he will wear himself out. One way to deal more adequately with the church's problem of losing members through the back door is to do a better job of counseling inquirers at the front door of the invitation. Every pastor, even those in the smallest churches, should have one or more persons whom he has trained as counselors to assist him when needed during the invitation.

Some denominations have prepared materials to assist pastors with such training.[17]

New members also need opportunities to use their spiritual gifts. The greatest employment agency in the world ought to be the church. That old saying about idle hands being the devil's workshop may be applied to church member conservation.

Once or twice a year, and perhaps more frequently for rapidly growing churches, a banquet ought to be held to honor all new Christians. Give them a dinner. Have a feast. Throw a party. Welcome them royally into your local assembly.

Conclusion

We all come to discipleship already formed to some extent. We are formed by our families, our friends, our churches, our culture. What we want in Christian discipleship is to be reformed into the image of Christ. In fact what we need is a transformation. That can't be done overnight or in a weekend. It takes time to be holy. Follow-up never ends. That's one reason God has given the church pastors. That's one reason God has made us priests to one another.

Suggestions for Further Reading

Walter A. Henrichsen, *Disciples Are Made Not Born* (Wheaton, Illinois: Victor Books, 1974).

Billie Hanks, Jr. and William A. Shell, eds., *Discipleship* (Grand Rapids: Zondervan Publishing House, 1981).

Sidney W. Powell, *Where Are the Converts?* (Nashville: Broadman Press, 1958).

Russel Bow, *The Integrity of Church Membership* (Waco, Texas: Word Books, 1968).

Waldo J. Werning, *Winning Them Back: New Life for Inactive Church Members* (Minneapolis: Augsburg Publishing House, 1963).

Waylon B. Moore, *New Testament Follow-Up* (Grand Rapids: William B. Eerdmans Co., 1970 rev. ed.).

Notes

1. George E. Sweazey, *Effective Evangelism* (New York: Harper & Brothers, 1953), p. 216.
2. W. Hal Brooks, *Follow Up Evangelism* (Nashville: Broadman Press, 1972), p. 21.
3. D. James Kennedy, *Evangelism Explosion* (Wheaton, Illinois: Tyndale House Publishers, 1977 rev. ed.), p. 113.
4. Billie Hanks, Jr., "The Vision for Multiplication," in Billie Hanks, Jr. and William A. Shell, eds., *Discipleship* (Grand Rapids: Zondervan Publishing House, 1981), p. 25.
5. See my article, "Solving the Inactive Resident Church Member Problem," *Church Administration*, October, 1972, pp. 24-26.
6. Waylon B. Moore, *New Testament Follow-Up* (Grand Rapids: Wm. B. Eerdmans Co., 1970 rev. ed.), pp. 100-102.
7. Lyle E. Schaller, *Assimilating New Members* (Nashville: Abingdon, 1978), pp. 16, 128.
8. Lyle E. Schaller, *Parish Planning* (Nashville: Abingdon, 1971), p. 219.
9. Cited in Joe L. Ingram's "Viewpoint," *The Baptist Messenger*, Vol. 71, No 3, Jan. 21, 1982, p. 8.
10. Dawson E. Trotman, "The Need of the Hour," in Hanks, Jr. and Shell, p. 188.
11. Chapter 19, especially the section on "A Combination Model," for further information. Also, Charles Shaver, *Conserve the Converts* (Kansas City: Beacon Hill Press of Kansas City, 1976), p. 81; and Kennedy, pp. 113-163.
12. Charles Shaver, *Basic Bible Studies* (Kansas City: Beacon Hill Press of Kansas City, 1972); W. Hal Brooks, *Your Life in Christ* (Nashville: Broadman Press, 1971); Gary W. Kuhne, *The Dynamics of Personal Follow-Up* (Grand Rapids: Zondervan Publishing House, 1976), esp. pp. 145-206; LeRoy Eims, *What Every Christian Should Know About Growing* (Wheaton, Illinois: Victor Books, 1976); Waylon B. Moore, esp. pp. 186-201; Carl Wilson, *With Christ in the School of Disciple Building* (Grand Rapids: Zondervan Publishing House, 1976), esp. pp. 79-167; and Ralph W. Neighbour, Jr., *Survival Kit* (Nashville: Convention Press, 1979). My students and I have over the past five years built a grid of some forty questions and examined these and other models by running them through that grid.
13. LeRoy Eims, *The Lost Art of Disciple Making* (Grand Rapids: Zondervan Publishing House, 1978); Gary W. Kuhne, *The Dynamics of Discipleship Training* (Grand Rapids: Zondervan Publishing House, 1978); and Waylon B. Moore, *Multiplying Disciples: The New Testament Method for Church Growth* (Colorado Springs: NavPress, 1981). Southern Baptists have developed *MasterLife* for advanced training in discipleship. The Navigators have a discipleship training course called the 2:7 series. Based on Colossians 2:7, the series consists of six twelve-week courses on biblical principles of Christian growth and practical applications. Usually three courses are held from September to June of

the first year and the other three during a comparable time the next year.
14. Arthur C. Archibald, *New Testament Evangelism: How It Works Today* (Philadelphia: The Judson Press, 1946), pp. 87-88, and 98.
15. Quoted by Sweazey, p. 214.
16. Ibid., p. 207.
17. See for example the booklet, *Counseling Guide,* prepared and distributed by the Evangelism Section of the SBC Home Mission Board, Atlanta, Georgia.

Epilogue:
Testing Your Evangelistic Health

Hosea 7:8-9; John 20:19-23

Introduction

Back in 1975, I had the privilege of being with one of the classes on the campus of The Southern Baptist Theological Seminary in Louisville, Kentucky. A question was raised which I had never heard. Someone wanted to know: "How can I test the evangelistic health of my church? How can I tell whether or not my congregation is sick or healthy in its evangelism?" I should like now to address myself to that question because I think it is a substantive question and one which ought to concern every one of us.

The Discipling Test

Let me suggest that we can use the discipling test to determine the evangelistic health of our churches. Ask yourself about your church: Is my church producing Christian disciples? Are we adding any new converts to the kingdom of God?

This is what A. C. Archibald in his 1946 volume, *New Testament Evangelism*, calls the "fruit test." He is writing about visitation evangelism, but he says: "Visitation evangelism, like all other methods, must stand the fruit test."[1] Recall how Jesus said, "You will know them by their fruits" (Matt. 7:20).

Methodist bishop, Edwin Holt Hughes, in his book *Are You an Evangelist?* tells about a certain institution which claimed that it was trying to create a climate for evangelism, which said that everything it did was evangelism. But upon close-up examination for the previous ten years, that so-called climatic regime had not produced one single convert.[2]

"I know churches that have not had a convert for decades," wrote John R. W. Stott. "They are not expecting converts and they are not getting converts."[3] We need a revolution of rising expectations that the Lord will add regularly to the church those who are being saved.

I have heard Chester Vaughn of Mississippi tell about a black Baptist preacher who attended New Orleans Baptist Theological Seminary. The student flunked Dr. Roland Q. Leavell's class in evangelism. His name was Famous McElhaney. Some of the students who knew McElhaney were kidding him about flunking Dr. Leavell's course in evangelism. McElhaney said, "Yes, that's right I did flunk the course," but he said, "you know I baptized 112 converts last year."

That pastor may have flunked a course in evangelism, but he and his church did pass the discipling test. They were, at least, doing something right. They were adding some new disciples to a local church.

Call it the fruit test, the new converts test, the numbers test, or whatever you wish. I call it the discipling test. We need to face up to this question: are we adding any new disciples to the kingdom of God?

Are we producing new converts and adding them to the kingdom of God? Are these converts joining some local churches somewhere? Are we integrating and assimilating these new disciples into our congregational life? Are some of these converts outsiders as well as insiders? Sometimes we are just reaching our own children. That's important. We surely ought to try to reach our own children. But if that is the only kind of evangelism we are doing, we may not be as healthy as we think. The kind of evangelism that reaches only insiders can be an ingrown evangelism. We have to make new converts in order to survive. We have to make new converts in order to fulfill the Great Commission. That's the first test I hope you will apply if you aren't now using this test in the congregation to which you belong.

I am so happy we've moved out of the dreadful decades of the sixties and seventies when some of us began to use a slogan to counteract talk about numbers. We began to say, "God wants us to be faithful not successful." In other words, we created a theology of waiting. Some of us are still tarrying in Jerusalem when we ought to be threshing in Gilead. We are waiting in our church buildings when we ought to be walking into citizens' homes and invading the devil's dens of our communities. We are contented with being a faithful remnant when we ought to be intent on becoming a fighting company for Jesus Christ.

I hope we can move out of this negative thinking about numbers and begin to do the kind of positive thinking that the Church Growth Movement people are trying to get us to do, where we think the unthinkable, attempt the impossible, and do the undoable. Authentic evangelism is always effective evangelism. Therefore, a defeatist mind-set will not do in our evangelism. A church with a pygmy complex is a pathetic sight, especially in a world where nearly three billion persons belong to what Peter Wagner calls the "Fourth World," that is, the world of the lost.

The Equipping Test

Another way you can tell whether your church is sick or healthy in its evangelism is to apply the equipping test. Don't just tell how many converts you baptized last year. Tell how many people you taught to win others to Jesus Christ. Don't think you have an evangelistic church just because you happen to have an evangelistic pastor in your pulpit. Oh, that's great! Woe betide the church that does not have an evangelistic pastor in the pulpit. But tell us how many persons in your congregation have been taught how to intentionally introduce others to Jesus Christ. That is a pretty acid test of the health of the evangelism in your congregation.

A. C. Archibald insisted that Jesus had an organization

for lay evangelism. He found the heart of that organization to be in the sending out of the twelve and the seventy, two by two. "He organized them into definite groups of two, that they might become systematic soul winners," said Archibald. Archibald even called Peter and John "a gospel team."[4]

According to Archibald, what the church needs is "a mental revolution" which will see the local church as the place and the instrument of evangelism. He said, "We profess that evangelism is our chief task; but with a few exceptions, our churches are organized for everything except for our central project."[5]

When I was director of evangelism for Southern Baptists in South Carolina, I invited James Kennedy to speak to one session of the annual South Carolina Baptist State Conference on Evangelism. Kennedy is pastor of the Coral Ridge Presbyterian Church in Fort Lauderdale, Florida. He is the originator of Evangelism Explosion, a widely used lay witness training program in churches of many denominations. "It is more important," said Kennedy, "to teach one how to win a soul to Jesus Christ than it is to win a soul to Jesus Christ."

That is a powerful statement. I agree with it wholeheartedly. It is great to win a person to Jesus Christ. It is more fruitful still to teach one how to win someone else to Christ. Spiritual multiplication and reproduction are more important to the evangelistic health of the church than are mere spiritual addition and production. Kennedy was bearing witness to the equipping test. He was saying something analogous to the proverb about the hungry: "It is better to show a person how to fish, than it is to give him a fish."

Pastors and all church staff members are in the equipping ministry. We have been called and commissioned by God to teach others how to share their faith. If we don't do it, it shows that we are unhealthy to that extent in our evangelism.

I know how great it is for the preacher to go out and win a lot of people to Christ every week. But if, as the pastor, you are doing all of the introducing of folk to Jesus Christ, your church is not too healthy in its evangelism. I believe that God is going to hold us responsible for teaching persons how to share their faith. There are many who want to know how. It is our responsibility to teach them and to equip them. So, apply the equipping test to your evangelism.

The Balance Test

Yet another way to tell whether your congregation is sick or healthy in its evangelism is to try the balance test. Is the evangelism which your church espouses characterized by that same beautiful balance, perfect proportion, and sweet symmetry that we see in the life and ministry of Jesus Christ?

This is of course not just something that's confined to the New Testament and to Jesus. We see it, for example, in the prophet Hosea when he says: "Ephraim is a cake not turned" (Hos. 7:8b). Ephraim is like a half-baked cake—burned on one side and raw on the other. Ephraim is out of balance, out of round, out of symmetry. The nation is asymmetrical. The people's religion was out of balance. Apply this test of balance to your church's evangelism.

Are you using balance in terms of your evangelistic methodology? I think some of our churches are putting all of their evangelistic eggs in one method, in one technique. If that's true, they're out of balance.

There are many ways to introduce lost persons to Jesus Christ. One way will not appeal to all of the persons in your congregation. Nor will one way reach all of the lost persons. There are many ways to fish for fish. We ought to be wise enough to have some balance, variety, symmetry, and proportion in our evangelistic methods.

Apply this idea of balance also to your converts. What about the converts you're making? Do they exhibit balance, symmetry, and proportion in their Christian living? If not, they may be chaff instead of wheat. That's the great test to apply to your converts.

Apply it to other functions of the church. There are other things the church ought to be doing besides evangelism. There is worship, education, the area of missions, and stewardship. Evangelism relates to all of these in some way. But, if all you are doing is evangelism and you are putting down these other functions of the church, it may well be that you are out of balance on the side of evangelism.

The case is not too much like that in most of our churches however. So many of us are willing to give far more attention to education, stewardship, worship, music, and to missions than we are to evangelism. I am asking you to apply this test of balance to all of the activities and functions of the church. Some of our churches are like half-baked cakes in their evangelism.

What about balance between the head and the heart? If you don't have balance between the head and the heart in your evangelism, there is something unhealthy about it. We need to love God with our minds as well as with our hearts.

What about balance between the word and the deed? Some of us are all talk and no action.

What about balance between biological growth and conversion growth, between go structures and come structures, between the other world and this world, the individual and the society, the personal and the corporate? Do you balance pulpit evangelism with personal evangelism? You run it on down. Apply this balance test to every aspect of your evangelism in order to see how healthy it is.

The Leadership Test

The leadership test may also be applied. That's a mighty big evaluation. Ask yourself how committed to evangelism are the members of the church staff and the major leaders of the church. How interested are they in evangelism? If you have a church staff, even with one member of that staff who doesn't care much about evangelism, you have a potential blockage. You are potentially unhealthy in your evangelism. You are already sick at that point in your evangelism.

I heard Chester Swor preach a sermon one time. I don't know what the title of it was, but he quoted from Chaucer's *The Canterbury Tales.* I had read that once while in college, or tried to read it; nobody I think can read Chaucer very well. Swor quoted his text from Chaucer: "If gold rusts, what shall iron do?"

Everybody knows that iron is going to rust, especially if it is exposed to the elements and doesn't have sufficient oil on it. It is the nature of iron to keep rusting until it's all rusted out and gone. But Chaucer said: "If gold rusts, what shall iron do?" Gold, too, will rust.

When we have preachers, ministers of education, ministers of youth, ministers of recreation, and ministers of music who are not committed to evangelism, the gold has begun to rust! We ought to try to see to that, as best we can by the help of God, every staff member and every major leader in the church, right on down to the last one, is committed to a wholesome and intelligent evangelism.

Ask of your church: are our church staff and our major church leaders committed to evangelism? Is *evangelism* a dirty word to our church leaders? Whether that staff be just one part-time pastor or a hundred specialists, if they are not all committed to evangelism, they may erode and block the evangelistic outreach of the congregation.

Furthermore, if the majority of the deacons and Sunday School teachers and other church program organization leaders are not committed to conscious intentional evangelism, that church may well become a museum or a mausoleum. It can write *Ichabod* over its doors because the glory of God will depart from its midst. We need all of the pulpit power and all of the pew power which we can get in order to have an evangelistically healthy church. I do not believe a church is necessarily evangelistic just because it happens to have an evangelistic pastor.

The Sending Test

A final test by which we may judge our evangelistic health is the sending test. "The strength of a church," said Stanley Mooneyham of World Vision, "is not revealed by how many people it seats, but by how many it sends."[6] Tell us how many persons you sent out to plant and cultivate and reap the field of the world. Did you send out one hundred, fifty, or none?

The sending test is really the missionary test. God authenticated his love for the world by sending his only begotten and beloved Son to die for us on the cross. The church validates her love for her Lord and the lost by sending out her finest sons and daughters to the ends of the earth to make Christian disciples and to plant Christian churches until her Lord returns to consummate history and to complete her salvation.

Surely it has not escaped our attention that the disciples were first called Christians in Antioch (see Acts 11:26) and that from Antioch Barnabas and Paul and John Mark were sent out as missionaries. A church which is not involved in world evangelization through sending out Christian workers to the ends of the earth is building its own kingdom rather than God's kingdom.

Christianity is a universal religion. It seeks church growth through extension and bridging growth, as well as through the expansion of individual churches. Every church must have a Judea in addition to its Jerusalem, and a Galilee in addition to its Judea. No church, however small or large it may be in its home base, is at liberty to neglect the uttermost parts of the earth.

I do not understand local churches which make no effort and have no intentionality about sending ambassadors for Christ to all the peoples and places of their planet. Does

God love one kind of people more than he does all other kinds?

One of the problems I have with some super aggressive churches today is that some of them appear to be more concerned with building their own kingdoms than with building the kingdom of God. Is it wiser to bus children into one huge church from a radius of ten to seventy-five miles or to start mission Sunday Schools and churches for those communities?

I have for years admired and learned from such churches as The Church of the Savior in Washington, D. C. When measured by the sending test, that church and comparable churches may exhibit a lack of evangelistic health. Where is their intentionality and their conscious strategy to duplicate themselves and to reproduce churches to the ends of the earth?

Jesse M. Bader wrote in 1957:

> The church is always within one generation of extinction. If every church were closed tomorrow; every Bible destroyed; no one ever taught or preached the gospel to anyone else again, and no one ever mentioned the name of Christ to another, the church would go out of existence in one generation. The church lives, grows, and thrives because it evangelizes.[7]

Suggested Study Questions

1. What is the difference between go and come structures in a local church? Give an example of each.
2. Apply each of the five tests to your local congregation. If each test were reduced to a scale ranging from a low of one to a high of ten, where would you position your church on each scale? Why?
3. How would you go about applying each of the five tests to

yourself as a microcosm of the church?

4. What can you say about applying each test to your denomination? To the boards, agencies, commissions, and institutions of your denomination? May these tests, indeed, be applied to the church in macrocosm as well as in microcosm?

Notes

1. Arthur C. Archibald, *New Testament Evangelism: How It Works Today* (Philadelphia: The Judson Press, 1946), p. 144.

2. Edwin Holt Hughes, ed., *Are You an Evangelist?* (New York: The Methodist Book Concern, 1936), p. 8.

3. John R. W. Stott, "Setting the Spirit Free," *Christianity Today,* Vol. XXV, No. 11, June 12, 1981, p. 20.

4. Archibald, pp. 42-43.

5. Ibid., pp. 44-47.

6. W. Stanley Mooneyham, "Getting More Hooks in the Water Is Not Enough: World Evangelization Requires the Right Tackle," *Christianity Today,* Vol. XXV, No. 16, Sept. 18, 1981, p. 20.

7. Jesse M. Bader, *Evangelism in a Changing America* (St. Louis: The Bethany Press, 1957), p. 20.

Annotated Bibliography

Anderson, Gerald H., and Stransky, Thomas F., eds., *Mission Trends No. 2: Evangelization* (New York and Grand Rapids: Paulist Press and William B. Eerdmans Publishing Co., 1975), 279 pp. Twenty-two essays that probe the mandate and strategies of proclaiming the gospel in today's world, with statements from Bangkok, Lausanne, Rome, Bucharest, and Taizé.

Archibald, Arthur C., *New Testament Evangelism: How It Works Today* (Philadelphia: The Judson Press, 1946), 156 pp. The best of the manuals on visitation evangelism, by a Canadian pastor who applied the first-century norm to American Baptist churches in the first half of the twentieth century.

Augsburger, David W., *Communicating Good News* (Scottdale, Pennsylvania, and Newton, Kansas: Mennonite Publishing House and Faith and Life Press, 1972), 113 pp. Prepared as a study course for lay Christians by a popular and powerful Mennonite pastor. Shows how to translate the language of Zion about evangelism into the language of the people.

Dayton, Edward R., and Fraser, David A., eds., *Planning Strategies for World Evangelization* (Grand Rapids: William B. Eerdmans Publishing Co., 1980), 537 pp. A cross-cultural approach to the process of world evangelization, done from a missiological perspective under the auspices of MARC (Missions Advanced Research and Communication Center).

Douglas, J. D., ed., *Let the Earth Hear His Voice* (Minneapolis: World Wide Publications, 1975), 1471 pp. The official reference volume of the 1974 International Congress on World Evangelization, Lausanne, Switzerland. Contains all papers and responses.

Fackre, Gabriel, *Word in Deed: Theological Themes in Evangelism* (Grand Rapids: William B. Eerdmans Publishing Co., 1975), 109 pp. Fackre, a United Church of Christ theologian, relates systematic theology to evangelism. He makes much of "story," and of the metaphors of light and darkness. All of his books intentionally relate to evangelism.

Green, Bryan, *The Practice of Evangelism* (New York: Charles Scribner's Sons, 1951), 258 pp. A collection of lectures and articles on evangelism by Canon Green, one of the most successful evangelists in the Church of England. Uses a homiletical style, but treats substantive theological questions in a popular manner.

Green, Michael, *Evangelism in the Early Church* (Grand Rapids: William B. Eerdmans Publishing Co., 1970), 349 pp. A very substantive survey by a New Testament scholar who is an evangelical Anglican.

Hunter, George G., III, *The Contagious Congregation: Frontiers in Evangelism and Church Growth* (Nashville: Abingdon, 1979), 160 pp. A former secretary for evangelism with the United Methodist Board of Discipleship, shows some of the interfaces between evangelism and church growth. Presents a new inductive model for evangelization correlated with Abraham Maslow's hierarchy of human motivation.

International Missionary Council, *Evangelism* (London: Oxford University Press, 1939), 450 pp. One of the seven volumes which came out of the 1938 meeting of the International Missionary Council held at Tambaram, Madras, India. Surveys evangelistic work in several areas of the world, and reveals some roots of the modern Church Growth Movement.

Krass, Alfred C., *Evangelizing Neopagan North America* (Scottdale, Pennsylvania: Herald Press, 1982), 250 pp. A United Church of Christ house church pastor and Christian social activist redefines evangelism from a kingdom of God perspective. The eleven appendixes contain the most ecumenically significant statements on evangelism made during the decade of the 1970s.

Pippert, Rebecca Manley, *Out of the Saltshaker & Into the World* (Downers Grove, Illinois: 1979), 188 pp. Represents the best which Inter-Varsity Christian Fellowship offers in publications on evangelism. Takes a relational and incarnational approach.

Quere, Ralph W., *Evangelical Witness* (Minneapolis: Augsburg Publishing House, 1975), 160 pp. A professor of history and theology in the American Lutheran Church discusses the message, medium, mission, and method of evangelism in theological perspective.

Read, David H. C., *Go & Make Disciples* (Nashville: Abingdon, 1978), 110 pp. Deals with the why and how of evangelism. Especially useful in creating a rationale for evangelism. This is the Jesse Bader Memorial lectures in June of 1976 to the College of the Bible in Melbourne, Australia, by the pastor of Madison Avenue Presbyterian Church in New York City.

Rice, John R., *The Soul Winner's Fire* (Wheaton, Illinois: Sword of the Lord Publishers, 1941), 114 pp. A representative collection of messages on evangelism by one of America's foremost Fundamentalist evangelists. Rice was editor of *The Sword of the Lord* until his death.

Sweazey, George E., *Effective Evangelism* (New York: Harper & Row, Publishers, 1976 rev. ed.), 288 pp. An excellent, general introduction to evangelism by a former secretary for evangelism in the United Presbyterian Church, U.S.A. Was first published in 1953. The revised edition has a four and one-half page annotated bibliography on evangelism.

Watson, David, *I Believe in Evangelism* (Grand Rapids: William B. Eerdmans Publishing Co., 1976), 190 pp. A well-written general introduction to evangelism by an Anglican pastor who practices what he writes. One of Eerdmans' "I Believe . . ." series under the general editorship of Michael Green.

Wirt, Sherwood Eliot, ed., *Evangelism the Next Ten Years* (Waco, Texas: Word Books Publisher, 1978), 165 pp. Thirteen essays presented to Billy Graham on his sixtieth birthday, written by well-known Evangelicals who are "world" Christians.

Author

Biblical References

Subject